ALL OF US TOGETHER

Love,
Greta

ALSO BY LARA POLLOCK

Together Is Home
The Healing Messages of
A Course in Miracles

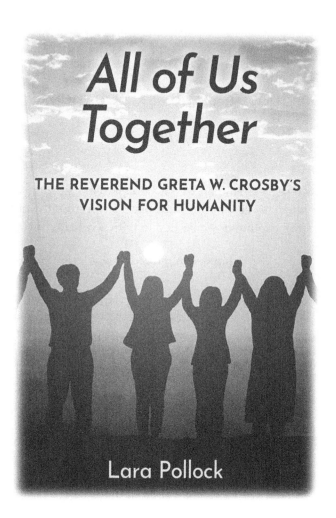

TOGETHER IS HOME PUBLICATIONS
WICHITA, KS

Copyright © 2024 by Lara Pollock

TOGETHER IS HOME PUBLICATIONS
Wichita, KS
larapollock.com

All rights reserved. No part of this book may be reproduced in any manner whatsoever without prior permission from the publisher, except for quotations embodied in critical articles or reviews.

ISBN: 979-8-9875932-8-8

LIBRARY OF CONGRESS CONTROL NUMBER:
2024917833

COVER ART
Provided by Shutterstock, modified by
Travis Foster — Tonight at Eight Studios
tonightateightstudios@gmail.com

PROJECT MANAGEMENT & PRODUCTION
D. Patrick Miller, Fearless Literary
www.fearlessbooks.com/Literary.html

Table of Contents

Opening Words .... *vii*
Preface 1

Section I: Introduction
Greta's Early Years and the 1950s 5

Ch 1: **Introduction to Greta W. Crosby & the 1950s** 7
Ch 2: **Spoken Essay Selection Process** 21
Ch 3: **"Mobile Deity"** 26
Ch 4: **The Late 1950s** 34

Section II: *The 1960s* 39
Ch 5: **The Early 1960s** 40
Ch 6: **"Justice Without a Blindfold"** 52
Ch 7: **Thus Spake Greta** 66
Ch 8: **"Fantasies on Blue"** 75
Ch 9: **The March on Washington** 92
Ch 10: **"Valley of the Shadow"** 100
Ch 11: **The Rest of the 1960s** 111

Section III: *The 1970s* 133
Ch 12: **The Early 1970s** 134
Ch 13: **"Beautiful Dreamers"** 142
Ch 14: **The Mid 1970s** 155

Ch 15: "A Celebration of Crows" 162
Ch 16: **The Late 1970s** 176

Section IV: *The 1980s* 183
Ch 17: **The Early 1980s** 184
Ch 18: "Lighting One Light with Another" 193
Ch 19: **The Mid 1980s** 202
Ch 20: "Shadows" 209
Ch 21: **The Late 1980s** 220
Ch 22: **Installation at Yakima, Washington** 237

Section V: *The 1990s to Current* 243
Ch 23: **The Early 1990s** 244
Ch 24: "First Things First: Dignity and Worth" 252
Ch 25: **The Mid 1990s** 262
Ch 26: "Fathers and Farewell" 272
Ch 27: **The Late 1990s** 284
Ch 28: **The Early 2000s to the Present** 304
Closing Words 316

List of Works Cited 317
Acknowledgments 322
About the Author 324

*This book is dedicated
to those who peacefully and lovingly
refuse to tolerate unjust treatment
of fellow human beings.*

Opening Words
June 4, 1961

"Lord of Welcome, who calls us into life and into fellowship one with another, it is your light that shines in our eyes and touches our hearts in every true greeting. Open the doors of our minds and hearts to welcome you in your surprising guises. Help us to reach out and go forth not only to meet you but to be you."

— Greta W. Crosby

Preface

My mother, Greta W. Crosby, was a Unitarian Universalist (UU) minister from 1959 until her retirement in 1996. Afterward, she continued to be a voice for social justice for years to come. At this printing in 2024, she is 93 and my husband and I currently live with her and care for her. While many memories of her years as a UU minister have faded from her mind, my mom still reads the newspaper every day. She stays informed on current issues, and she still cares deeply about the human condition.

Her dedicated ministry was characterized by her humanitarianism, her social activism and her highly intelligent compositions. Though she referred to her Sunday presentations as 'sermons,' she felt the term had a bit of a preachy connotation to it. Early in her career, she sometimes called her compositions Spoken Essays; then later in her ministry, she preferred to call them Commentaries.

My mom's sermons consistently reflect her main philosophy of life, which is to see the potential good in every person. Her Vision has always been to affirm and promote the worth and dignity of every person. She asserts that everyone should be afforded equal protection under the law, and everyone has the right to work and to earn a living wage. And most important is her encouragement to exercise empathy for people living in different circumstances.

It can be so easy for someone to say, "Well I don't have to worry about 'this or that,'" such as poverty, discrimination, abuse, or disenfranchisement. Then it seems so easy to express short-sighted, egocentric opinions or to enact inappropriate policies based on these entitled circumstances. Yet my mom has always taken time to understand a situation from many different perspectives, which allows compassion for others to naturally flow from within.

Over her years of service as a UU minister, she composed and presented well over 1,200 insightful Commentaries, often presenting a Vision of a better way for all of us to thrive together. Idealistic, perhaps, but without a Vision of how it could be, it's harder to see past our present dissatisfaction. Rather than staying stuck bemoaning the ways of the world, Greta empowered people to envision a better way to live together, collaboratively and cooperatively.

After she retired, I shared a collection of her early Spoken Essays with the Rev. David Carter, who was the minister of our church at that time. He was so impressed with her poetic prose that he called it 'High Literature.' When he described her collection in this way, I realized that the content could genuinely be likened to the philosophical essays of Emerson and Thoreau.

This brings attention to the concept of the sermon as an art form. It's not commonly viewed in this way, but there is much to be appreciated about sermons/Spoken Essays/Commentaries from any minister. Their insights reflect the current issues of the time, as well as the timeless relevance of messages of Love and compassion shared throughout the ages. Yes, more and more I am learning that the sermon as art form is a valid and valuable conceptualization.

I credit my father, Robert J. Crosby, for planting the idea of saving my mom's sermons for eventual publication. My father was brilliant, yet unhealed childhood traumas contributed to his mental illness and clinical depression. I would describe him as a dysfunctional genius. This caused difficulty with all of his relationships over the years.

My parents were married in 1961, and there were some good times together, but eventually Dad's dysfunction became too much to bear, and they were divorced in 1984. Likewise, I was estranged from him for many years. Fortunately, due to my husband Danny's encouragement, my relationship with my father improved in the later years of his life. During the time of his passing in 2015, through the miracle of heart-felt forgiveness, all of my grievances against him fell away, and there was only Love left between us.

I now find that Dad's messages about many things have proven true even if he sounded crazy at the time — he was far ahead of his time. One of his important messages was, "Save Greta's sermons, they are deeply meaningful, share her legacy with the world."

Now I have finally reached the time in my life where I can accomplish this goal. Thankfully, the self-publication process has made it feasible to begin the journey, with this book as the first step, and more to follow after that. Now is the time to publish my mom's profoundly insightful works, and I am grateful for the opportunity. For me, it's not a matter of the marketability of the content or selling a certain number of books, it's about providing access to thought-provoking, compassionate messages of hope for humanity.

For those who feel prompted to explore these pages, I say, "Yes! Thank You!" It will be well worth your time to sit with these insights, and in doing so, to gracefully share Greta's Vision of unity for *All of Us Together*.

With Gratitude, *Lara Pollock*

Section I: Introduction
Greta's Early Years and the 1950s

As we embark on our exploration of Greta's ministry, let's begin with one of her Opening Prayer-Meditations:

Let us join in meditation.

Honoring the diversity of our spiritual heritage and the unity of our human condition, I invite you to call upon what is highest and deepest by the name you hold sacred and dear.

Creating, sustaining, renewing spirit, we open our hearts and minds to you. We welcome you as the messenger of peace and the friend of justice. Be with us in our gathering as the gladness and gratitude we feel in this company. We rejoice that we are not alone in desiring merciful and just resolutions to the conflicts and conditions that affect us all, where we live and throughout the world.

Temper our anxieties and enlighten our fears as we seek to understand what is happening and how we may be helpful in bettering this world. Then quicken our steps on our way, the steps we will walk today, and the steps we will take with renewed courage and greater understanding toward a peaceful world of caring people.

And now let us bring our meditation to a close, each in our own way, resolving to embody in our lives the Spirit of Love and Truth.

— Greta W. Crosby

REV. GRETA W. CROSBY, 1991

Chapter 1

Introduction to Greta W. Crosby & the 1950s

As mentioned in the Preface, my mother, Greta W. Crosby, was a Unitarian Universalist minister from 1959 to 1996. Throughout her career, she was a trailblazer for women and an advocate for people who've been marginalized and treated unjustly. She gave a voice to those who had no voice.

I have conservatively estimated that Greta composed over 1,200 sermons in her forty-year career, and I wouldn't be surprised if it was closer to 1,500. I intend to anthologize these at a later date, but it will take years for me to methodically curate her legacy. The scope of this book is to provide a retrospective overview of her life's work with a collection of ten sermons. The first is from Greta's last year in theological school in 1959, then three from 1963, and two from the 1970's, 1980's and 1990's respectively. The final Commentary included here is actually the last one she delivered before retiring in 1996.

Nestled between each sermon are little gems, various items either written about Greta, like newspaper articles or letters from church members, or items written by Greta such as letters to the editor, poems, meditations, etc. Additionally, between each sermon, I'll fill in the blanks with narratives of her life and her corresponding career pathway.

Before reading her first sermon, it might be helpful to learn about her life-path that led to her becoming a UU minister. It was not an easy one, and the more I delve into the details, the more proud I become of her. Every parent has lived lifetimes within their lifetime — many of which we are unaware. They often deserve much more credit and honor than we ever realized, and that is certainly the case for my mom. Here is how my mother's lifelong career of service to humanity began.

Greta's Early Years

Greta Worstell Crosby was born Greta Marie Worstell in Iowa City, Iowa on April 19, 1931. Her mother, Emma Jane, was born in 1900 to German immigrants. Her given name was Empke Johanna Vietor. My Aunt Paula explains that their mother spoke only German in her younger years, but once WW I occurred, the family downplayed their German roots due to anti-German sentiment. Hence Greta's mother went by Emma Jane and she no longer spoke the mother tongue of her family's homeland.

Education was important to Emma Jane's family and they sent her to business college after her high school graduation in 1918. She then attended Coe College in Cedar Rapids. She traveled and worked as a secretary in several places, including working for the mayor of Toledo, Ohio. She also worked in an office down the hall from Franklin D. Roosevelt when he was Secretary of the Navy. Starting in 1924, Emma Jane worked for several years in the offices of the University of Iowa Hospitals and Clinics in Iowa City.

Greta's father, Dr. Henry Paul Worstell, was born in 1899. His ancestors had emigrated from Great Britain in the late 1600's or early 1700's. He grew up on a farm in Knoxville, Iowa, but he did not like farm life. When World War I began, Paul was too young to join the military, so he lied about his age to enlist in the Navy. Once he returned from the war, he was able to go to college at the University of Iowa with a scholarship for his service in WW I.

I'm not sure how Paul and Emma Jane met, but I recall my mom mentioning that Emma Jane's family was not too thrilled with Paul's prospects; and this is what prompted Paul to continue his education, pursuing the profession of physician. Paul and Emma Jane were married on June 3, 1927. Then according to a July 7, 1927 article in *The Gazette* in Cedar Rapids, H.P. Worstell of Knoxville, Iowa, received a scholarship to attend medical school at the University of Iowa.

When Greta was born in April 1931, Paul was working on his internship as an orthopedic surgeon at the University of Iowa Hospitals and Clinics. In 1932, after her father completed his medical training in Iowa City, the family moved to Columbus, Ohio, for a job opportunity.

Over the next few years, Paul and Emma Jane had two more children, Nancy and Paula. Greta loved her sisters very much, however, she also loved reading in her room. She spent a great deal of time self-sequestered there, voraciously consuming books like a hungry baby bird.

World War II induced a temporary move for the Worstell family. In 1942, her father, who was a Lieutenant Commander in the Navy at the time, felt compelled to participate as a physician to support the allied forces' defensive efforts. The family moved back to Iowa City where Paul assisted in setting up the Pre-Flight Training Program for cadets. He helped establish the medical training unit and he also coached recruits in boxing to promote physical fitness.

Before Paul shipped out overseas, they were surprised to

learn that Emma Jane was pregnant with their fourth child. Once he went overseas, Aunt Paula explained that their mother hired a man to drive the family back to Columbus because she didn't drive. A few months later, Emma Jane delivered their son John. I can only imagine how difficult it must have been worrying for Paul's safety, managing a household with three girls, and caring for a newborn baby! Fortunately, Paul returned safely when the war was over and the Worstell family was reunited and complete.

Once back in Columbus, Greta attended University Middle School and then High School. Being a very bright student, she completed her required credits by the time she was a Junior in 1947, so she was eligible to graduate early.

Through a serendipitous series of events, she was then afforded an opportunity to live and study in France for a year from July 1947 to July 1948. Concurrently, Claudine, Greta's French family's daughter, traveled to Columbus, staying with Greta's family for the year. I am tickled by the notion that they were foreign exchange students in the literal sense. [NOTE: My next project will be compiling Greta's letters back and forth to her family during this enriching experience.]

The 1950s

When Greta returned from her world travels, she attended Ohio Wesleyan where she majored in political science, Spanish and unrequited love — but more on that in a bit. She spent the summer of 1950 enrolled in college courses in Mexico, and this immersive experience improved her fluency in Spanish. Not too surprisingly, she completed her college credits in three years and she was awarded her Bachelor of Arts degree in 1951.

For many years, the trajectory of Greta's life was to work toward acceptance into the foreign service, possibly working as a diplomat at a U.S. Embassy overseas. The next step in this preparatory process was to attend law school. Remarkably, she was admitted into Harvard Law School in 1952. It was only the second year that women were permitted entrance into their hallowed halls. In 1954, she completed her Doctor of Jurisprudence degree and she was subsequently admitted into the Ohio bar in that same year. Then she worked for a few years in the Legal Section at Battelle Memorial Institute in Columbus.

Greta was well on her way to qualifying for admittance into the foreign service, however, even while in law school, something wasn't sitting well with her. With deepening concern, she'd begun to realize that working in the foreign service would entail her upholding government policies, some of which she did not agree with. In fact, she had become more and more certain that she did not wish to be beholden to the government in such a way.

This was deeply disappointing and unsettling for her. It was important to her to do meaningful work in service to humanity, but neither the foreign service nor practicing law were resonating with her as her life's calling. It was then that she found her calling in the ministry — but not in a mainstream denomination — her singular aspiration was to become a Unitarian Universalist (UU) minister. The reason for this is because UU's have a much different approach to religion than many other denominations.

The Unitarian Universalist Association website (*uua.org*), describes the denomination as follows: Unitarian Universalist congregations "affirm and promote seven Principles, which we hold as strong values and moral guides. We live out these Principles within a 'living tradition' of wisdom and spirituality, drawn from sources as diverse as science, poetry, scripture, and personal experience."

The Seven Principles which we affirm and promote are:
1. Honoring the inherent worth and dignity of every person;
2. Upholding justice, equity and compassion in human relations;
3. Acceptance of one another and encouragement to spiritual growth in our congregations;
4. Supporting a free and responsible search for truth and meaning;
5. Encouraging the right of conscience and the use of the democratic process within our congregations and in society at large;
6. Progressing toward the goal of world community with peace, liberty, and justice for all;
7. Respecting the interdependent web of all existence of which we are a part.

Though these statements have been modified over time, this is the foundational framework which attracted Greta from the time she was in her teens. When she joined the Unitarian church in the 1940's, Unitarians and Universalists were separate denominations. In 1961, they consolidated into one denomination and it took a while for Unitarian churches to implement the name change. This is why whenever I have sourced documents from the 1960s, they will often simply say Unitarian.

I've outlined Greta's educational path with broad brushstrokes, but there is much more to the story. Let's look at her detailed account of how this discovery process transpired, drawing from her own wonderful wordsmithing ways. The following is an excerpt from a letter written on April 2, 1956 to Dr. Wallace Robbins as part of her application for admission to the Meadville

Ch 1 - Introduction to Greta W. Crosby and the 1950s

Theological School, which is an affiliate of Chicago University. Dr. Robbins had asked Greta, who was twenty-four at the time, to describe her "religious pilgrimage." She responds:

> The word "pilgrimage" is my clue to your question, Dr. Robbins. It implies at least a purpose, a method, and a certain amount of on-goingness. In one sense, my 'pilgrimage' must be equated with my life experiences; 'purpose' with my desire to lead a worthwhile life, i.e., of value to others and worth my while to live it; 'method' with the trial-and-error, hit-and-miss way I use a bit of thinking here, a bit of feeling there, and a bit of habit everywhere, hoping that as I grow older, I shall be able to plot more and plod less; and 'on-goingness' with the days I have seen, today, and the days I shall see.
>
> I suspect, however, that you used 'pilgrimage' in a more narrow sense with reference to the specific question: Why in the world does she want to become a minister?
>
> My religious pilgrimage began in a background of American Protestant not-very-church-going parents and of childhood attendance first at a Presbyterian and later at an Episcopal Sunday school. I still remember somewhat ruefully a statement I made to my teacher at Episcopal Sunday school; I declared with all the dignity of my eight or nine years that Darwin must be wrong about the apes since the Bible says that God made Adam and Eve. I also remember rendering my first bit of exegesis a year or two later when, at a choir convention, the local bishop asked for one of the children to tell him what Jesus meant by keeping your light under a bushel (aptly illustrated by the bishop, with a candle under a bushel basket).
>
> At the age of eight I began to take a voracious interest in

the stories of Greek mythology, with some overlap into Norse and Egyptian legends. I also read the Bible, somewhat less voraciously, but I had it down to a system of about a chapter a day when I was ten or eleven. I think Deuteronomy broke the system. It was at some point during this period that my father made the remark which changed the orientation of my religious life. In response to my insistent chant, "Ask me a question about Greek mythology, Daddy." He said, "What about Jewish mythology?" I didn't understand him at first, but when he mentioned Noah, I knew what he meant, and I informed him that those stories were all true.

During the next few years, I began to compare the Bible stories with the myths, and at some moment, I realized that Noah was a myth, too. It happened very naturally, and since I had to rebel against neither parental disagreement nor against church authority (World War II having moved our family to Iowa in time to save me from First Communion and also from further church attendance), I managed to leave strict orthodoxy in a painless manner. My interest, my faith, if you will, in God was not weakened, but my allegiance to the churches I had known was dead.

The next important event in my religious pilgrimage was a chance conversation with one of my high school classmates. We were both crawling on our hands and knees in a field, thinning lettuce or bunching radishes or some such activity shortly after the war. My friend told me about her church. That fall I began to attend the services of her church. There was only a small congregation, and services were held at the local Hillel Foundation because there was not yet a church building for the group. I knew that I had found my church.

Two years later, at the age of seventeen, I officially became a Unitarian. (Recently, someone remarked that I was a convert to Unitarianism. I was rather shocked as I do not consider myself to be a convert. I merely found the external church which corresponded to my internal church.)

The full effect of Unitarianism on my life is difficult to analyze. I believe that one important thing I have gained is a unity of outlook and an enjoyment of diversity. By unity of outlook, I mean that I do not have to look out of different windows in my mind when viewing religious matters, or scientific matters or joking matters. By enjoyment of diversity, I mean that I can welcome and appreciate experiences in every field without the secret fear that some experience will shatter my faith or will at least require special measures of rationalization or relegation to avoid cracking that faith. I regard my faith not as a delicate vessel assailed by experiences but as a living, developing creature nourished by experience. This attitude has enabled me to receive with interest, rather than with stunned disillusionment or automatic disbelief, the revelations of college courses such as astronomy and religion, chemistry and sociology, and of professional legal training.

Before turning to the specific circumstances of my decision to enter the ministry, I should speak to you of my attitude toward what is called God. Briefly, I can say that I am a humanist in my understanding of the world in human terms. I see the world with human eyes, I think human thoughts, I care for human beings, and I judge by human standards. I cannot escape and do not wish to escape my human heritage, for I find no basic conflict and no sharp dividing line between humanity and divinity.

This is not to say that I am satisfied by the status quo of humanity. I find conflict within humanity, but I do not find value in labeling all the dissonances 'human' and all the harmonies 'divine.' I can also say that I am a theist in my appraisal of the fact that man is not the whole orchestra and the whole audience, much less the sole composer and the sole conductor of the universe. I want the self-respect and the down-to-earth vision of the humanist together with the humility and the up-to-the-universe vision of the theist — in short, I want a humanist rudder and a theist compass.

Many factors entered into my decision to enter the ministry, not the least of which was the background of interest and value I had always found in the field of religion. Let me first explain, however, that throughout high school and college, the orientation of my training was toward an eventual career in the foreign service. I must emphasize that this goal was always more in the nature of an assumption on which I acted rather than an ideal to which I was dedicated. How can I truly express the distinction I wish to make here? I mean that since I was thirteen, it was just taken for granted that I would train for the foreign service, that college would follow high school, that law school would follow college. Occasional re-examination of the goal only revealed that foreign service work would probably suit my aptitudes, my love of languages, and my desire for a varied experience. Yet I know now that I lacked the most important thing in a person's relationship to a goal: Commitment.

My discovery of this lack grew out of a very complex situation. The major factor was a deep dissatisfaction with law school, or more precisely, with my experience of law school.

The fatigue and pressure of the system were not in my case made bearable by the promised goal of a much-desired profession, either in law or in the foreign service, nor did I find my courses of such great intrinsic interest or inspiration that I was sustained by the pure joy of 'finding out.' I did not break under the system — I managed to graduate, at least — but I was shaken to the foundations of my life.

At one point I turned in despair to someone who then turned away from me — a person with whom I was affianced. Thus came my lesson in anguish as well as despair. I cannot overstate the situation. Ordinarily, I might have turned from study to human warmth, or from human coldness to study, but in the downward spiral from despair to anguish to despair, I found for a long time, only the black night of the soul.

I did not run away, asking religion to kiss my hurt and make it well. I did begin a rigorous re-examination of the bases of my life. I discovered first the lack of real commitment to my stated goal and how this had contributed to my difficulties. I rediscovered then the fact that throughout my life, from the time of Greek myths, through Bible study, philosophy, humanities, and even law studies, how strong ran the current of my interest in things called religious. It occurred to me that I should make use of my natural bent (Gide says that it is good to follow your bent so long as it is upward), that I should couple my interest with what talents I have.

Finally, the idea of entering the ministry began to form in my mind, not as a refuge from the world — how can I emphasize this enough? — not as a place to bury my head, but as a place to be useful in the world, the place where I could use my energies and abilities in a manner which interested and satisfied me, the place where I could use my head, and my heart, too. Now that I have made this choice, the only thing about the matter which seems strange to me is that I had not made the choice many years before.

Well, Mr. Robbins, perhaps you disapprove of my burning bush. If I could have selected my bush, I assure you that I would have found something more dramatic than dissatisfaction with legal studies, compounded by a human rejection, leading to an ultimate reappraisal of what I was doing with my life.

Eventually, very eventually, my hope is to be the minister of a small church. I do not underestimate the difficulties here. I have never found it necessary to apologize for being a woman, but I do understand that this fact presents difficulties and perhaps impossibilities. But I believe that with good training, and much work, and by gently capturing opportunities, I might succeed. And even if I never succeed, I shall find some corner in which to work, and I promise to be a cheerful failure.

What a letter from twenty-four-year-old Greta! As mentioned previously, she earned her law degree as a credential for admittance into the foreign service. It's important to note, however, even though she did not wish to pursue a career as an attorney, she has always held a great respect and admiration for the law. She sees the law as a defining benefit to our society. If a law is just, and if it is upheld appropriately, it will provide protections to citizens, which is critically important for the equitable functioning of society. If the law is not just, or if the law is not upheld appropriately, correction is called for. As we will see, this is quite relevant to Greta's core values and practices.

Next, it may not be surprising that once she arrived at her decision to become a Unitarian minister in the mid-1950's, Greta met with resistance on many fronts. One argument against her pursing this career was that no one would want to hire a woman minister. In the last lines of her letter to Dr. Wallace she states, "Eventually, very eventually, my hope is to be the minister of a small church... even if I never succeed, I shall find some corner in which to work, and I promise to be a cheerful failure."

Well, I can assure you that she did not fail in her ministerial endeavors, not in the least. She was admitted to the Meadville Theological School, and she completed her studies in May 1959. A few months later, she was called to The Church of the Reconciliation in Utica, New York, where she was ordained as a Unitarian minister in 1960.

As it turns out, Greta had the honor of being called to serve five churches in her ministerial career, which spanned five decades, from her admittance into Meadville in 1956 to her retirement in 1996. Her years of active ministry were highly rewarding, yet also incredibly challenging — and nearly impossible at times. Nevertheless, she persisted.

In her ministerial journey, Greta always maintained her timeless messages of compassion. She consistently encouraged people to think outside their self-limiting belief systems. For this, she encountered extreme controversy along the way. She never sought it out, her natural disposition is that of a genteel introvert. However, when she observed an unjust situation, she followed her inner voice of integrity. She would rally the strength within herself to name that injustice, and to make her "No" visible, in order for people to understand the need for change.

As she followed her calling, the ripple effects of her dedicated ministry touched many thousands of lives. These selected sermons from Greta's legacy are confirmation that she genuinely fulfilled her life's purpose in service to humanity.

Chapter 2

Spoken Essay Selection Process

For the early years of Greta's ministry, I relied on a helpful resource to determine which sermons to include in this book. In 1972, she compiled sixteen of her Spoken Essays for submission to the Beacon Press in Boston, which is a non-profit publisher affiliated with the UUA. This was quite fortuitous for me because I could rely on her own selection of her quality works. Three of the Spoken Essays in *All of Us Together* came from the manuscript that she submitted in 1972: "Mobile Deity," "Fantasies on Blue," and "Valley of the Shadow."

At the time she submitted her collection, the Director of the Beacon Press declined to publish it because he felt that sermons don't effectively translate into written form and he believed it wouldn't sell. I can understand his hesitation, however, I don't agree with his decision — though I freely admit I am biased. Fortunately, with easy access to self-publication venues, that decision is being righted in this very moment. As mentioned in the Preface, for me it isn't a matter of selling books, I'm just delighted that those who are meant to experience Greta's elegant compositions now have access to them!

The following is her letter to the Director of the Beacon Press when she submitted her collection of Spoken Essays in 1972.

Though there are a few dated references, I include Greta's letter here because she lists a number of reasons why they may be of interest and these reasons are just as relevant to our current edition. I love her thought process and her enthusiastic wit. [NOTE: I removed the name of the person she was writing to for the sake of anonymity.]

Greta W. Crosby
Star Route Box 10B
Helotes, Texas 78023
June 21, 1972

Director
Beacon Press
25 Beacon Street
Boston, Massachusetts 02108

Dear (Director),

What a good omen to see you not only at May meetings but at the other end of this letter! Writing nearly paralyzes me unless I can "see" someone at the other end, which is perhaps why I am condemned to the sermon as my art form.

Well, here it is. I know, I know: "Vanity, vanity, all is vanity," in both the transitory and the egoic sense. I know, I know: a book is the verbal-type's idea of the perfect tombstone. But still, a book is a more sharing tombstone than most, giving out light and warmth as well as reflecting the phosphorescence of the dead.

Lord knows, Beacon Press must have a consecrated burial ground for old sermons, or a potter's field for the shards. But against all the odds, I seem impelled to offer these relics under the hallucination that they might be of interest in one of the following categories, or perhaps as an unusual combination of diverse categories:

1. WOMAN'S WORK

No one could have cared less a few years ago for a woman's work product, but now some do. These writings were not critically composed for publication in the ordinary sense but grew out of the course of a work, a ministry. Much is now published by women "on women," mainly studies and polemics. Perhaps there is a place now for a woman's work product as such, a woman's work not so much "on women" as out of the working life of a person who is a woman.

2. DECADE

These writings involve a weaving of the themes of a decade, the sixties. Once a decade is over, it suddenly becomes an activity to look back on what people cared about then: quaint, but interesting to some.

3. SERMON AS ART FORM

The less said here the better, but it is strange that there is so little recognition of the sermon as an art form. Though set periscopes are "out," thematic interweaving is still the thing, always remembering that the words will be spoken more in an asking than a commanding way. In that respect, the sermon approaches the prayer. It also approaches the song, though somewhat epic in length.

4. DENOMINATIONAL UTILITY

The denomination needs something now that Mendelson's "Why I Am A Unitarian Universalist" is out of print. While not specifically an introduction to liberal religion, most of these writings arose in the context of the liberal church and often reflect its premises, problems and promises.

5. LOVE STORY

This category will kill Beacon's interest, perhaps, but there it is: these writings also constitute a love story, or several.

A word on the selection of the sermons: These are the most "public" and the most "private" of my writings. I began with a nucleus of five chapel talks at Hollins College, Virginia. These were made over a period of years in the chapel series of the college, which included everything from Samuel Terrien to Grace Ty-Atkinson. The chaplain regularly invited me to participate, I suspect, as an alternate role model for the young women (this, before the surge of women's liberation) as well as for anything I might say. The remainder sound my typical themes and also touch on personal "story."

I played with titles, rejecting such pleasantries as "Jill-in-the-pulpit;" "Thus Spake Greta;" and "Rev-Elations," for the dull but accurate SPOKEN ESSAYS. And I like the hidden meaning of "essay" — to try, to test, to weight and balance.

So here is my try.

Greetings to the old crew at 25 Beacon Street. I told you then I would look back upon my times in the Bookroom with you all as the Golden Age.

Cordially,
Greta W. Crosby

Along the lines of Greta's 'try' I want to comment here that this book is my 'try' in capturing and sharing the essence of her many talents.

To put Greta's life journey into context, there will be several references to historical events throughout the book. Within certain paragraphs I've included optional information links or

YouTube links for additional details about those events.

If you have a Smartphone, you don't need to input each character of the link. Depending on your phone, there may be different ways to do this, but here is how to use Google Search:

1. Open Google App on your phone.
2. To the right of the search line, click the photo icon.
3. Take a photo of the page in the book where the link appears.
4. Select & follow the highlighted link.

Including these links for historical context is one aspect of my 'try' in conveying Greta's life story. This is because there are many details that I do not know about her experiences — I'm quite curious about the many untold stories in her life that will remain unspoken. Due to her fading memory, I can't retrieve those details from her. In some cases, she won't say because of her utmost commitment to confidentiality. I've super-sleuthed some of her more public stories, through her own sermons, newspaper articles and church histories, and I hope I've gotten the details right. What is in this book that I know is right, is the inclusion of her high-quality Spoken Essays.

Introduction to "Mobile Deity"

This brings us to Greta's first Spoken Essay in our collection, which happened to be her last sermon she presented as a theological student before her graduation in May 1959. She presented it at Hull Chapel in Chicago, which was Meadville's training ground for students to present their assigned sermons. Greta was 28 years old at the time of her final student presentation entitled "Mobile Deity."

Chapter 3

"Mobile Deity"

Greta M. Worstell
Meadville's Hull Chapel
Chicago, Illinois
May 1959

[The following biblical readings were incorporated in an earlier portion of the church service, then Greta referred back to them within her Spoken Essay.]

Genesis 32:24-30 (ESV)

And Jacob was left alone. And a man wrestled with him until the breaking of the day. When the man saw that he did not prevail against Jacob, he touched his hip socket, and Jacob's hip was put out of joint as he wrestled with him. Then the man said, "Let me go, for the day has broken." But Jacob said, "I will not let you go unless you bless me." And the man said to him, "What is your name?" And he said, "Jacob." Then the man said, "Your name shall no longer be called Jacob, but Israel,[1] for you have striven with God and with men, and have prevailed." Then Jacob asked him, "Please tell me your name." But the man said, "Why is it that you ask my name?" And there the man blessed Jacob. So Jacob called the name of the place Peniel,[2] saying, "For I have seen God face to face, and yet my life has been delivered."

1. Genesis 32:28 — Israel means He strives with God, or God strives
2. Genesis 32:30 — Peniel means the face of God

Luke 24:13-18 & 28-32 (ESV)
(On the Road to Emmaus)

That very day two of them were going to a village named Emmaus, about seven miles from Jerusalem, and they were talking with each other about all these things that had happened. While they were talking and discussing together, Jesus himself drew near and went with them. But their eyes were kept from recognizing him. And he said to them, "What is this conversation that you are holding with each other as you walk?" And they stood still, looking sad. Then one of them, named Cleopas, answered him, "Are you the only visitor to Jerusalem who does not know the things that have happened there in these days?".... So they drew near to the village to which they were going. He acted as if he were going farther, but they urged him strongly, saying, "Stay with us, for it is toward evening and the day is now far spent." So he went in to stay with them. When he was at table with them, he took the bread and blessed and broke it and gave it to them. And their eyes were opened, and they recognized him. And he vanished from their sight. They said to each other, "Did not our hearts burn within us while he talked to us on the road, while he opened to us the Scriptures?"

Greta's Spoken Essay: "Mobile Deity"

To the two legends you have heard in the readings, I shall add a third from my pagan past. Perhaps you remember the Greek myth of Baucis and Philemon? This elderly couple lived a meager existence on the outskirts of a town. One evening, two travelers came to their door. The strangers had just crossed town. The townspeople refused them shelter, in an age when hospitality was a prime moral obligation, part of the structure of human survival.

Some of the townspeople had joined together to drive out the strangers. The people shouted and mocked and threw stones while the dogs barked in imitation of their masters. Baucis and Philemon, however, opened their door and shared their food and home with the travelers.

Strangely, as they served the meal, they found that the pitcher of wine was always full. And when they looked out to see the town, they saw only a lake. Then realizing that their guests were gods (Zeus & Hermes), they were afraid. But the gods willed only blessings for them. They asked the couple to choose the gift that they most desired. Baucis and Philemon quickly agreed that what they wanted most was to live out their lives together in serving the gods and to die at the same instant to spare each one the sorrow of surviving the other. And so it was. Their house became a shining temple and they, its priest and priestess. Many years later, as they walked on the temple grounds, their feet ceased to move. As they said goodbye, one transformed into an oak tree, the other into a linden tree, with branches intertwined, as though they were holding hands.

In the Jewish legend found in Genesis, Jacob meets a stranger and strives with him for his blessing. When dawn comes, and Jacob has prevailed, Jacob realizes that he has seen God, face to face. In Christian legend, the disciples travel a road and meet a stranger, and at last it dawns on them that they have been in the presence of their friend and savior.

Throughout the world, gods in disguise travel through myth and folklore, bestowing gifts on those who receive them humanely and dealing swift justice to the inhumane. Our TV Western is only a late and sometimes strident variation on the theme of the wandering divinity, the cosmic Lone Ranger, the mobile deity.

In liberal churches, we frequently adopt the metaphor of pilgrimage. We think of ourselves as pilgrims on a journey to a great city, the City of God or the City of Man; or, as seekers of the way, sometimes lost, sometimes found, but at least on the go — like the apocryphal telegram reporting a minor train derailment in Ireland: "Off again, on again, gone again, Finnegan." Of course, we are not stodgy pilgrims but singing and story-telling pilgrims, perhaps a bit more like the spinners of the Canterbury Tales than the Puritanical landers on Plymouth Rock.

The pilgrim or seeker image is so basic to us that my meek suggestion that another image might also be in order, should not be construed as a demand for carting away the pilgrim. On the contrary, it was only in clutching firmly my pilgrim's staff that it ever occurred to me that the wandering god might be a pilgrim, too, in search, not of a City, but of the citizens. Those citizens who will bid welcome when a knock is heard upon their door.

Without the hope of visitation from the god, however fleeting, the religious pilgrim engages in a search for reward in the never-never land of the future, whether in form of terrestrial paradise or in seeking Utopia. If we inherit life only at the end, we are in danger of acting like poor relations, plotting for inheritance and fighting amongst ourselves in the meantime.

And what of non-pilgrims? Suppose we are not on our way to anywhere, just living out our days in a tiny orbit, or else revolving in intricate frantic circles? What is our hope except the visit of the god in disguise? What is our chance of life and meaning in those moments when we lose all hope, if not the chance of meeting that which sparks life and meaning? And what of those of us who have chosen to be nomads and have imposed the shape of the nomadic life on the lives of those attached to us by links of affection and responsibility? What can we promise each day to them, and to ourselves, but the possible gifts of the mobile deity; the fruits of the Spirit that bloweth where it listeth?

The classical list of the fruits of the Spirit includes: love, joy & peace, patience & kindness, tolerance & generosity, integrity & self-discipline. I have no quarrel with this list — it covers the waterfront. But I prefer to note that the gift of the wandering god to Baucis and Philemon was a pitcher of wine that could not run dry, a life of service, and a death without sorrow — and, to the dejected disciples, the wandering god gave nothing less than himself.

I do not know what gifts the mobile deity has given you. Perhaps you will tell me one day. For myself, I will mention one not usually listed. When the god asked me what I wanted most, I said: "A talent for serenity." In my case, however, the gift wandered, as well as the god, and I received instead a penchant for serendipity. My mobile deity is at least consistently mobile! I still have a hankering after serenity, but it really cannot compare with serendipity, the finding of unexpected joy when you are doing something else.

For example, one time I was busily writing a sermon in a swan boat on the pond in the Boston Public Garden. I was very intent, you know, busily crossing out everything I had written. Suddenly, one of the smaller passengers in the row ahead of me asked his mother, "Mommy, is that bird a fish?" "No," said his mother patiently, "that's a duck." "Then, Mommy, why does it have eyes on its nose?" It almost makes sermon-writing worthwhile.

I also remember an incident that occurred when I was working as an attendant in a psychiatric ward to eke out my existence during my last year in theological school. One evening I was assigned to a patient who was seriously disturbed. She was to stay in her room and not mingle with the other patients on the ward because she frightened them. I was to remain with her while she was hallucinating. It was carefully explained to me that her strange actions were due to fear, that she was presently suffering from terrifying hallucinations, and that what she needed most was a reassuring presence instead of fear, anger or desertion in return.

I sat in her room, a small bare detention room that had been stripped of all but bed and chair. I was aware of much white, a bright light in the high ceiling; the stark white linen; even my pale green uniform seemed almost a shade of white. Only her head was dark on the pillow as she writhed and moaned and cried out. For a long while I sat watching her twist and turn, listening to her voice, unable even to understand the words, for in her delirium she spoke in her native tongue, Chinese. I thought of the fearful apparitions she must be seeing and struggling against. And once I wondered whether they were patterned on ancient oriental demonry, or, on the grotesque creatures of modern civilization.

While I watched, her agitation grew more intense until some kind of crisis-point was reached. She stiffened for a moment. Then she was still. She slept quietly, breathing slowly and deeply, as if she were a child in gentle slumber. After some minutes she awoke and looked at me with lucid eyes and said two words in English: "Thank you."

And yet it was *I* who would have gone down on my knees, had I dared, to thank her for the two intertwined serendipities I had witnessed that night. First was a strength in myself. I had felt no fear whatsoever, allowing my calm presence to be a comfort for her. And the second was a strength in the woman, and I had watched the signs of it: I had seen a woman lost in a terrifying, far-away hell come back to herself. Mysterious strength, welling up from within us — unexpected gifts of the mobile deity.

The principle of the mobile deity has many implications. Take education, for example, religious and otherwise. Like pilgrims, we must have roads to follow and goals to draw us on, but we must always resist being 'educated' into rejection of the god wandering in disguise. The penalty for ignoring or rejecting the mobile deity is simply stated in the story of Baucis and Philemon. We must either remain hospitable to the unknown messenger, or we, jointly and severally, will die a stagnant death and perhaps submerge even the City we seek in a new flood.

We have explored many aspects of the mobile deity, but finally I want to say something about its guise or disguise. It is perfectly clear that the mobile deity we are called upon to welcome does not come as a mighty king, thrower of banquets, much less as a deity robed in unearthly glory, but as the stranger who asks to share our table.

The stranger comes to us daily in the only form that is meaningful to us, in human form, in human ideas and needs, and most particularly, in human beings seen — not as anonymous humanity — but as you see me and others by name. As one of my favorite ministers, Karel Botermans, once said: "I don't give a damn about brotherhood." The damn you give is for the guy in front of you, in person, built on flesh and blood. And the damn is given not only for what makes him tick but what makes him ache. Giving a damn is the response the mobile deity asks, and the reward is simply your response, itself transmuted by the touch of the wandering god, into abundance of life.

May we be grateful for the gift of life: the life of the body, the life of the mind, and the life of the Spirit. And, may we show forth our gratitude in strong, joyful and ingenious endeavor, churchly and unchurchly, that all may live more abundantly.

Amen

CHAPTER 4

The Late 1950s

Follow-Up on "Mobile Deity"

WHAT A delightful exploration of the wandering deity. Something I've noticed in many of Greta's Spoken Essays are certain themes that she touches on in her word weavings. We'll see references to pilgrimages, the symbolism of a city and its citizens, as well as basic human survival rights. She often advocates for access to provisions for a decent life — reasonable opportunities to work and to gain access to food and shelter.

Though they didn't appear in "Mobile Deity," she also refers to shadows, with various connotations associated with them, some darker-themed and some more whimsical. She sometimes references one of her foundational religious ideals from childhood, that of not hiding our light under a bushel. Another theme that she occasionally incorporates is the concept of 'taming.' She uses the idea in terms of intimately knowing someone or something — learning something significant about them. The symbolism of taming, particularly in her later years, has deep meaning for Greta.

The one theme that comes up in nearly every Spoken Essay, interview, or letter to the editor, is her emphasis on turning the tables, to be able to see and understand the life circumstances that our fellow human beings are experiencing. She models how to extend compassion for every individual, even if they're displaying defensive or short-sighted behaviors. She overlooks appearances, finding the shining Light within people, even if they cannot see it in themselves. What a gift that is! In her 1959 Spoken Essay, "Mobile Deity," Greta is already wise beyond her years, sharing the gift of humanitarian Vision in her final sermon before graduation.

Finding Placement

In her last year of theological school, she presented her Spoken Essays at various Unitarian churches around the country, mostly in the eastern states. Among others, these locations included Decatur, Illinois; New London, Connecticut; Greenfield, Massachusetts; Boston, Massachusetts; and Utica, New York.

As a woman minister, it did take a little longer for Greta to find placement, so after her graduation in May 1959, she worked in Boston at the UUA's headquarters and in the bookroom at Beacon Press. A few months later, she was called to The Church of the Reconciliation in Utica to be their first female parish minister. And it was there that she was ordained in 1960. (At the time, the church was called The Church of the Reconciliation, and because of the Unitarian and Universalist consolidation in 1961, it is currently called the Unitarian Universalist Church of Utica.)

Unrequited Love

On a more personal note, my mom has said that she spent the majority of her twenties majoring in unrequited love. Either someone was interested in her, but she did not feel the same way; or she was smitten with another who did not return the affection. I recall a story she told about a time when she was at home on a college break, Greta was so preoccupied with the man in her life, she cracked an egg and plopped it into her coffee cup. She apologized to her mom, saying, "Oh, I'm sorry, it's just that I'm in love." Her mom replied, "So am I still just as in love with your father."

As mentioned in her application to Meadville, a young man had proposed to her while she was in law school, she had accepted and she was over-the-moon with excitement. But after a few months, it became clear that his commitment to marrying had dwindled. This deep disappointment contributed to Greta's dark night of the soul and it took quite a while for the light to return.

A little while after being ordained in Utica, Greta met my father, Robert Crosby. He was originally from Boston where he had earned a degree in electrical engineering from Tufts University. He was working for General Electric and he had been transferred to Utica for a time. After attending her services, he decided to call and ask her out on a date. They courted for a time and then they were married on January 28, 1961.

A 1962 newspaper article quotes Greta describing her time at Utica's Church of the Reconciliation as "the most marvelous experience of my life."

The following is an excerpt from an email from Sally Carman, who was a church member at that time:

> Yes, I remember Greta Worstell. We started at the church on Oneida Square in 1960 when she was minister and when we had first moved to this area. I came from a Presbyterian tradition, and my husband came from no tradition. I remember I liked her very much. She was a favorite of the matriarchs of our church...I remember that Verna Carncross kept up

correspondence with her and used to tell me about her.

So life was going well for Greta, she had found both a beloved church and a husband with an intellect that matched her own.

However, a change was around the corner — a change that would be severely challenging. My vibe tells me that Greta's messages of compassion for humanity were desperately needed elsewhere. Though she may not have chosen the next stepping-stone in her career path, I believe it chose her, and as we will see, she was needed in this new location for very important reasons.

Section II

The 1960s

This poem by Greta was included in the UU hymnal, Singing the Living Tradition, as a responsive reading:

"Winter"

Let us not wish away the winter.
It is a season unto itself,
Not simply the way to spring.
When trees rest, growing no leaves, gathering no light,
They let in sky and trace themselves delicately against dawns and sunsets.

The clarity and brilliance of the winter sky delight.
The loom of fog softens edges, lulls the eyes and ears of the quiet,
Awakens by risk the unquiet.
A low dark sky can snow, emblem of individuality, liberality, and aggregate power.
Snow invites to contemplation and to sport.

Winter is a table set with ice and starlight.
Winter dark tends to warm light: fire and candle;
Winter cold to hugs and huddles; winter want to gifts and sharing;
Winter danger to visions, plans, and common endeavoring —
and the zest of narrow escapes;
Winter tedium to merrymaking.

Let us therefore praise winter,
Rich in beauty, challenge, and pregnant negativities.

— Greta W. Crosby

Chapter 5

The Early 1960s

The Move to Virginia

GRETA knew when she married Bob that they would be moving to Virginia, where he would work at General Electric. He also planned to study biomedical engineering at the University of Virginia. In June of 1961, they moved from Utica, New York to Lynchburg, Virginia, and she applied for placement at various Unitarian churches in the area.

The Roanoke Valley Unitarian Church (currently called the Unitarian Universalist Church of Roanoke, UUCR) was a growing community. Being established in 1954, they moved into a building in 1960, then they purchased the building in 1961. They didn't have a minister at the time, so they had a rotation of guest speakers coming in each Sunday. They invited Greta as a guest speaker on September 17, 1961.

According to their historical record, which was written by William H. Hackworth, they were genuinely impressed with her. Subsequently, they decided to take a giant step forward by retaining her as the first minister of their church, on a part-time basis, on January 1, 1962. She was formally installed on March 11, 1962. Here is a description of their appreciation for her Spoken Essays:

Rev. Crosby's sermons were thoughtfully prepared, idealistic, and poetic. She had a very special way with words and could turn everyday happenings into something beauti-ful. Members found listening to her to be an enriching experience.

Then on May 20, 1962, she was also installed as a half-time minister at the First Unitarian Church of Lynchburg (currently called the Unitarian Universalist Congregation of Lynchburg, UUCL). She spoke once a month at Roanoke, twice a month at Lynchburg, and for the remaining week of the month, she often traveled to other locations as a guest speaker.

Gradually she developed her ministries in both Roanoke and Lynchburg. In Roanoke, Greta stepped up as editor of the church's monthly newsletter, which she called "The Roanoke Unitarian." Her home was about 50 miles away from Roanoke. When she was in Roanoke for her Sunday sermon, she would stay the weekend with a different family for an opportunity to get to know them better. She conducted Saturday evening discussions when she was in town, which were enthusiastically attended. The UUCR history also notes that at least once a week she drove to Roanoke to attend a meeting or an activity to maintain a presence in their church.

The UU Congregation of Lynchburg's historical documentation, written by Mary Frances Williams, describes some innovations that Greta brought to their congregation. Since Bob and Greta lived in the country near Lynchburg, she was able to hold Sunday evening discussions with college students, as well as a mid-week adult discussion session.

Greta encouraged the use of orders of service for Sunday services, which had not been utilized before. She updated educational materials for the Church School. Additionally, she reached out to other colleagues in the community and surrounding areas, forming friendships and professional bonds. This broadened the list of guest speakers who came to speak at their church on the weeks that Greta was not in the pulpit. She also provided supportive pastoral care to both of her congregations in the years of her ministry with them.

Challenging Times

Though there were numerous fulfilling aspects to her ministries in Virginia, Greta's life journey in the early 1960s marks a time of emotional controversy and important life lessons. We tend to say that the 2020's are unprecedented times of fear, conflict and polarization. I wouldn't exactly agree. I believe the 1960s bore as much if not more intensity and controversy, particularly with regard to the Civil Rights Movement, as well as the Vietnam War.

With her move to Virginia, Greta had more exposure to the appalling racial injustices practiced in the segregated South. The Civil Rights movement was beginning to build momentum, but there was profound resistance to change. Greta recalled that transformative time in a service she conducted in 1989, in honor of Dr. Martin Luther King, Jr.'s national holiday. Her sermon was entitled "Remembering," and in it she recounts how she was impacted by Dr. King's inspiring messages in the early 1960s:

> I remember hearing Dr. Martin Luther King, Jr. I heard him first in a public meeting in Lynchburg, Virginia, in the early sixties as he traveled from place to place speaking the word of dignity, the word of hope, the word of change, the word of love impelled by spirit with power. He spoke aloud the word that was written in the hearts of people who did not want to live any more under the codes of inequality. We who heard

Ch 5 - THE EARLY 1960s

our unspoken word spoken aloud, realized that together we could change those codes, first in ourselves and then in our shared world.

As we will see in this section, that powerful experience directly influenced Greta's ministries in Virginia in the 1960s. I've included three of her Spoken Essays in this section, all from the year 1963, and all of which uniquely address the Civil Rights Movement. The first is entitled "Justice Without a Blindfold" — March 3rd; next is "Fantasies on Blue" — July 28th; and finally, "Valley of the Shadow" — November 10th.

The reason these compositions are included here is because "Fantasies on Blue" and "Valley of the Shadow" were in Greta's 1972 Spoken Essays manuscript. What I did not know for several years is that "Valley of the Shadow," which was presented at Roanoke's Hollins College in November 1963, is actually a toned-down version of an impassioned Commentary, "Justice Without a Blindfold," which she boldly delivered to her congregation at the First Unitarian Church in Lynchburg in March 1963.

I was not aware of this until May 2021, when I was contacted by Dale Brumfield, an author who has written over ten books on criminal justice reform and other social justice matters (see *dalebrumfield.net*). His book project in 2021 involved researching the history of activists supporting the abolition of the death penalty in Virginia. He informed me that in the early 1960s, Greta was among the very first people in Virginia to strongly advocate for the abolition of the death penalty. He said that she and a few other religious leaders formed a multi-racial abolitionist organization in Virginia called "Death to Death," to advocate for criminal justice reform.

Then he described what motivated the organization to forge a path of change into Virginia's corrupt criminal justice system. Brumfield explained that in 1963, a black teenager named Thomas Wansley had been sentenced to death after being wrongfully convicted of rape and robbery.

This caused me to search Greta's 1963 files for any reference to the Death to Death initiative. I did not find any specific references to the organization, but I did find something quite surprising to me. I discovered her sermon from March 3, 1963, "Justice Without a Blindfold," which was an impassioned Commentary on Lynchburg's segregationist practices, where she specifically referred to Thomas Wansley's case.

With more research, I found out that the reasons Greta had for delivering this powerful Commentary were genuinely monumental. Before exploring her 1963 Spoken Essays, let's go over Thomas Wansley's controversial case, which will put the study of "Justice Without a Blindfold" and "Valley of the Shadow" into context.

The Thomas Wansley Story

Virginia is a mid-South commonwealth, and in the times leading up to the 1960s, segregation and vitriolic racism was alive and rampant in the Lynchburg community. In my research I have found several references to 1960s Lynchburg as a 'sick community,' very resistant to integration, and the following accounts corroborate this assessment.

The Foreword to Part 1 of Dale Brumfield's book, *Closing the Slaughterhouse*, is entitled, "The Thomas Wansley Story — A textbook case of Corruption and Racial Injustice in the 20th Century."

On December 14, 1960, a sit-in was staged at Patterson's Drug

Store, protesting racial segregation at the lunch counter — four white students and two black students were present. Interestingly, the organist for the Unitarian Church of Lynchburg, Mary Edith Bentley, was one of those who participated in the protest. Brumfield explains, "They were arrested, and a hostile judge, Joseph McCarron, sentenced them to 30 days in jail, where they served 21 days total. Afterward, the students faced ostracism from their friends, families, and churches."

According to a February 15, 1961 article in the *Daily Advance*, on February 13th there was another sit-in at Patterson's Drugstore with eight people arrested. Then on February 14, 1961, a picket line formed in front of Patterson's Drugstore in protest of the arrests. In subsequent months, the community continued to experience heightened racial tension as the legal appeals process ensued.

Brumfield explains that as a result of these events, several local white male leaders in positions of power retaliated against the rising Civil Rights Movement by arresting, convicting and sentencing 16-year-old Thomas Wansley to death for crimes he did not commit. This systematic "railroading" was deliberately orchestrated in order to send a message to the black community that sit-ins and such protests would be put down quickly, painfully, and with dire consequences to the entire black community.

Thomas Wansley's case was handled so corruptly that it took fifteen years to finally resolve. As we review some of the historical details, and Greta's Spoken Essay in response to this case, please keep in mind that the term 'Negro' was commonly used at that time. Brumfield describes in his Foreword:

> The page-one headline seemed almost a benign afterthought—'Preliminary Hearing Set for Negro Charged in Rape Cases.' However, the accompanying story, cynically created

by the publishers of the Lynchburg *Daily Advance* in the Dec. 10, 1962 edition, contained particular buzzwords, loaded phrases, and flat-out false assertions, such as that Wansley had confessed to four attacks. It seemed intended less to report the capture of a suspected rapist but more to embarrass, intimidate, and send a message to Lynchburg's Black Community.

And this was just the beginning. The Lynchburg courts, law enforcement, and the white-owned local press would go on to meticulously construct a public and personally damning narrative about this Black teenager with no prior records, criminalizing him long before his first 1963 trial and long afterward.

Thomas was a dishwasher at the Virginia Grill and he was arrested at his place of work on December 8, 1962. Even though numerous newspaper articles list Thomas as 18, he was 16 years old when he was arrested. To me it seems that his age was misquoted to make that fact that he was being tried as an adult look more acceptable. Brumfield's description continues:

> After a short questioning, they charged and arrested him for the Dec. 5 rape and robbery of a white woman named Annie Carter and the mid-November rape of another Japanese-American woman, Kyoko Fleshman. They also charged him with a third attempted rape and the robbery of $1.37 in bus change.
>
> Wansley had no prior arrests and had never been in any trouble. What led the police to him?
>
> Wansley told his attorney, Reuben Lawson, that he had been having a consensual affair (consisting of two previous liaisons) with Fleshman, who lived not far from where he

worked. One night her husband unexpectedly came home and almost caught them. Wansley escaped through a window, and Fleshman told her husband she had been raped.

Fleshman tried to get Wansley to resume the affair a few days later, but he prudently declined her invitation. But when the attack on Carter occurred, Fleshman threatened to tell police that Wansley had raped her and probably the other woman if he refused to resume the affair. Still, Wansley declined, so she contacted the police and told them she knew who raped her and Ann Carter. That ID led to his subsequent arrest, trial and conviction.

After his arrest, because he was 16, he was booked in the Juvenile Court where he was interrogated for five hours without a lawyer present. Even before his hearing, a judge illegally declared that Thomas Wansley would be tried as an adult. On Dec. 18, he was briefly questioned by a physician and he was deemed competent to stand trial.

Then in January 1963, it was ruled that Wansley would be tried as an adult. Brumfield points out, "This decision was significant because in Juvenile Court, Wansley could not get a death sentence — but being tried as an adult assured he would."

Brumfield also reveals that, "Five weeks before the trial, a vital defense witness, Sylvester Dickerson, who was to testify that he was also an acquaintance of Fleshman's and had supposed proof of Wansley's innocence, was found stabbed to death."

The trial was held on Feb. 7, 1963, but no court reporter showed up to record the notes of the trial. For this reason, Wansley's attorney requested a continuance, and in a distinctly inappropriate ruling by Judge Raymond Cundiff, the continuance was denied.

This ensured that no transcript of the trial existed, and not surprisingly, there were other legal side-steps throughout the trial.

One important aspect was that Annie Carter, the 59-year-old woman who had been raped and robbed on December 5th, had been unable to pick Thomas Wansley out of a lineup. Then at the trial she testified that she was "not too sure" that Wansley was her attacker.

And yet, Brumfield explains that Thomas Wansley was convicted and sentenced by an all-white jury "to death for the Carter rape and twenty-years imprisonment for a robbery of $1.37 from her. Five days later, Wansley was found guilty of raping Fleshman and received a second death sentence." He was scheduled for execution on June 7, 1963.

This series of blatant, racially-motivated maneuvers was greatly upsetting to Lynchburg's black community. Adding insult to injury was the fact that only a few months before Thomas Wansley's case was tried, another case had been handled by the same judge. Police officers had arrested a white man, George Brooks, 37, who was in the act of raping an 11-year-old black girl — yet Brooks had been treated completely differently. He was released on bond and he was given the benefit of a thorough mental examination that delayed his trial for several months.

At his trial, Brooks was found guilty of statutory rape and perjury, and then the same judge, Raymond Cundiff, who subsequently mishandled Wansley's trial, sentenced Brooks to five years in prison (but he ended up serving only two years). Typically, statutory rape is considered as having consensual sex with a post-pubescent person who is still under-age, and it usually implies a lesser crime than the act of rape. An 11-year-old is still a child — she would not be post-pubescent and she would not be capable of consenting to sexual relations with a 37-year-old male.

Lynchburg's black community was understandably concerned about Wansley's extreme punishment of death for falsified rape convictions, especially in light of the Brooks case that was handled by the same judge. This caused black leaders to stand up and draw attention to the injustice that was inevitably unfolding for Thomas Wansley. Brumfield explains what happened next:

> As news of Wansley's case spread, white people started speaking out. One of them was Rev. Greta Crosby, who was also the secretary of the Lynchburg Council on Human Relations. In response she and others founded a local, interracial death penalty abolition group called, "Death to Death."

Reflections on Capital Punishment

Now I'd like to step back for a moment to reflect on Greta's belief that the death penalty is a primitive, outdated form of punishment that should be abolished. Others may or may not agree with this, however, my opinion is completely aligned with Greta's. First and foremost, in the example of execution for murder, my question has always been, 'If killing is wrong, how can more killing in the form of execution, be right?' The logic is irrational.

In addition, innocent people have been executed, and that is an enormous flaw in the practice. That's the deal-breaker right there. Another reason is that an imbalanced number of people of color, specifically black people, are executed. For example, Brumfield's book states that from the year 1908 to 1962, the commonwealth of Virginia performed 236 executions, and of those 236 executions, 201 were black Virginian citizens.

Later in his book, Brumfield includes excerpts from Greta's Spoken Essay entitled "The Sequel to Punishment," which she first presented in Roanoke, Virginia, on October 29, 1961, well before Thomas Wansley's trial occurred:

> I think that vengeance, like all evil, has its origin in good. I think it began as a part of the impulse to self-defense... but somehow, as man left animalhood and developed mind and memory and then machines, he twisted and exalted this aggressive tendency all out of proportion to the need of self-defense; he carefully nurtured within himself the cancer of vengeance and called it ennobling. What began in the power of life was bent back upon itself and became death-dealing...
>
> ...Let me then speak for myself and say that to my sorrow, I have often felt the unwelcome white heat of vengeful anger within me. It is my unwilled first reaction to various situations. It contradicts my knowledge and understanding, but there it is... My first reaction to the report of a heinous act, one that outrages by horror, such as molesting and murdering a child — my first reaction is that boiling oil is too good for the malefactor. And yes, I know better. I know that as a general rule, the more bizarre and horrible the act, the less responsible the actor is for the act.

Greta's call was for careful consideration of what would cause a person to perform a heinous crime. She called for justice in terms of compassion for all parties involved. And even though she may not have been aware of all the factors that proved Thomas Wansley's innocence, she still advocated for him because she knew with every fiber of her being that executing him was entirely unjust.

Introduction to "Justice Without a Blindfold"
This brings us to Greta's bold Commentary she delivered to

the First Unitarian Church of Lynchburg on March 3, 1963, when she was 31 years of age. I find it eloquent, passionate, and well-reasoned — with loads of subtle yet powerful messages to be gleaned from in-between-the-lines. Near the end of her Commentary, she refers to both Thomas Wansley's and George Brooks' cases and speaks of the details as if the congregation is aware of them, which most of them very likely were.

That portion of her composition is not as polished, but I feel this is because the details of Thomas Wansley's case, and the efforts of the Death to Death organization, were unfolding minute-by-minute. With regard to the systemic illegal subterfuge practiced in Thomas Wansley's case, keep in mind that Greta holds a law degree and she has a great respect for the laws of our society, and great expectations of the law to provide equal protections to our citizens. But when the law is not upheld, when due process is contaminated with deliberate corruption, she *will* feel compelled to stand up and speak out.

And now we are ready to experience Greta's powerful Spoken Essay, "Justice Without a Blindfold."

Chapter 6

"Justice Without a Blindfold"

Greta W. Crosby
The First Unitarian Church of Lynchburg
Lynchburg, Virginia
March 3, 1963

[The following readings were incorporated into the church service before the sermon, then Greta referred back to them within her Spoken Essay.]

Greta's Reading for Meditation:
From A. Powell Davies, *The Urge to Persecute*

Most of you have heard of A. Powell Davies, who was the long-time minister of All Soul's Church in Washington D.C., the Unitarian church that John Calhoun helped found in 1821. Here are his words for contemplation in context of today's service:

A minister of religion has many duties, some of which are quiet and inconspicuous, and no one minds if he is zealous in attending to them. If, however, he performs with equal zeal the duty of applying religion to a public issue and is widely heard, he will be sharply criticized. This he expects — not because he thinks he has overstepped the boundaries of his ministerial obligations, but because he knows that religion, if it be authentic, is greatly feared and widely misconstrued.

The reason for this is not obscure. Religion measures all things by its claim for righteousness. Since such a claim, to many folks, seems too exacting, they try to set a limit to it. Religion must be walled in, preferably beneath the roof of churches.

The Kingdom of God must be a prayer, not a program; justice must be an aspiration, not an intention; and love must be a mood and not on any account, a motivation. If, therefore, a minister applies his religion to the factors which are shaping history, rebuking unrighteousness where it is most damaging, he is told that this is not his province.

The answer is, in the first place, that such an argument does not make sense and whatever does not make sense is bad religion. How could it make sense that a minister should plead for righteousness in his own parish and keep silence when righteousness is being mocked in the total sum of all the parishes that constitutes a nation? Moreover, no minister is confined within the boundaries of a single parish. He vows himself to serve the brotherhood of man. Wherever, then, the brotherhood of man requires his service, he must try to serve it.

There are those who say that this may be, but still the duty of a minister is to 'stay out of politics' and 'preach his sermons from the Bible.' Without conceding this, I feel bound to point out that those who demand it, have very little knowledge of the Bible. What do they think of the preacher Nathan, who went to King David, and pointing his finger at him said, 'Thou art the man'? What do they say of Elijah, who publicly condemned Queen Jezebel? Or of Amos, a preacher self-ordained, who went to the capital city of Samaria to tell the nation's rulers that God has grown weary of their sins? Or of Isaiah, a preacher from an aristocratic family who was nevertheless a reformer and who told King Hezekiah that religion had a place in foreign policy? Or of Jeremiah, who foretold of the doom of a nation that forsook its moral principles? Or — about cleansing the Temple, but who took 'a whip of cords' and drove the grafters from its precincts in complete defiance of the alliance of priests and politicians?

Any minister worthy of his ordination will take these as his examples, and knowing the Bible better than his critics, will pray for the wisdom and courage to be as forthright and as faithful as the Bible preachers. Even, however, if the Bible tradition were otherwise, and if there had never been any John Knoxes, Savonarolas,* or Theodore Parkers, the condition of the modern world requires that preachers deal with public questions. We live at a time of indescribable peril and with almost no margin of error. Even at best, we may not avoid calamities. We do not know. But we do know — or should — that only through calm, deliberate wisdom, inspired by benevolent justice and an unflagging zeal for righteousness, can we hope to be saved. That, above all, is why religion, even though its spokesmen are fallible, and make no other claim than that they speak what conscience has commanded, must be extended to the uttermost. Less than that would be betrayal.

*Girolamo Savonarola (1452–1498) was a Dominican friar active in Renaissance Florence who denounced clerical corruption, despotic rule and the exploitation of the poor.

Amos 5: 21-24

I hate, I despise your feasts, and I take no delight in your solemn assemblies.

Even though you offer me your burnt offerings and cereal offerings, I will not accept them; and the peace offerings of your fatted beasts, I will not look upon.

Take away from me the noise of your songs; to the melody of your harps, I will not listen.

But let justice roll down like waters, and righteousness, like an ever-flowing stream.

Reading From Simone Weil's *Intimations of Christianity Among the Greeks* (1958):

There are three mysteries in human life of which all human beings, even the most mediocre, have more or less knowledge.

One is beauty.

Another is the work of pure intelligence applied...to the understanding of the world...

The last are those flashes of justice, of compassion, of gratitude which rise-up sometimes in human relationships in the midst of harshness and metallic coldness.

Here are three supernatural mysteries constantly present right in human nature.

From *St. Joan of the Stockyards* by Bertolt Brecht (1931) — Joan is dying, and as she comes to the end of her life, she looks back with regret:

One thing I have learned and I know it in your stead
Dying myself: How can I say it —
there's something inside you
And it won't come out! What do you know in your wisdom
That has no consequences?
I, for instance, did nothing.
Oh, let nothing be counted good,
however helpful it may seem
And nothing considered honourable, except that

Which will change this world once and for all:
that's what it needs.
Like an answer to their prayers I came to the oppressors!
Oh, goodness without consequences!
Intentions in the dark!
I have changed nothing.
Swiftly vanishing without fear from the world
I say to you:
Take care that when you leave the world
You were not only good, but are leaving
A good world!

Greta's Spoken Essay: "Justice Without a Blindfold"

The last few times I have been with you, we have been discussing various things related to the general theme of expiation, the need to make right the wrongs of the past. We have spoken of the religious liberal's possible release from traditional guilt-centered or legalistic religious systems, but we have also affirmed his participation in the basic human needs underlying traditional systems.

We have said that so long as the religious liberal holds anything at all to be of value, there will always be ways of preserving, enhancing and manifesting what he holds to be of value — and on the contrary, there will also be ways of destroying what he holds dear. Since wrongdoing is our possibility — in fact, our actuality — we, too, have need of reflection and self-examination in order to become more aware of ourselves and of the nature and consequences of our actions; we, too, have need of expiation, that is, of finding ways to enter into a more living rather than deadening relationship with what we hold to be of value; we, too, have need to invite renewal of spirit.

Last time, I spoke of some of the functions of the outward and visible signs of Lent and other established seasons of penitence. I hoped to evoke appreciation even, for the methodology of these seasons, without suggesting mass imitation of the particular customs involved. I did, however, suggest that we recognize the need of our children for appropriate outward and visible signs of their own, for tangible manifestations of their developing values and their participation in a religious community.

This morning, I wish to share with you a meditation in the Lenten vein. I shall not be concerned only with wrongdoing, but also with saving graces. Herein, I reflect on encounters with the Lynchburg community, the part that lives in shadow. What casts the shadow? Monumental crimes of the past; cowardly ones of the present. Who casts the shadow? All those who perpetuate the crimes; all those who consent to the crimes; all those who acquiesce in the crimes; all those who blindly benefit from the crimes; all those who benefit from the crimes *even* if they engage in active and apt expiation of them, and so, add to the shadow a mite of light.

You and I, without exception, cast the shadow.

I know that in the minds of some, I have neither birthright nor seniority-right in this city and therefore no right to tell forth what I have seen. Let me claim, then, only the child-right of new eyes — have you never seen an old world made new through the eyes of a child? Or perhaps it is Lynchburg that is like the child for me, a chosen child, an adopted child, a child for whom I have passionate hopes for *growth* in wisdom and in spiritual stature. To others I must leave uncritical reverence for Lynchburg, the honored parent, and to others yet, I must leave affectionate toleration for Lynchburg, the friend of a fullness of years.

For me the valley of the shadow began at the foot of Monument Terrace. My husband had brought me to see this church. He had told me long before of the beauty of its setting. I loved the stairway at first sight, its impracticality even, its ancient symbolism of the hard ascending pilgrim's path.

And then, the shadow fell across my way. Have you ever stopped to see the World War I memorial at our feet? Have you ever followed the names of the men who died in that preparatory carnage, and then paused due to a blank space on the slab, and then read the word "colored," then, two more names? Segregated *names*, segregated in a common cause, and on stone, and in death.

That was the cold baptism that sealed all my previous catechismic education in books and newspapers and stereotypic jokes. And still I resisted. I said to myself; but I *must not judge* on the basis of a World War I memorial — World War I was my father's first war. That was a long time ago.

The spell of my baptism was still upon me, however, when I ascended the steps and walked to the *newly-constructed* courthouse. Perhaps that was why I shuddered when I saw the figure of Justice over the door. Justice — *without* a blindfold.

Why is Justice blindfolded in ancient symbolism? Justice wears a blindfold in sign of *impartiality*. Justice does not look to see whether the parties in controversy are richly attired or in rags, native or immigrant, male or female, white or Negro. Again, I resisted. Perhaps it means that Justice has her eyes wide open, carefully considering all the evidence with wisdom? But this Justice turned away from the scales of evidence and was preoccupied with the sword. She even grasped the sword by the blade below the hilt, so that in executing her judgments, she would injure *herself*.

Between the old war memorial and the new law memorial, there is another monument at Monument Terrace — a spirit memorial (The First Unitarian Church of Lynchburg). This is the monument to freedom and responsibility in religion. For me, it was the saving grace of the day, a reminder of Simone Weil's third mystery: that there *are* "flashes of justice, of compassion, of gratitude which rise up in the midst of harshness and metallic coldness." And more, this monument became the very holy ground on which I stood when I experienced such a mystery. Not that the monument sponsored this mystery, but at least let it happen here.

There was a long preparation for this mystical experience:
- My mother's attitude when I was four and startled by the unaccustomed sight of a dark-skinned woman who was helping her. "Now, Greta, don't be afraid, she's just the same as we are."
- My school and college textbooks, carefully dealing with 'racial theories' and their distortions in racist doctrines.
- A few classmates and friends of friends, but at such a distance!
- The *obvious* corollaries of religious doctrines of brotherhood, political theories of democracy, and psychological concepts of human development.
- The personal decision that I *would not* consent or quietly acquiesce in the division and torment of fellow human beings.

But still the preparation had not sufficed to carry me through my first encounters with groups of Negroes and whites together without an acute awareness of duality: black and white. In part, this was the familiar phenomenon of becoming acutely aware of anything that you are trying particularly hard to forget. And also, it was a function of being a stranger when *any* new group seems somewhat blurred into non-individuality; the difference here is that there were two contrasting non-individual blurs. But mainly it was the symptom of the inner force of actual segregation which had long shaped my customs and expectations, and even what I saw.

I cannot tell you what it meant to me one evening in this very place when I suddenly realized that I no longer saw a checkerboard, but a rainbow; not black and white but a spectrum of color; pink and beige and gold and tan and brown, with highlights and shadows of all colors — and this was only in the outer eye; the inward eye was beginning to distinguish *persons*. For me, it was a burning bush, the birth of the Christ child, the descent of the tongues of flame.

What *is* religion but the fall of false barriers, the rending of the veil of temples? All the rest is commentary.

And I *am* called to the office of commentary.

I would like to have you meet some of the persons in the valley of our shadow. Many of us outwardly see a few who inhabit the valley, mainly those in the lower reaches of economic peonage, those who are counselled to work hard, be thrifty, be moral, and to live and support a family on a pittance. But how many of us have ever asked, "What kind of a life can such a material basis support in our day?"

Here is a remarkable woman in the shadowed valley. By the grace of dedicated parents and the grace of her talent and effort, she was enabled to follow a profession: dentistry. It is not simply her means of living; it is her *vocation*. She was called to it. She remembers the day in college when it came to her — not as a wishywish or as an hallucination, but as a certainty — that she was to be a dentist.

Thirty years later, she is still practicing her profession, conscientiously, with great gentleness. Her gentleness of nature being confirmed by long experience with school children in the dental chair. And what does she think about segregation? "When I was growing up," she said, "My mother used to comfort me, saying, 'Things will be better by the time you're grown.' But they weren't better by the time I was grown. And now I'll die before they are much better." And again, "Sometimes I think I just can't stand it, it *nauseates* me so." And this woman is one of the quiet ones, a veritably Southern lady in constitutional aversion to open controversy — although she did once stand on a picket line.

Another woman of the valley — a French teacher by *vocation*, Master's from Columbia, special training in teaching French to children, several years' experience in France teaching American studies to children and American educational methods to teachers in a French school. In Lynchburg, this woman teaches seventh grade in a Negro school. Why not French? This is the reason given to her: There is no similarly well-qualified French teacher in the white schools, therefore, she may not teach French in a Negro school. It goes without saying that she has not been asked to teach French in a white school. Note the special segregation logic: Perhaps something about separate but equal? Lynchburg Justice hurts her own hand when she executes her judgment.

Another woman, a poet. Langston Hughes and Arna Bontemps tell a little about her in their book *The Poetry of the Negro, 1746-1949*:

> Anne Spencer was educated in the Virginia Seminary in Lynchburg, Virginia, the city in which she spent most of her

life. She is the librarian of the Dunbar High School there. Recently, she developed a pink, candy-striped Chinese peony, eight years from seed. This fact, perhaps, tells as much about her life as anything — with the exception of her poems... And here is one of her favorite poems:

For Jim, Easter Eve
If ever a garden was Gethsemane,
With old tombs set high against
The crumpled olive tree — and lichen,
This, my garden, has been to me.
For such as I, none other is so sweet;
Lacking old tombs, here stands my grief,
And certainly its ancient tree.

Peace is here and in every season
A quiet beauty.
The sky falling about me
Evenly to the compass...

What is sorrow but tenderness now
In this earth-close frame of land and sky
Falling constantly into horizons
Of east and west, north and south;
What is pain but happiness here
Amid these green and wordless patterns, --
Indefinite texture of blade and leaf;

Beauty of an old, old tree,
Last comfort in Gethsemane.

For over twenty-five years, Mrs. Spencer was the librarian at Dunbar, when books were made available there for Negroes from the

Jones Memorial Library. When the school came to have a modest library of its own, access to the Jones branch was discontinued, and Negroes can no longer use the resources of the Jones Memorial. Mrs. Spencer, in view of her work of a quarter of a century, and of her contributions to literature, was offered the special privilege of continuing to use books from Jones Memorial. She refused. Why? She will tell you quietly, "I have *some* conscience."

Another example, a visitor to this spirit memorial, a man with little formal education, much less degrees. He had questions. Would I tell him something about the Jews? He was interested because he knew that they had often suffered much and been oppressed in many places. He had become interested in them because of his own experiences. He had asked a member of the local synagogue about his religion, but the latter thought he should talk to the Rabbi. The man did not want to 'bother' the Rabbi until he at least knew something about the Jewish religion.

Soon, it became apparent that the man was asking something more. He was really asking for himself: "How can I be faithful, even unto death, to what I believe without betraying what I believe in? How can I actively resist the whole shape of this Lynchburg world that would press me down to something less than a man, and how do I resist without hate — no, how do I resist with *Love* that will withstand *anything*, without running away and without giving way to violence?"

What does this have to do with religion? To ask such a question with your whole heart *is* religion. Have you and I ever asked *any* question with our whole heart?

And what of the teenage boy (Thomas Wansley)? If he had been your son or mine, do you think he would now be awaiting his execution? Would he not have been tried as a juvenile? Would he not have spent a long time in a mental institution under observation?

I do not rely particularly on the comparison between the white man (George Brooks) sentenced to five years for the statutory rape of an eleven-year-old Negro girl and this instance of the Negro youth sentenced to die for rape of an adult white woman — with a twenty-year sentence for stealing a purse, added for good measure. Statutory rape means that the woman appeared to give consent but that the consent was not valid because the woman was not a woman but a child. In the case of the white man accused of statutory rape, the prosecutor himself requested and was granted a mental examination for the white man, involving several weeks under observation in a mental hospital. No such action was afforded to Thomas Wansley.

And again, I do not make too much of this, since the legal question of insanity is scarcely the medical one of severe mental illness. First, there are inconsistencies in his case — we do not know if he actually was the perpetrator. Second, for those who have committed the crime of rape, the commonwealth of Virginia asks only 19th century questions of the doctors: "Did the defendant know he was doing the act?" and "Did he know it was wrong?" Until the law is changed, the 20th century question cannot be asked: "Was his condition such that he *could* keep from doing what he did?" The case of the white man does reveal something else, however, about the valley of our shadow: the prostitution of a child of eleven.

No, I am only asking, would a son of yours or mine, under the same accusation and conviction, be waiting to die by our hand?

In my brief pilgrimage through this valley, I have asked myself these questions: "Do I consent to cast the shadow?" "No." "Do

I *acquiesce* in the casting of the shadow?" This is a harder question. In myself, I do not consent, but unless this refusal to consent is made manifest, unless some outward and visible sign of the inward decision is given, then I do, in fact, acquiesce in the casting of the shadow.

What are ways of refusing to acquiesce? In other words, how do I *say* the "No" that ends acquiescence? There is no other way but simply to *begin* to say, or to do "No," even if I have to begin in a whisper or with the flicker of an eyelid. I can do this for a while, in private, with close friends; it is at least a beginning, a tiny raft of "No" in a vast sea of acquiescence.

Later, I may hesitantly inscribe my name upon the records of an organization — a mild one, such as the Virginia Council on Human Relations. I may progress in knowledge and courage toward activity in such an organization, and perhaps beyond to other groups such as the NAACP, or the Southern Christian Leadership Conference — in other words, I shall begin to find my way into more vigorous expressions of "No" until it becomes at least a sturdy *island* in the sea of acquiescence.

And then, if you will join me, we can make an archipelago.

This morning I have shared with you a Lenten meditation concerned not only with wrongdoing, but with saving graces. May we put on the blindfold of justice long enough to right our wrongs and then put it off again when we have been granted the grace to see clearly in the Light of Love.

Amen

Chapter 7

Thus Spake Greta

Follow-Up on "Justice Without a Blindfold"

Wow! It is at this point that I would like to say: My mom is the gentlest bad-ass I know!

Greta noted in her Spoken Essay, "...this monument became the very holy ground on which I stood when I experienced such a mystery. Not that the monument sponsored this mystery, but at least let it happen here."

There is an interesting meaning here. The UUCL history explains in a section entitled "Blacks and Whites" that the Unitarian Church of Lynchburg was the only building in Lynchburg where regular meetings between blacks and whites could take place. In 1958, by unanimous vote, church members made "the Church available for the Virginia Council on Human Relations to hold a meeting for the purpose of organizing a branch of the Council in the Lynchburg area."

As it turned out, this was the only facility that approved such meetings. The church leadership also felt it would be wise to increase their building insurance coverage from $20.00 annually in 1958 to $200.00 in 1960, in case of vandalism, or worse, in retaliation for these multi-racial meetings. Fortunately, they did not experience any damage to their building in that controversial time.

March 10, 1963 — Lynchburg *News and Advance* **— Letter to the Editor: "'Issues' in the Wansley Case Receive Discussion"**

One week after delivering "Justice Without a Blindfold," Greta submitted a detailed letter to the editor of the Lynchburg *News and Advance*. It stated in part, "No white man has been executed for rape in the Commonwealth of Viriginia since the first decade of this century...such a pattern does raise the question in the Wansley case...would Wansley now be awaiting execution if he were white?"

Brumfield reports that between 1900 and 1963, Virginia executed 68 black men for rape or even attempted rape, *but not one white man* — and because of railroading tactics, a number of those executed were innocent men. Brumfield explains that the practice of "protecting the Southern white woman from black men" was more a cruel method of oppression than any form of legal justice.

The UUCL history explains that before submitting the March 10th letter to the editor, Greta had shared it with the Board of Trustees for approval. "Advised by the Church's Board, Greta had signed only her name, but her association with the Unitarian Church was soon discovered. Her views, apparently in defense of the rapist, were assumed to be those of her congregation."

The UUCL history goes on to state that her letter to the editor soon became labeled 'the Wansley Letter,' and it had "angered many Unitarians, because they sensed the disapproval of Southern friends and the public."

That last sentence points to a disturbing pattern in 1960s Lynchburg — guilt by association. Thomas was not a rapist, he was innocent, but he had been convicted and sentenced to die. Greta spoke out at the injustice of his impending execution, and by association she was accused of defending 'the rapist,' as if she was condoning rape. A few months later, this sickening pattern of guilt by association became even more serious.

In the early 1960s, damaging fallout from the McCarthy era's "Red Scare" was still occurring. One way politicians and the press would discredit social activists was to accuse them of having communist affiliations. In regard to Thomas Wansley's unjust death sentence, Carl Braden, a staff member from the Southern Conference Educational Fund (SCEF) said that he would make the case a "national issue." Unfortunately, Congressional Committees had cited Braden, and also the SCEF as a 'communist-front organization,' and the Lynchburg press used this to besmirch Braden's reputation. The UUCL history then describes how in late May 1963, Greta unwittingly exacerbated the press's accusations of Braden's communist ties:

> Even more damaging to the Unitarian peace of mind was Greta Crosby's action as secretary of the Virginia Council on Human Relations (VCHR). To avoid the awkwardness of typing notices (of upcoming meetings) on postcards, she issued a one-page newsletter called *The Hill City Hummingbird*. Thinking it would be interesting to the membership, she enclosed with the May, 1963 issue, an article by Dr. Howard Schomer from *The Christian Century* about Carl Braden... (who) had been imprisoned for refusing to answer questions from Senator McCarthy's committee about the communist leanings of people he knew. The article pointed out that Carl and his wife Anne had worked for integration and were *not* motivated by communism. Nevertheless, *The News* printed a headline four columns wide: "Rape Case Takes on Commie Shade."

I suspect that Greta had no idea that simply sending an article to members of the VCHR would be weaponized so perversely by the press. The accusations of guilt by association caused backlash on Greta, on the Virginia Council on Human Relations, as well as members of the Unitarian church. To make matters worse, these events unfolded in the week right before the church's annual meeting, and emotions were running high. The UUCL history states: "Angered by the injury she thought Mrs. Crosby had done to the image of the Unitarian Church, one woman moved at the annual meeting on May 26, to have her dismissed."

This action was blocked by the Board, but they requested letters from the members who were 'for' or 'against' Greta's removal, to be submitted over the summer. The letters would be then discussed in the fall of 1963. We'll go over those results later in this section as they come up in our chronological timeline.

Developments in Thomas Wansley's Case

Despite the upsetting controversy at the Lynchburg church, Greta's efforts, along with several others in the Lynchburg community, in Virginia, in the U.S. and even around the world were making a difference in Thomas Wansley's case. However, as evidenced by Greta's experience, the process was wrought with struggle and strife.

I'll touch on a few more details in Thomas Wansley's case that occurred after Greta's March 3rd Commentary and her March 10th letter to the editor. I recommend reading the full account in Dale Brumfield's book, *Closing the Slaughterhouse.*

On March 23, 1963, an odd and rather suspicious event occurred in Thomas Wansley's case. His black defense attorney, Reuben Lawson, died suddenly and unexpectedly. This caused serious problems with the case, especially because there was no transcript of the original trial. Thomas Wansley's new attorney,

Leonard W. Holt, affiliated with the Southern Conference Educational Fund, was at a huge disadvantage.

As Thomas Wansley's June 7th execution date approached, his new attorney Leonard Holt worked diligently to obtain a stay of execution while they awaited a hearing before the Virginia Supreme Court of Appeals. Fortunately, this was achieved on May 2, 1963.

On May 7, 1963, Brumfield explains in his Foreword that Greta led a delegation to Richmond to confront Governor Albertis Harrison regarding the Wansley case, as well as the abolition of the death penalty:

> Rev. Crosby told the June 6, 1963 edition of *Jet* magazine of their meeting that "we prepared to tell the governor that we were not asking for the execution of a white man (Brooks) or the saving of one Negro (Wansley), but the abolishment of all capital punishment." She added that the death sentence was a carry-over from the primitive 'eye for an eye' concept. "How can you apply that to rape?"
>
> *Jet* reported that Gov. Harrison promised to look into the Wansley case and surprisingly urged the Death to Death organization to go public to encourage the General Assembly to repeal all capital punishment laws.

Gov. Harrison was pro-death penalty, and 'promising to look into the case' was a common gaslighting tactic. Additionally, the sincerity of his suggestion to 'go public' to the General Assembly encouraging the repeal of all death penalty laws is also questionable, however that is *exactly* what the organization did.

Miraculously, the dedicated efforts of several social justice organizations, as well as state, national and international public outcry, brought about an unexpected change in Virginia's death penalty practices in 1963 — a moratorium was established on executions in the commonwealth, which ended up lasting through 1981, though it was controversial and hotly debated over those years.

According to Brumfield, this was Virginia's "first intentional multi-year pause in executions since the practice began in 1608. Virginia joined an informal, multi-state moratorium on executions in 1963 as part of a declining trend in jury-imposed death sentences that started in the 1950's."

Additionally, the means of execution, the electric chair, was being called into question for possible technical malfunctions. "The pause in executions was not just for internal and technical reasons — many foreign countries expressed indignation at the United States over their wholesale and seemingly arbitrary use of capital punishment, especially in those cases where Blacks received death penalties for non-homicidal crimes."

This historic moratorium on executions reminds me of Margaret Mead's words of wisdom: "Never doubt that a small group of thoughtful citizens can change the world; indeed, it's the only thing that ever has."

We'll revisit Thomas Wansley's case later in this section.

Introduction to "Fantasies on Blue"

Along with her efforts to save Thomas Wansley, her work on the Death to Death initiative, and her work with multi-racial social justice organizations, Greta was also actively promoting attendance at the March on Washington for Jobs and Freedom on August 28, 1963.

Several newspaper articles in July 1963 quote Greta as encouraging attendance at the March on Washington, not as a march on Congress, but as a Civil Rights rally. However, the articles also mention that she is unsure whether she herself will be able to attend. On July 25th, the Lynchburg *Daily Advance* explains:

> Mrs. Crosby said she did not know at this time whether she would be able to participate in the march, but that she supported the stand taken by the Commission (on Religion and Race of the UUA) of which she is a member. She noted that her church was supporting the demonstration because it supported the civil rights legislation proposed by President Kennedy.

I'm intrigued by her slightly evasive response to whether she will attend the March. This is because the leadership of the Lynchburg church did not want her to go to Washington. I'm unsure what the reasoning was, all she would say is that they didn't want her to go. Perhaps they were concerned about her safety? Or maybe it would increase the anger of those who wanted her dismissed? Or perhaps they were concerned about retaliation from Lynchburg's powers-that-be for their minister's participation in the rally? The July 25th article in the Lynchburg *Daily Advance* also states:

> Commission Chairman, the Rev. Walter Royal Jones, Jr., said the more than 1,000 Unitarian Universalist churches and fellowships in the U.S. and Canada will be urged to send delegates to the rally. Jones noted that "on the preceding Sunday, churches will be asked to give notice of the impending demonstration. Ministers will be encouraged to speak on the issue of Civil Rights, and laymen will be urged to give local support through letters to editors and congressmen, local meetings, etc."

This dovetails into the next sermon in our collection. In "Fantasies on Blue," which Greta presented to the Roanoke Valley Unitarian Church on Sunday, July 28, 1963, she gracefully invites people to attend the March on Washington. I particularly enjoy her uniquely whimsical approach to this Spoken Essay.

There is also the eerie but imaginative symbolism of the children's story Greta selected, which was 'Sand Flat Shadows' from Carl Sandburg's *Rootabaga Stories*. The 'Sand Flat Shadows' story reminds me of the Island of the Misfit Toys, from the 1976 version of Rudolph the Red-Nosed Reindeer. The Island of the Misfit Toys is a secret island where 'defective' toys live because they've been rejected and thrown away due to their mistaken shape or function. But in Sandburg's imagination, what's been thrown away are the distorted shadowy practice-shapes that form in the eastern sky as the morning light of sunrise shifts from dawn into day.

When I first read "Sand Flat Shadows," I found it unsettling and I didn't care for it. I didn't like the implication of throwing away mistakes. What are mistakes anyway? Who gets to define them? One person's seeming deformity can be another person's treasure. Yet as I contemplated the symbolism of the rejected practice shapes, I related it to the disturbing tendency of our society to discount and discard what doesn't conform to our tidy little rules and our societal norms.

Particularly in that era, people born with congenital deformities or with Down's Syndrome, the mentally ill and the poverty-stricken were regarded as mistakes to be thrown away, to be avoided or to be locked up. Additionally, those of differing religions, races, or nationalities, people with differing ideologies or sexual preferences were often rejected and cast out from mainstream society because, "You're not one of us." Anyone deemed 'different' must dwell in shadow, on the periphery, in the no-man's-land of the Sand Flat Shadows.

Since that era, as a society, we've broadened our acceptance of many walks of life, however, we still have a long way to go. Perhaps I didn't like "Sand Flat Shadows" because of the truth that it revealed and I didn't want to see it. Once you read this Rootabaga Story, I'd be interested to know what your take is on this 'children's story' that is not really a children's story.

After "Sand Flat Shadows," Greta includes selected portions of a poem called "The Man with the Blue Guitar." When I mindfully read this poem, I picture that it is coming from the inner-voice of Greta-as-minister, describing the problems within the fabric of segregated Southern society, yet not being well-received. Through the stanzas of the poem, Greta, who was 32 years old in July 1963, is essentially saying in a satirical way, "I've got something to say about the way things are, it may not be well-received, but here it is."

She also has examples of learning to see things differently embedded within her poetic prose. I like to savor the words and really sit with each of her service elements: "Sand Flat Shadows," "The Man with the Blue Guitar," and her Spoken Essay. Let's now experience Greta's "Fantasies on Blue."

Chapter 8

"Fantasies on Blue"

Greta W. Crosby
Roanoke Valley Unitarian Church
Roanoke, Virginia
July 28, 1963

[The following readings were incorporated into an earlier portion of the church service, then Greta referred back to them within her Spoken Essay.]

Children's Story: Sand Flat Shadows
from *Rootabaga Stories*, by Carl Sandburg (1922)

Fire the Goat and Flim the Goose slept out. Stub pines stood over them. And away up next over the stub pines were stars.

It was a white sand flat they slept on. The floor of the sand flat ran straight to the Big Lake of the Booming Rollers.

And just over the sand flat and just over the booming rollers was a high room where the mist people were making pictures. Gray pictures, blue and sometimes a little gold, and often silver, were the pictures.

And next over the high room where the mist people were making pictures, next just over were the stars.

Over everything and always and highest of all were the stars.

Fire the Goat took off his horns. Flim the Goose took off his wings. "This is where we sleep," they said to each other, "Here in the stub pines on the sand flats next to the booming rollers and high over everything and always last and highest of all, the stars."

Fire the Goat laid his horns under his head. Flim the Goose laid his wings under his head. "This is the best place for what you want to keep," they said to each other. Then they crossed their fingers for luck and lay down and went to sleep and slept. And while they slept the mist people went on making pictures. Gray pictures, blue and sometimes a little gold but more often silver... and over everything and always last and highest of all, were the stars.

They woke up. Fire the Goat took his horns out and put them on. "It's morning now," he said.

Flim the Goose took his wings out and put them on. "It's another day now," he said.

Then they sat looking. Away off where the sun was coming up, inching and pushing up far across the rim curve of the Big Lake of the Booming Rollers, along the whole line of the east sky, there were people and animals, all black or all so gray they were near black.

There was a big horse with his mouth open, ears laid back, front legs thrown in two curves like harvest sickles.

There was a camel with two humps, moving slow and grand like he had all the time of all the years of all the world to go in.

There was an elephant without any head, with six short legs. There were many cows. There was a man with a club over his shoulder and a woman with a bundle on the back of her neck.

And they marched on. They were going nowhere, it seemed. And they were going slow. They had plenty of time. There was nothing else to do. It was fixed for them to do it, long ago it was fixed. And so they were marching. Sometimes the big horse's head sagged and dropped off and came back again. And sometimes the club on the man's shoulder got bigger and heavier and the man staggered under it and then his legs got bigger and stronger and he steadied himself and went on. And again, sometimes the bundle on the back of the neck of the woman got bigger and heavier and the bundle sagged and her legs got bigger and stronger and she steadied herself and went on.

This was the show, the hippodrome, the spectacular circus that passed on the east sky before the eyes of Fire the Goat and Flim the Goose.

"Which is this, who are they and why do they come?" Flim the Goose asked Fire the Goat.

"Do you ask me because you wish me to tell you?" asked Fire the Goat.

"Indeed it is a question to which I want an honest answer."

"Has never the father or mother nor the uncle nor aunt nor the kith and kin of Flim the Goose told him the what and the which of this?"

"Never has such of this which been put here this way to me by anybody."

Flim the Goose held up his fingers and said, "I don't talk to you with my fingers crossed."

And so Fire the Goat began to explain to Flim the Goose all about the show, the hippodrome, the mastodonic cyclopean spectacle which was passing on the east sky in front of the sun coming up.

"People say they are shadows," began Fire the Goat. "That is a name, a word, a little cough and a couple of syllables.

"For some people shadows are comic and only to laugh at. For some other people shadows are like a mouth and its breath. The breath comes out and it is nothing. It is like air and nobody can make it into a package and carry it away. It will not melt like gold nor can you shovel it like cinders. So to these people it means nothing.

"And then there are other people," Fire the Goat went on. "There are other people who understand the shadows. The fire-born understand. The fire-born know where shadows come from and why they are.

"Long ago, when the Makers of the World were done making the round earth, the time came when they were ready to make the animals to put on the earth. They were not sure how to make the animals. They did not know what shape animals they wanted.

"And so they practiced. They did not make real animals at first. They made only shapes of animals. And these shapes were shadows, shadows like these you and I, Fire the Goat and Flim the Goose, are looking at this morning across the booming rollers on the east sky where the sun is coming up.

"The shadow horse over there on the east sky with his mouth open, his ears laid back, and his front legs thrown in a curve like harvest sickles, that shadow horse was one they made long ago when they were practicing to make a real horse. That shadow horse was a mistake and they threw him away. Never will you see two shadow horses alike. All shadow horses in the sky are different. Each one is a mistake, a shadow horse thrown away because he was not good enough to be a real horse.

"That elephant with no head on his neck, stumbling so grand on six legs — and that grand camel with two humps, one bigger than the other — and those cows with horns in front and behind

— they are all mistakes, they were all thrown away because they were not made good enough to be real elephants, real cows, real camels. They were made just for practice, away back early in the world, before any real animals came on their legs and to eat and live and be here like the rest of us.

"That man — see him now staggering along with the club over his shoulder — see how his long arms come to his knees and sometimes his hands drag below his feet. See how heavy the club on his shoulder loads him down and drags him on. He is one of the oldest shadow men. He was a mistake and they threw him away. He was made just for practice.

"And that woman. See her now at the end of the procession across the booming rollers on the east sky. See her the last of all, the end of the procession. On the back of her neck a bundle. Sometimes the bundle gets bigger. The woman staggers. Her legs get bigger and stronger. She picks herself up and goes along shaking her head. She is the same as the others. She is a shadow and she was made as a mistake. Early, early in the morning she was made, for practice.

"Listen, Flim the Goose. What I am telling you is a secret of the fire-born. I do not know whether you understand. We have slept together a night on the sand flats next to the booming rollers, under the stub pines with the stars high over — and so I tell what the fathers of the fire-born tell their sons."

And that day Fire the Goat and Flim the Goose moved along the sand flat shore of the Big Lake of the Booming Rollers. It was a blue day, with a fire-blue of the sun mixing itself in the air and the water. Off to the north the booming rollers were blue seagreen. To the east they were sometimes streak purple, sometimes changing bluebell stripes. And to the south they were silver blue, sheet blue.

Where the shadow hippodrome marched on the east sky that morning was a long line of blue-bird spots.

"Only the fire-born understand blue," said Fire the Goat to Flim the Goose. And that night as the night before, they slept on a sand flat. And again Fire the Goat took off his horns and laid them under his head while he slept. And Flim the Goose took off his wings and laid them under his head while he slept. And twice in the night, Fire the Goat whispered in his sleep, whispered to the stars, "Only the fire-born understand blue."

Greta's Reading for Meditation: "The Man with the Blue Guitar"
by Wallace Stevens, from *Poems by Wallace Stevens* (1937)

"The Man with the Blue Guitar" is a collection of thirty-three short poems on the theme of, in Stevens own words, "The incessant conjunctions between things as they are and things imagined." I shall read the first four and the thirty-second.

I.
The man bent over his guitar,
A shearsman of sorts. The day was green.

They said, "You have a blue guitar,
You do not play things as they are."

The man replied, "Things as they are
Are changed upon the blue guitar."

But they said then, "But play, you must,
A tune beyond us, yet ourselves.

A tune upon the blue guitar
Of things exactly as they are."

II.

I cannot bring a world quite round
Although I patch it as I can.

I sing a hero's head, large eye
And bearded bronze, but not a man,

Although I patch him as I can
And reach through him almost to man.

If to serenade almost to man
Is to miss, by that, things as they are,

Say that it is the serenade
Of a man that plays a blue guitar.

III.

Ah, but to play man number one,
To drive the dagger in his heart,

To lay his brain upon the board
And pick the acrid colors out,

To nail his thought across the door,
Its wings spread wide to rain and snow,

To strike his living hi and ho,
To tick it, tock it, turn it true,

To bang it from a savage blue,
Jangling the metal of the strings...

IV.
So that's life, then: things as they are?
It picks its way on the blue guitar.

A million people on one string?
And all their manner in the thing,

And all their manner, right and wrong,
And all their manner, weak and strong?

The feelings crazily, craftily call,
Like a buzzing of flies in autumn air,

And that's life, then: things as they are,
This buzzing of the blue guitar.

XXXII.
Throw away the lights, the definitions,
And say of what you see in the dark

That it is this or that,
But do not use the rotted names.

How should you walk in that space and know
Nothing of the madness of space,

Nothing of its jocular procreations?
Throw the lights away. Nothing must stand

Between you and the shapes you take
When the crust of shape has been destroyed.

You as you are? You are yourself.
The blue guitar surprises you.

— Let us join in the exercise of silence —

Greta's Spoken Essay: "Fantasies on Blue"

There are seven sermons this morning; seven separate stanzas for my blue guitar. It is the only way I can strike my "living hi and ho, to tick it, tock it, turn it true. To bang it from a savage blue, jangling the metal of the strings..."

There are seven sermons this morning, one for each string of the blue guitar. How many strings to a guitar? Only six, you say? But you forget to count the one you cannot see. How could you strike a living hi and ho without a seventh, without a heart string?

There are seven sermons this morning, and my living hi and ho are to blame. In autumn, winter, and spring, my hi and ho are somewhat civilized. They think long thoughts together. They paint long pictures together. I don't know about your hi and ho, but in summer, mine run wild. They think in hopscotch. They paint in Picasso. Sometimes my ever-living hi doesn't even know what my ever-loving ho is doing! Do you ever have that trouble?

There are seven sermons this morning, one for each bone in the neck of a giraffe or in the neck of a whale, even though the whale doesn't have a neck; and for each bone in your neck or in mine — just in case we are ever tempted to think we have nothing in common with giraffes or whales or with each other.

There are seven sermons this morning, which would be cause for great alarm on account of the wooden church benches, except for one thing. Each sermon is only one-seventh as long as what you think of as a sermon.

There *were* seven sermons this morning, but now there are six. The first one just left. It was called: "And the Spirit Blew Where It Listed."

II.

When I read the Rootabaga story earlier this morning, what did you think about? Did you think that animals can't talk, that they don't take off their horns or wings to sleep at night, that there aren't any artistic mist people, that dark clouds *couldn't* be practice shapes for us, and that nobody can 'understand' a color anyway? These are true thoughts, but they don't hurt the truth of the story at all.

Where is the truth of the story? Everywhere and to spare! Truth is in the way our mind can see the stub pines and white sand and hear the Booming Rollers away under the silent stars while the words go by, and afterwards. It's in the way we *feel* what Fire the Goat and Flim the Goose feel when they are together without talking, or when they ask questions without their fingers crossed, questions to which they want honest answers. Truth is in the way a heritage from kith and kin is solemnly shared when the heart is kin. And truth is in the shiver of recognition you give when you hear the words: "Only the fireborn understand blue"— is there one among us who has not been rejected in some way? Felt misshapen or mistaken, or dejected? Is there one among us who is not fire-born in some way, to understand some kind of blue?

But the meaning of the story goes even beyond its truth. For instance, whenever I read a Rootabaga Story, I think of my mother reading one to me. I don't remember hearing about Fire and Flim, but I do remember hearing about the Iowa and Nebraska corn fairies, and how you could tell them apart by the number of stitches in their corn cloth clothes — the farther west you go, the more stitches — and one year in Minnesota they wore a blue sash of corn flowers. Carl Sandburg is to blame if my living hi and ho grew up in a fireborn Midwest, and it was no other than Carl

Sandburg who first baptized the Southern sun in blue fire for me.

It was the summer before my last year in theological school, I went to the Blue Ridge Assembly near Asheville, North Carolina, at the time of the summer migration of Unitarians. There were Unitarians as far as the eye could see — it was wonderful! One morning in a fit of madness brought on by the exuberance of seeing so many birds of a feather, I got up at 3:30 in the morning and climbed High Top Mountain with about forty liberal lights of high school age and fortitude. High Top is climbable by anyone by the clutch, crawl and scoot school of mountain climbing; but it does go marvelously up. When we had achieved the summit, we observed the custom of the place — silence until the sun had risen. And it was there, above the valley mist and the pinked tops of the Blue Ridge crest — there was the hippodrome, the spectacular circus, the patient dark practice shapes marching on across the dawn!

And so ends the second sermon, "Only the Fireborn Understand Blue Ridge."

III.

But I am not quite through with Blue Ridge. This year at the time of liberal religious migration, I was the morning worship leader and the "bookie," the manager of the Blue Ridge Bookery, also the source of this morning's book array in our foyer.

My passion for book-dealing is not the subject of this sermon, however. It is even more uplifting because it is about balloons.

One day the children at Blue Ridge gathered on the front lawn of the main hall. Each held a balloon on a string. They were filled with helium — the balloons, that is. These children were filled with other things: big appetites, affection, joy, sadness, madness, bright ideas and not so bright ideas, and so on until they were full of themselves. Tied to the string of each balloon was a postcard on which was written the child's name and address and a note asking the finder to mail the card. Then the balloons were released, up, up, into the mountain air and carried away, who knows where, unless a finder did mail back a card.

Have you ever done something like this? When I was a child, we used to put notes in bottles and throw them into a river named the Olentangy, or sometimes into one called Scioto. But no one ever sent back a message.

If you were to send a message now into the sky or the water for someone on Earth to find, what would you say? Besides asking for the return of the word? What are some of the things you would like to tell the stranger?

My trouble of course is that I can think of too many things to say. Once I thought that I would say, "You are better than you think," because a lot of people need encouragement. But the trouble is, that's not the whole truth, and it's not fair to a stranger to send him a mysterious message with only part of the truth. After all, even people who are better than they think, are often worse, too; and part of getting even better is finding out the worse without letting it make you forget the better that is, and may be. And even more important than things anyone can call better or worse, there is so much that we just *are*, that we can't or don't think about, at least not very often.

And so, perhaps, I would say, "You are *more* than you think."
Here ends the third sermon on "B'loons Away!"

IV.

In the next sermon, I'm the one who's going up in the air, into what is sometimes called the "wild blue yonder." As you probably guessed, I didn't go up by helium balloon but by airplane. Even without being an astronaut, you only have to spend three hours well-aimed in the air to go to Boston, Massachusetts, one of the places where Unitarians grew up in this country. Of course, you have to spend almost as much time in between on the ground getting ready to go, but that's always the way. It's known as groundwork.

Anyway, I was in Boston last week for the first meeting of the Commission on Religion and Race of the Unitarian Universalist Association. The commission came about as a result of a great concern in the matter of Civil Rights, shown in an overwhelming vote of the delegates at the General Assembly last May. The commission decided to do a number of things, the first of which was to urge Unitarians to participate in the Washington March on August 28th. This is not to be, as some have said, a march on Congress. It will go the other way from the Washington Monument to the Lincoln Memorial. There is to be no civil disobedience. I would call it a religious pilgrimage, an urgent public prayer for liberty and justice for all.

Religious liberals who go to Washington will not only have the opportunity to walk a long way with many people, there are plans for meeting with Congressmen and also for an open hearing of the Commission when suggestions and observations from religious liberals will be received on the matter of its concern, Religion and Race.

But this morning I would mainly like to tell you a story Professor Thurmond, one of the Commission members, brought to our meeting. He had been sent to Canada to study Indian adjustment to Canadian life. There he met, among others, three men, and three ways of meeting the situation. The first Indian felt that his Indian ties were the chief obstacle to his life in the Canadian situation, and he strove with all his might to get rid of his Indian ways and memories. He felt that this was the only way to become all Canadian.

The second Indian told the professor that he wanted the young of his tribe to grow up in the Indian ways so that they would have a 'center' inside them. And he expected the Canadian to grow up in Canadian ways and so to have a 'center,' too. When Indian and Canadian met, they would *both* have centers, and so they could come together in peace and truth, each having what he needed and something to share from his center.

Lastly, the professor met a man who lived near the arctic circle. For about ten minutes, the man and the interpreter went back and forth over the professor's question: Whether the man thought of himself as Indian or Canadian. The interpreter grew exasperated and finally turned to the professor. "He's stupid," he said. "I just can't make him understand the question. He says in summer he lives with the long sun and the earth and the flowers, and in winter he lives with the stars and the ice and the snow. He doesn't know the meaning of "Indian" and "Canadian."

> Throw away the lights, the definitions,
> And any of what you see in the dark
> That it is this or that it is that,
> But do not use the rotted names... Nothing must stand
> Between you and the shapes you take
> When the crust of shape has been destroyed.

You as you are? You are yourself.
The blue guitar surprises you.

So ends the fourth sermon, "Wild Blue Yonder and You".

V.

I'm still up in the airplane, but coming down, down in the dark. The city is beautiful. First appearing as a jeweled pin for evening wear — but no, there are too many jewels moving. It is perhaps a living, phosphorescent animal at the bottom of the sea of air.

I remembered looking at pictures of deep-sea shells in a magazine when I was six. There was one picture of a sea monster that covered the whole page. There was a gigantic eye, and worse, a mouth open all the way back, and its teeth caught things. I used to skip that page because it frightened me. I would turn each page just a little to see if it was coming next, and when it was, I would hold two pages together and turn them as one. When I was twelve, I found the magazine in the attic. I wanted to see the old monster again, perhaps because I had never had a good look at it. There it was, big eye and big mouth, but down at the very bottom of the page was another tiny picture. "Actual size," it said, and there, just barely visible was my little old monster. It was about *this* big ( ). Has anything like that ever happened to you?

And so ends the fifth sermon entitled, "Out of the blue."

VI.

At last the feet are on the ground, but you can't keep the eyes from looking higher yet. "Over everything and always last and highest of all, were the stars."

Lately I've been reconnoitering the heavens again with some

seriousness — constellation-hunting. Until a few months ago, in my whole life I had tamed only four or five constellations, and even these were not fully tamed since I included only part of their stars. Imagine having Orion as a good friend for three-fourths of your life and not even knowing he had a shield! I had even seen the nebula in his sword through a telescope, but I had never known about his plain-as-night star shield; I had never seen it with my lone eyes until someone came along to help. This other person couldn't do my seeing for me, but what he did was to make new patterns out of the old star dots in the constellations. And now I see it.

In a book called *The Stars*, H.A. Rey has drawn the constellation lines to make new pictures as much like the meaning of the constellation names as he could. For example, in linking the stars of the constellation Gemini, which means twins, he has made two men-type stick figures side-by-side, without losing a star. Now, in season, at least, there they are, bigger than life, whole and brotherly in the sky, instead of just being two head dots in the sky.

I tell you about this because someday you may need someone to help you tame the night-sky — and also because this shows how people often help each other — not by changing what is, but by seeing it in a new way and sharing the view.

So ends the sixth sermon, or "Whose Blue Guitar is the Sky?"

VII.

The stars and constellations of the sixth sermon herald the birth of the seventh in baby blue. Earth has stars and constellations, too. I think of the birth of my sister Nancy's seventh child into a welcoming family constellation.

By sheer force of number, the children know their importance in that family. The love of the parents expands with each one, but, of course, their time cannot. Fearful that some child might feel lost in the shuffle, they do what they can to make special occasions on which each child, in turn, has supreme attention. They make much of birthdays, for example. The birthday child past infancy either presides at a small party of neighborhood friends, or else goes out to dinner alone with his parents. He can order anything he wants to eat. Even the birthday request of the four-year-old fourth child was honored: at the restaurant, he ordered "coffee and rolls." How he wanted to be grown up!

Once the oldest child, in third grade at the time, was asked to describe herself in a composition. It came home nonchalantly in a batch of school papers, and her mother had the joy of reading it. The girl began by telling how she looked, the color of her hair and eyes, and what she was wearing. Then she told about her family, her six brothers and sisters (she was counting herself among them, for there were only six all together at the time), even her four uncles and four aunts — I was flattered to be included in her description of herself, of course! Then she confided that she knew all the secrets of her parents, (about holidays, she explained), and ended with her love for her mommy and daddy.

A million people on one string?
And all their manner in the thing.
May we, too, find ourselves not only as one but as many.
Who is not
Something old, something new,
Something borrowed, something blue?

And so ends the seventh indigo sermon, "Love in Bloom."

Amen

Chapter 9

The March on Washington

Follow-up on "Fantasies on Blue"

There are many aspects of these brilliant little ditties that I love. First, it took me a couple of read-throughs to notice that each sermon-title weaves either 'blue' or the sound of 'blue' into it — such as, B'loons Away (Blue-ns Away), and Love in Bloom (Love in Blue-m).

I'm impressed with how Greta weaves the symbolism found within each of the service elements — the children's story and the poem — into her Spoken Essay. What goes unspoken speaks volumes, as do all her allusions to 'blue,' layered one over the next, just waiting to be unpacked by receptive minds.

I love her personal references, making her discoveries and experiences relatable, showing us what makes Greta tick — and tock, and turn it true, to her own inner-voice of Truth; navigating treacherous waters with her humanist rudder and her theistic compass, guiding her profound choices of conscience.

Primarily, how to enact both her commitment to integrity as a minister, pointing to how things are in the segregated South, and, how to encourage a better way for all. How to truly embody the Unitarian Universalist's second principle of "Upholding justice, equity and compassion in human relations." How is a minister to do this without incurring the wrath of the fearful ones resistant to change? Those stubbornly stuck in the quagmire of 'Old Dominion' — quite an apt nickname for the commonwealth of Virginia. How, indeed?

Then there is her invitation to join the March on Washington for Jobs and Freedom, nested precisely smack-dab in the middle of her "Fantasies on Blue." Greta still didn't know if the Lynchburg leadership would approve her going, but she could at least encourage attendance.

Then exactly one month later, on August 28, 1963, despite admonitions to the contrary, my mom, the gentlest bad-ass I know, made her "No" to racial oppression visible by attending the March on Washington — along with approximately 250,000 progressively-minded people. What a powerful experience that must have been!

I had the honor of attending the Women's March in Washington D.C. in 2017 with my daughter and her best friend. I treasure the experience of that gathering, which resonated with a uniquely cohesive energy of 'All of Us Together.'

For years I've been curious about my mom's experience at the March on Washington, so I was delighted to locate this little gem in her 1989 sermon I referenced earlier entitled "Remembering."

"I remember hearing Dr. Martin Luther King, Jr. speak the dream at the Washington March, August 28, 1963. I remember King speaking and Odetta singing. But what I remember most of all was the *feeling* of being a joyful dot in that sea of more than 250,000 people of all colors — black and brown and beige — from all over the country. I remember the smiles. Imagine the kinship feeling of a gigantic church picnic or family reunion combined with the exhilarating sense of history moving, turning under your feet. And then I remember the miracle of the Civil Rights Act of 1964..."

YouTube link: *I Have a Dream* speech
by Martin Luther King .Jr HD (subtitled)
https://youtu.be/vP4iY1TtS3s?si=L30NU7owopQZOMwV

[NOTE: The Civil Rights Act of 1964 outlawed discrimination based on race, color, religion, gender and national origin: https://www.history.com/topics/black-history/civil-rights-act]

'For' or 'Against' Input from Lynchburg Church Members

As described in the follow-up on "Justice Without a Blindfold," in the summer and fall of 1963, Greta was still at the center of controversy at the Lynchburg church for her actions defending Thomas Wansley and her activism encouraging the integration of Lynchburg. As described by the UUCL history, one woman called for her dismissal at the May 26th Annual Meeting. The action was blocked, but letters were to be written by members over the summer 'for' or 'against' her dismissal.

On September 17, 1963, a meeting was held without Greta being present and twenty-two letters were reviewed. One letter said in her defense, "If some of our members persist in pushing for her removal, I think it is an indication that the CHURCH is sick."

Whether 'for' or 'against' her dismissal, many members did agree that she "should, however, realize that every public and private appearance she makes is interpreted to some extent as representative of the church."

On November 2, 1963, Greta met for three hours with the Board and the executive secretary of the Thomas Jefferson UU Council, going over the views expressed by the Lynchburg church members. Then a Laison Committee was formed for better communication with their minister. The UUCL history goes on to say:

Thus a year and a half of dissension ended without either the dismissal of the minister or the split of the congregation into two groups. Certainly it was Greta's knowledge of the law that obliged such a gentle woman to offend Southern sensibilities by pointing to the injustices in Lynchburg.

The history concludes the section on Greta's ministry at UUCL with an important insight that she shared about her experience two decades later:

When I think of the Lynchburg Church, it is with the memory of the individual people who come to mind, each unique, each still amazingly distinct in image and feeling and voice for all these years. I cannot forget how angry some Church people were with me in the atmosphere of anxiety and change in the early sixties. I learned from those difficulties and had the important experience of continuing to be with and coming back together again with many who had known anger.

Reflections on the UUCL History

I want to step back at this point and look at what was coming up for me as I studied the history provided by the UUCL. I will admit that I was not too pleased when I read some of the details in this account. So Greta, a Northerner, offended Southern sensibilities when she pointed out Lynchburg injustices? Yet the alternative would be to remain silent while an innocent black teenager was unjustly executed? To be 'good' and to maintain the church's 'good standing' in the community was to tacitly approve the inhumane treatment of fellow human beings.

My inner-voice told me to take time to contemplate this, so I did exactly what Greta would do, I turned the tables and looked at the situation from the perspective of the angry church members. What I saw from their perspective was fear. Based on the systemic corruption demonstrated just in Thomas Wansley's case alone, we can see that sympathizers could be harmed in any number of ways. The sick 1960s Lynchburg segregation system was intimidating and powerful. It was not right to acquiesce, but when I put myself in their place, I do see why they were afraid when Greta spoke out.

Putting this into perspective, though she was a Northerner who spoke her mind, she was not a radical loose cannon, acting brashly on her own. As evidenced by the July 25, 1963 article in the Lynchburg *Daily Advance*, thousands of UU churches across North America were activating and participating in the national Civil Rights Movement. It just so happened that Greta's placement at the Lynchburg church put her on the precarious edge of the envelope of change. Based on a June 5, 1963 newspaper article, there's a fine point here that I have started to grasp about mid-South and deep-South states.

The article by Anne Braden appeared in *The Gazette and Daily* in York, Pennsylvania, entitled "The Wansley Case: Seeing Injustice Whole." The tag line showed the story originated in Lynchburg, Va., and the subtitle stated, "For the First Time a Locally Initiated Campaign." I'm surprised at what the article says in support of the Civil Rights movement as well as Thomas Wansley's case, and I commend Anne Braden for writing it. She explained that the local black leadership in Lynchburg was speaking out and she lists Greta as an example of the white Lynchburg citizens who were joining the cause.

Braden described similar cases in Mississippi where black men had been sentenced to death for allegedly raping white women,

"...but few if any persons in Mississippi have spoken out about it." Segregationist practices were pretty much deadlocked in the deep South but Braden explains:

> The difference reflects the sharp contrast between a Deep South state and this one (Virginia) in the mid-South. In Mississippi, Negroes are still struggling for the most elementary rights of free speech and the vote, and white liberals are still silenced by fear.
>
> Here in Virginia, although many battles against segregation remain, the basic right to protest has been won in the last few years. A new Negro leadership has emerged which feels confident in its right to speak its mind.
>
> The atmosphere has become relaxed enough that white people can dare raise their voice on controversial issues. Having found they can talk about integration, they find that it's also possible to speak of other civilized goals like abolishing capital punishment.
>
> It is an indication that where the South is breaking loose from the strait-jacket imposed when segregationists are able to stifle all dissent, the doors are opening to free discussion of all important social issues.

I'm not sure how 'relaxed' the Lynchburg environment was, considering Greta's job was put at risk when she spoke out. However, this article reveals that the city of Lynchburg was a pivot point, truly on the edge of the envelope of change. Controversial though it was, Greta's Vision was leading the UU community into new ways of thinking, of acting, and of embodying the Seven Principles of Unitarian Universalism.

Forgiveness as a Saving Grace

The saving grace of the UUCL historical account is Greta's beautiful reflections on the healing process that gradually unfolded over time with many of the church members: "I learned from those difficulties and had the important experience of continuing to be with and coming back together again with many who had known anger."

This line resonates right into the depths of my soul. So many people will shut down and lock-down grudges against another over disagreements like this. But with time, several members were able to come back together again and heal their grievances with her. As uncomfortable as it was to go through, these valuable forgiveness lessons for so many people, including Greta, would not have resulted without those difficult challenges.

Introduction to "Valley of the Shadow"

Our next Spoken Essay, "Valley of the Shadow," is a redux of "Justice Without a Blindfold," that Greta prepared for the guest lecture series at Hollins College, in Roanoke, on November 10, 1963 — just eight days after her three-hour meeting with the leadership of the Lynchburg church. The main parts of the sermon are the same as "Justice Without a Blindfold," so there will be some repetition. However, I have found that every time I reread it, I glean more meaning from it.

Since this was not delivered in Lynchburg, Greta removed the comments near the end about Thomas Wansley's and George Brooks' cases. She neutralized some of the more charged language, and she added some examples of positive progress in the area.

It was a good idea to compose her Spoken Essay with care,

in light of who her audience might have been. Though Hollins College was an institution of higher learning, many opinions would be represented, some supportive, and some still stuck in the old apartheid paradigms. Without losing her passion for her subject, she tailored her Spoken Essay to a more general audience, and in doing so, I think she found the perfect balance. Her elegantly crafted sermon has an emphasis on meeting people where they are in their own belief system with respect to what she calls the Emancipation Movement, echoing Dr. Martin Luther King Jr.'s reference at the March on Washington.

In the Introduction of this book, I remarked that our parents live several lifetimes in their lifetime, many of which we are unaware. When I compare "Valley of the Shadow," which she presented eight months after "Justice Without a Blindfold," I think 32-year-old Greta had lived at least one of those lifetimes in the time in between. Her intentions are so purified by this time, purified through the crucible of tumult and controversy. Everything else was burned away, and only the pure message remained, titrated into her Spoken Essay very precisely, which was conveyed from deep within her heart of hearts.

Chapter 10

"Valley of the Shadow"

Greta W. Crosby
Jessie Hall, DuPont Chapel
Hollins College
Roanoke, Virginia
Nov 10, 1963

[The following readings were incorporated into the church service before the sermon, then Greta referred back to them within her Spoken Essay.]

Reading for Meditation

Amos 2: 6-7 — They sell the innocent for silver, and the needy for a pair of sandals. They trample on the heads of the poor as on the dust of the ground and deny justice to the oppressed...

Amos 5: 1 & 7-12 — Hear this word, Israel, this lament concerning you...There are those who turn justice into bitterness and cast righteousness to the ground... There are those who hate the one who upholds justice in court and detest the one who tells the truth. They levy a straw tax on the poor and impose a tax on their grain... There are those who oppress the innocent and take bribes and deprive the poor of justice in the courts.

1 John 2: 9-11 — Anyone who claims to be in the light but hates a brother or sister is still in the darkness. Anyone who loves their brother and sister lives in the light, and there is nothing in them to make them stumble. But anyone who hates a brother or sister is in the darkness and walks around in the darkness. They do not know where they are going, because the darkness has blinded them.

1 John 3:11 — This is the message you heard from the beginning: We should love one another.

Greta's Spoken Essay: "Valley of the Shadow"

To the ancient words of Amos and John on justice and love, I would like to add two modern readings for your reflection. The first is from Simone Weil's *Intimations of Christianity Among the Greeks* (1958).

"There are three mysteries in human life of which all human beings, even the most mediocre, have more or less knowledge. One is beauty. Another is the work of pure intelligence applied...to the understanding of the world... The last are those flashes of justice, of compassion, of gratitude which rise-up sometimes in human relationships in the midst of harshness and metallic coldness. Here are three supernatural mysteries constantly present right in human nature."

The second is from St. Joan of the Stockyards by Bertolt Brecht (1931). Joan is dying, and as she comes to the end of her life, she looks back with regret:

One thing I have learned and I know it in your stead
Dying myself: How can I say it —
there's something inside you
And it won't come out! *What* do you know in your wisdom
That has no consequences?
I, for instance, did nothing.

Oh, let nothing be counted good,
however helpful it may seem
And nothing considered honourable, except that
Which will change this world once and for all:
that's what it needs.
Like an answer to their prayers I came to the oppressors!
Oh, goodness without consequences!
Intentions in the dark!
I have changed nothing.
Swiftly vanishing without fear from the world
I say to you:
Take care that when you leave the world
You were not only good, but are leaving
A good world!

Today, I want to share with you a portion of the pilgrimage I have made in the last two and a half years. Every spiritual journey is difficult to talk about because words never quite match what happens and how it *feels*—and even the best-matched words never strike exactly the same spark in others. As I go along, then, I shall need the help of every imagination to eke out the meaning of the journey — and because of the nature of this particular pilgrimage, perhaps I shall need your indulgence as well. Walk with me then through a valley of the shadow in the nearby city where I make my home. For part of my community *does* live in shadow.

In the center of my city, there is a steep stone staircase bordered by orderly processions of magnolia and dogwood trees. This is Monument Terrace. Various war memorials are placed there at intervals. At one side, on different levels, are found several city buildings, such as the city hall and the courthouse. On the other side, about two-thirds of the way up the hill, is the chapel of the church I now serve in that city.

For me, the valley of the shadow began at the foot of Monument Terrace. My husband had brought me to see the chapel for the first time when we were visiting the city we would be moving to. He had told me of the beauty of the chapel's setting. I loved the stairway at first sight, its impracticality even, its ancient symbolism of the hard, ascending way of the pilgrim's path — And then, the shadow fell across my way.

At the foot of the Terrace stands an imposing World War 1 memorial. I read the list of men's names who died in that preparatory carnage — then there was a blank space — and then I read the word "colored," then, two more names. Segregated *names*, segregated in the common cause, and on the stone, and in death.

That was the cold baptism that sealed all my previous catechismic education in books and newspapers and stereotypic jokes. And still I resisted. I said to myself, I *must not judge* on the basis of a World War 1 memorial—World War 1 was my father's first war, so many decades ago.

But I will admit that the spell of my baptism was still upon me when I had ascended the steps and walked to the *newly-constructed* courthouse. Perhaps that was why I was so startled when I saw the figure of Justice over the door. Justice — *without* a blindfold! Why is Justice blindfolded in ancient symbolism? Justice wears a blindfold in sign of impartiality. Justice does not look to see whether the parties in controversy are richly attired or in rags, native or immigrant, male or female, white or Negro. Again, I resisted. Perhaps it means that Justice has her eyes wide open, carefully considering all the evidence with wisdom? But this Justice turned away from the scales of evidence and was preoccupied with the sword. She even grasped the sword by the blade, below the hilt, so that in executing her judgment she would injure *herself*.

Between the old war memorial and the new law memorial there is, as I have said, another monument on Monument Terrace — a spirit memorial, the chapel of the church where I serve, dedicated to freedom and responsibility in religion. For me, it was the saving grace of that day, a reminder of Simone Weil's third mystery: that there *are* "flashes of justice, of compassion, of gratitude which rise up in the midst of harshness and metallic coldness."

And more, this very monument became the holy ground on which I stood when I experienced such a mystery.

There was long preparation for the experience: my mother's attitude when I was four and startled by the unaccustomed sight of a dark-skinned woman who was helping her at the counter. "Now, Greta, don't be afraid. She is just the same as we are!" My school and college textbooks carefully dealt with racial theories and their distortions in racist doctrines. A few classmates and friends of friends, but at such a distance! The *obvious corollaries* of religious doctrines of brotherhood with all people. Of political theories of democracy; of psychological concepts of human development. The personal decision that I *would not* consent or quietly acquiesce in the division and torment of fellow human beings.

But still the preparation had not sufficed to carry me through my first encounters with groups of Negros and whites together without an acute awareness of duality: black and white. In part, this was the familiar phenomenon of becoming acutely aware of anything that you are trying particularly hard to forget. But mainly it was the symptom of the inner force of the actual segregation that had long shaped my customs and expectations and even what I saw with my eyes.

I cannot tell you what it meant to me one evening at a meeting held in that chapel. Suddenly I realized that I no longer saw a checkerboard, but a rainbow, not black and white, but a spectrum of faces: Pink, and beige and gold and tan and brown, with highlights and shadows of all colors — and this was only in the outer eye: the inward one was distinguishing *persons*. For me, it was a burning bush, the birth of the Christ child, the descent of the tongues of flame.

And what does this have to do with religion? What *is* religion but the fall of false barriers, the rending of the veil of temples? All the rest is commentary.

And I *am* called to the office of commentary.

I would like to have you meet some of the persons in this valley of our shadow. Many of us know outwardly a few who inhabit such valleys, mainly those in the lower reaches of economic peonage to whom we give 'good advice,' but from whom we withhold the minimum material basis of a hopeful life. But what of others?

Here is a remarkable woman in the shadowed valley. By the combined grace of dedicated parents and of her own talent and effort, she was enabled to follow a profession: dentistry. It is not simply her means of living: it is her *vocation*. She was called to it. She remembers the day in college when it came to her — not as a wish or as an hallucination, but a certainty — that she was to be a dentist. Thirty years later, she still practices her profession with great gentleness and patience.

And what does she think about segregation? "When I was

growing up," she said, "my mother used to comfort me, saying 'Things will be better by the time you're grown.' But, they weren't better by the time I was grown. And now I'll die before they are much better. Sometimes I think I just can't stand it, it *nauseates* me so." And this woman is one of the quiet ones with a constitutional aversion to open controversy — although she did once stand on a picket line.

Another woman of the valley — a French teacher by *vocation*. Master's degree from Columbia, special training in teaching French to children, several years' experience in France teaching French to children and American educational methods to teachers in a French school. In my city, this woman teaches seventh grade in a Negro school. Why not French? This is the reason given to her: There is no similarly well-qualified French teacher in the white schools, therefore, she may not teach French in the Negro school. Note the special segregation logic: something about separate but equal? Justice hurts her own hand when she executes such judgments.

Another woman, a poet. Langston Hughes and Arna Bontemps tell a little about her in their book, *The Poetry of The Negro 1746-1949*:

> Anne Spencer was educated in the Virginia Seminary in Lynchburg, Virginia, the city in which she has spent most of her life. She is the librarian of the Dunbar High School there. Recently she developed a pink candy-striped Chinese peony, eight years from seed. This fact, perhaps, tells as much about her life as anything — with the exception of her poems...

And here is one of her own favorites among her poems:

For Jim, Easter Eve

If ever a garden was Gethsemane,
With old tombs set high against
The crumpled olive tree — and lichen,
This, my garden, has been to me.
For such as I, none other is so sweet:
Lacking old tombs, here stands my grief.
And certainly its ancient tree.

Peace is here and in every season
A quiet beauty.
The sky falling about me
Evenly to the compass...

What is sorrow but tenderness now
In this earth-close frame of land and sky
Falling constantly into horizons
Of east and west, north and south;
What is pain but happiness here
Amid these green and wordless patterns, —
Indefinite texture of blade and leaf;

Beauty of an old, old tree
Last comfort in Gethsemane.

Mrs. Spencer was for over twenty-five years librarian in my city's Negro high school when books from the private library in the city were made available to Negroes through the high school. When the school came to have a modest library of its own, access to the branch of the private library was discontinued, and Negroes no longer have access to its resources. This is a serious deprivation because there is no public library in my city. Mrs. Spencer, however, in view of her work of a quarter of a century, and of her own contribution to literature, was offered the special privilege of continuing to use books from the private library. She refused. Why? She will tell you quietly, "I have *some* conscience."

A visitor to my church office, a man, with little formal education, much less academic degrees: he had questions. Would I tell him something about the Jews? He was interested because he knew that they had often suffered and been much oppressed in many places. He had become interested in them because of his own experiences. He had asked a member of the local synagogue about his religion, but the latter thought he should talk to the Rabbi. The man did not want to "bother" the Rabbi until he at least knew something about the Jewish religion.

Soon it became apparent that the man was asking something more. He was really asking for himself in his participation in the Emancipation Movement. "How can I be faithful, even unto death, to what I believe without betraying what I believe in? How can I actively resist the whole shape of this city that would press me down to something less than a man? And how do I resist without hate — no, how do I resist with *love* that will withstand anything and will help me to withstand anything without running away and without giving way to violence?"

What does this have to do with religion? To ask such a question with your whole heart, as this man asks, this *is* religion.

The account of my pilgrimage would not be complete if I failed to tell you of another statue of Justice to be found in my city. It stands in a coffee house, a Christian coffee house where all are welcome. She stands out of time in an atmosphere of love. The blindfold lies lightly on her already closed eyes. Her sword rests by her side. She holds the scales near her heart as she considers her verdict. Let *this* Justice then stand as a sign of hope for my city and others like it, for my city is changing now. The shadow is still deep, but lighter than it has been in centuries.

Now a Negro child, albeit with great difficulty, may go to the same school as his white peer. And he may dream his dreams of glory at a movie without first passing under a yoke of humiliation. Negro parents may visit their daughter in college and have a place to stay and a place where they can take her for that precious meal away from the campus. And in a few churches no one asks your race when you would worship.

In my brief pilgrimage through this valley, I have asked myself these questions, or rather, these questions have arisen unbidden in commanding form, from the source of all questions: "Do I consent to the casting of the shadow? Do I want my shadow to be a part of the darkness that falls across the path of another?" "No."

"Do I *acquiesce* in the casting of the shadow?" This is a much harder question. In myself, I do not consent, but unless this refusal to consent is made manifest, unless some outward and visible sign of the inward stance is given, then lo, I do in fact acquiesce in the casting of the shadow.

And what kind of world will I leave if, echoing the words of St. Joan, I am good but do nothing?

Well, what are the ways of refusing to acquiesce? How do I say the "No" that ends acquiescence? There is no other way but simply *to begin* — to say or to do "No." Even if I have to begin in a whisper or with a flicker of an eyelid. I can do this for a while, in private, with close friends; it is, at least, a beginning, a tiny raft of "No" in a vast sea of acquiescence.

Later, I may hesitantly inscribe my name upon the records of an organization — not a very active one, perhaps, but where at least my name will be a vote against acquiescence and where I may further my education as a human being among others regardless of our racial labels.

Then I may progress in knowledge and courage toward activity in such an organization, or in others more to the forefront of the Emancipation Movement, until I find my own level of energy and commitment. In other words, I shall begin to find my way into more vigorous expressions of "No" until it becomes a sturdy *island* in the sea of acquiescence.

And then, if you will join me, we can make an archipelago.

Now in all the days and ways of our life, may we put on the blindfold of justice long enough to right our wrongs, and then put it off again when we have been granted the grace to see clearly in the light of love.

Amen

Chapter 11

The Rest of the 1960s

Follow-up on "Valley of the Shadow"

This toned-down version includes a profound insight at the opening of the sermon. Greta's heart-felt description conveys not only her struggle of standing up for Civil Rights, but she elegantly articulates what we all may experience when on a challenging learning path:

> Every spiritual journey is difficult to talk about because words never quite match what happens and how it *feels*—and even the best-matched words never strike exactly the same spark in others. As I go along, then, I shall need the help of every imagination to eke out the meaning of the journey...

Notice in this November talk, that Greta did not even mention that she had been to the March on Washington in August. She didn't mention that she had written letters to editor, or met with the Governor of Virginia in an effort to save Thomas Wansley's life. She never said she was a leader in the Death to Death initiative, or that she was an active participant on the Commission on Religion and Race and the Virginia Council on Human Relations.

None of that came up in this talk. Why? Her final paragraphs become the pivot-point where Greta brings her message home. She first discerns how she was complacently and complicitly tolerating these injustices. Then in first person she asks, "Do I consent to the casting of the shadow? Do I want my shadow to be a part of the darkness that falls across the path of another?" "No."

But as the next question arises, there is much more to consider, "'Do I *acquiesce* in the casting of the shadow?' This is a much harder question. In myself, I do not consent, but unless this refusal to consent is made manifest, unless some outward and visible sign of the inward stance is given, then lo, I do in fact acquiesce in the casting of the shadow."

Though she uses first-person here, she is also gently encouraging everyone present to look deeply within themselves, anchoring themselves in their own sense of integrity. And then, the message, the call for others to *begin* to say "No" and to make their "No" visible. She downplays her own impressive record of activism so she can gently encourage people to start slowly, *if* that is how they need to begin.

The one line that stands out to me as the essence of Greta's message is: "I shall begin to find my way into more vigorous expressions of 'No' until it becomes a sturdy island in the sea of acquiescence."

How beautiful! How elegant! I love her wordsmithing ways.

A Shadow Cast Across the Country

Thirteen days after Greta delivered "Valley of the Shadow" at Hollins College on November 10th, John F. Kennedy was assassinated in Dallas, Texas, on November 23, 1963.

A shadow was cast across the heart of the nation and around the world. Yes, it was dangerous to bring progressive changes to a world stuck in an old, horribly dysfunctional paradigm. Yet, in my opinion, Greta's words were that much more meaningful in light of this tragic event. It took courage to side with powerful internal integrity, and with losses like this, it was even more important to do so.

The Rest of the 1960s

The rest of the 1960s continued to experience periodic tumultuous conflict. Riots occasionally erupted across the country due to the enforced poverty and untenable living conditions for many people of color.

>Race Riots of the 1960s | Encyclopedia.com
>https://www.enclyclopedia.com/history/encyclopedias-almanacs-transcripts-and-maps/race-riots-1960s

June 30, 1962 — *Richmond Times Dispatch* — Letter to the Editor: "Unitarian Minister Sees Ruling Justified"

In addition to the Civil Rights movement, another controversial topic in the 1960s was prayer in schools and the preservation of the separation of church and state. In late June 1962, the U.S. Supreme Court ruled that prayer in publicly-funded schools is unconstitutional. It is important to note that the first clause in the First Amendment of the U.S. Constitution's Bill of Rights states, "Congress shall make no law respecting an establishment of religion." As unpopular as the ruling was, Greta wrote a letter to the editor in support of the Supreme Court's decision:

>Count my vote in your clerical poll in favor of the six justices who ruled the commonwealth (of Virginia) out of bounds in prescribing a prayer in public schools. Students of church-state matters have expected this decision at least since the McCollum case (1948), in which the Supreme Court declared sectarian religious education on public school property in school time to be strictly unconstitutional.

Much of the criticism of the recent decision, I believe, stems from misunderstanding of several basic points.

First of all, it must be understood that the public school is the instrument of the state. If religious devotions are held in connection with the public school, the state is sponsoring them. Far from expressing hostility toward religion, the decision protects religion from state interference when it declares that the state must not prescribe an act of worship for the school children under its care.

Secondly, it is important to realize the wide divergence of conscientious religious opinion in this country. Religious freedom means that one is free to hold his own honest convictions in the area of religion whether or not his neighbors would call them 'religious.'

Some have urged the nondenominational nature of the regents' prayer. Even if the prayer were acceptable to all denominations, which it obviously is not, it is still a prayer. Any prayer, no matter how simple, rests on certain ideas and assumptions about God, man, and prayer itself, and these ideas are not shared by everyone. Furthermore, the state is not only prohibited from acts tending to establish 'denomination,' but from those tending to establish 'religion.'

Finally, the fact that the separation of church and state is ignored in matters such as legislative prayers and mottos is not a reason for approval of public school prayers but a reason for further investigation to determine whether these practices are consistent with the separation of church and state.

I believe that many who now criticize the Supreme Court's decision will, upon reflection, come to see that it is an important clarification of the classic American principle of the separation of church and state — the separation largely inspired by the example of Virginia in its Statute of 1786 based on Thomas Jefferson's Bill for establishing religious freedom.

Greta W. Crosby
Unitarian minister in Lynchburg & Roanoke
Lynchburg

Greta submitted a total of three letters to the editor in support of this ruling in 1962. The above letter went to the *Richmond Times* on June 30th, another was printed in the Lynchburg *News and Advance* on July 8th, as well as one to Roanoke's *World-News* on July 18th. Greta also delivered several sermons in the 1960s on the topic of maintaining the separation of church and state.

In 1964, Greta declined to participate in Roanoke's local high school Baccalaureate ceremony. One reason was because she was going to be out of town. However, it also was because she was concerned about leading the audience in a prayer for the public school-related event. The local newspaper sensationalized this with the following article:

April 10, 1964 — Roanoke's *The World-News*
"Pastor Declines Speaking Offer"

A minister has declined to make a graduation day address to the Cave Spring High School seniors. Greta W. Crosby, who occupies Unitarian Church pulpits in Roanoke and Lynchburg, cited her belief in separation of church and state as grounds for refusing.

Cave Spring Principal Con Davis declined to discuss the refusal today. Mrs. Crosby could not be reached for comment.

A student committee of seniors planning graduation day ceremonies asked her to speak.

Another article appeared in *The Roanoke Times* on April 11th with similar wording. A few days later, a follow-up article was printed:

> **April 14, 1964 — Roanoke's *The World-News***
> **"Pastor Explains Action in Rejecting School Bid"**
>
> A Unitarian minister says she rejected an invitation to speak at Cave Spring High School's baccalaureate service because of 'my own conception' of the principle of separation of church and state.
>
> The Rev. Greta W. Crosby, who serves Unitarian churches in Roanoke and Lynchburg, said today that her action related only to her own participation in the religious service...
>
> She declined the invitation in a letter to the chairman of the school's graduating committee composed of students. The letter said:
>
> "I am honored by your invitation to give the baccalaureate sermon for the graduating class of Cave Spring High School on Sunday, May 31, 1964. I regret, however, that I must decline the invitation. I am to participate in various denominational activities on the West Coast during the month of May. I do not plan to return to Virginia until the first or second week of June.
>
> "For the sake of conscience, I must also be forthright in stating that I have religious scruples concerning my own participation in a religious service held under the auspices of a public school.
>
> "I do heartily thank you for your confidence in me and I do wish you well in fulfilling the responsibilities you have undertaken for the class."

Advocating for the separation of church and state is a prime example of Greta taking an unpopular stand. The U.S. Constitution's protection of religious freedom is in place for important reasons. As harmless as it may seem to be to incorporate prayer or religious instruction in public schools, we really do not want that to be mandated by our government. Historically, imposing religion on citizens has ended very badly for the citizens.

Simply because the majority of a population has a certain set of religious beliefs, this does not give them the right to impose those beliefs onto others. Throughout her life, Greta has consistently affirmed the Constitutional right of each person to follow their own religious or non-religious path.

December 26, 1964 — Roanoke's *The World-News* "Woman Pastor Has Yule Baby"

In mid-1964, Bob and Greta moved from Lynchburg to Keswick so Bob could attend the University of Virginia in Charlottesville. On December 25, 1964, they became the parents of a strikingly handsome baby boy. As announced in Roanoke's *The World-News*:

> The Rev. Greta W. Crosby, part-time pastor of the Roanoke Valley Unitarian Church, can mix motherhood and ministry after the birth on Christmas day of a son, Paul Jefferson Crosby.
>
> The child was born in Charlottesville, where the minister and her husband, Robert J. Crosby, have lived since moving from Bedford County recently.
>
> Mr. Crosby is a graduate student at the University of Virginia and the boy, their first child, was named partly for Thomas Jefferson, who was also a Unitarian.

Paul's first name was given in honor of Greta's father, Henry Paul Worstell, and Jefferson was her most respected Unitarian Founding Father. Bob and Greta were delighted to welcome their Yule Baby into their family.

As the newspaper article mentioned, Bob had been admitted to a Ph.D. program for biomedical engineering. This would have been a great credential for Bob to achieve, however, his mental health was already in decline and he dropped out of the program after a short time. Greta was now about an hour and a half from Lynchburg, and she reduced her Sunday sermons to once a month. She was over 2 hours from Roanoke, but she still maintained her once monthly Sunday sermons, and she still traveled to both churches as often as she could.

March 1965 — Tragedy in Selma, Alabama

Unfortunately, another tragedy unfolded in March 1965. As told by the UU Church of Roanoke (UUCR) history book:

> The 1960s of course was a period of social action against the segregationist policies in many areas. Unitarian Universalists were at the forefront of this movement. In March 1965, Selma, Alabama became the focal point of this action.
>
> On March 6, for the first time, white Alabamans in numbers, demonstrated for racial justice in Selma. Of the approximately 70 whites, approximately one-half were members or ministers of UU churches in Alabama. On March 7, Selma to Montgomery marchers were brutally beaten and gassed by possemen of the county sheriff and state troopers. Dr. Martin Luther King, Jr., put out a call for ministers of all faiths to converge on Selma to make possible the march on Montgomery to protest police brutality and the non-registration of black voters

(because of corrupt voting practices, less than two percent of Selma's eligible black citizens were registered).

Rev. Crosby wrote the UUA on March 9, expressing her anguish at not being able to go to Selma because of her unweaned infant, and pledging an amount equal to the airfare to Atlanta to the Freedom Fund. By March 9, forty-five UU ministers were among the hundreds present in Selma (the UUA estimates that one-fifth of all UU ministers went to Selma and Montgomery). Among them was 38-year-old James Reeb, (who was working with American Friends Service Committee in Boston at the time), in addition there were many lay members who enabled the march to proceed.

Following the march, Rev. Reeb and two other white UU ministers, the Rev. Clark Olsen and the Rev. Orloff Miller, were viciously attacked by four or five white men when they were walking on a street that went past a whites-only restaurant in Selma. (Three of these men were later charged but acquitted by an all-male, all-white jury.)

Reeb was so severely injured that it was decided to take him by ambulance the 90 miles to Birmingham. En route, the black driver and physician and the two other injured ministers were intimidated by whites when the ambulance broke down. Reeb died on March 11, 1965 (he was survived by his wife and four children).

Police in Selma prevented a march to a prayer meeting and observance of Reeb's death, so a vigil was kept at a place called 'Selma Wall.' President and Mrs. Lyndon B. Johnson sent flowers to Rev. Reeb's wife and arranged for a presidential airplane to return Mrs. Reeb and James Reeb's father to Boston.

March 12, 1965 — Roanoke's *The World-News*
"Slain Minister Is Remembered for Enthusiasm"

During one of his four visits to Roanoke, the Rev. James Reeb gave a sermon he called 'Sin Bravely.' He told those who attended the service at the Roanoke Valley Unitarian Church that they should have the courage to act on what they believe is right even if such action is not acceptable to the majority...

...Jack Goodykoontz, at whose home Mr. Reeb usually spent the weekend when he spoke here, remembered that the Unitarian minister liked Roanoke and enjoyed coming down from Washington... Goodykoontz said he was most impressed by the minister's youthful enthusiasm. "He was the friendliest type of man. He seemed to love living." He recalled that Mr. Reeb often discussed his summer vacations when he would go on camping trips out West to pursue his hobby of fossil hunting. The minister once brought with him to Roanoke the fossil of the head of an ancient horse to show the children here.

Mrs. Goodykoontz remembered a letter from Mr. Reeb following the death of President Kennedy in which he said the people of this country must dedicate themselves to preventing such a thing from happening again. "He was such a fine person. You felt as if you had always known him." She said, "He laughed so hard and was not pious for being as dedicated as he was. He seemed so young in spirit."

John A. Cunningham, president of the Roanoke Valley Unitarian Church remembered Mr. Reeb as "a very warm person. He was humorous and vital."

The Rev. Greta Crosby, minister of the Roanoke Church on a part-time basis, wrote a statement for the members of the church.

"What I remember about Jim Reeb was his seriousness of purpose and his gaiety of heart," she said. "The most important thing about Jim Reeb is not the way he died, but the way he lived. He had turned his whole life, not just his leisure, toward people whose lives are stifled by the pressures of economic and psychological want. Now he is dead by private violence encouraged by public violence done or condoned by the official representatives of the people of the state of Alabama.

"Jim Reeb knew what he was doing and risking when he went to Alabama. His death was in keeping with his life. It is not a consolation for being dead, but it is something for your death to count for what you have lived for. How his death will count depends on what we will do in the light of it."

The UUCR historical document continues:

On March 15, at Brown's Memorial Chapel in Selma, a memorial service was held, with Dr. Martin Luther King, Jr. delivering the principle eulogy and Dr. Dana McLean Greeley, president of the UUA, giving the prayer...(100's of UU's and others attended and funds were set up to aid his family).

That evening, President Johnson delivered his "We Shall Overcome" speech to a joint session of Congress, proposing the Voting Rights Act. The President invited Rev. King to attend, but he remained in Selma to deliver Reeb's eulogy.

The following is the first several lines of President Johnson's landmark speech in support of Civil Rights. On March 15, four days after Rev. Reeb's death, President Johnson began:

I speak tonight for the dignity of man and the destiny of democracy. I urge every member of both parties, Americans of all religions and of all colors, from every section of this country, to join me in that cause.

At times history and fate meet at a single time in a single place to shape a turning point in man's unending search for freedom. So it was at Lexington and Concord. So it was a century ago at Appomattox. So it was last week in Selma, Alabama.

There, long-suffering men and women peacefully protested the denial of their rights as Americans. Many were brutally assaulted. One good man, a man of God, was killed.

There is no cause for pride in what has happened in Selma. There is no cause for self-satisfaction in the long denial of equal rights of millions of Americans. But there is cause for hope and for faith in our democracy in what is happening here tonight.

For the cries of pain and the hymns and protests of oppressed people have summoned into convocation all the majesty of this great government — this government of the greatest Nation on earth. Our mission is at once the oldest and the most basic of this country: to right wrong, to do justice, to serve man...

The entirety of President Johnson's compelling speech, "We Shall Overcome," can be found at:
https://www.pbs.org/wgbh/
americanexperience/features/lbj-overcome/

Five months later, on August 6, 1965, Congress passed, and President Johnson signed, the Voting Rights Act into law. It is considered to be among the most comprehensive Civil Rights legislation in U.S. history. It provided far-reaching protections to minority voters — until two cases decided by the Supreme Court, one in 2013, and one in 2021, greatly weakened the law. Recalling Greta's prophetic words from "Justice Without a Blindfold":

> We have said that so long as the religious liberal holds anything at all to be of value, there will always be ways of preserving, enhancing and manifesting what he holds to be of value — and on the contrary, there will also be ways of destroying what he holds dear.

AND

> I shall begin to find my way into more vigorous expressions of 'No' until it becomes a sturdy island in the sea of acquiescence.

Vietnam War Protests

Another cause of unrest was outrage at the atrocities of the Vietnam War and emotional protests were emerging. Greta wrote in the Lynchburg church newsletter in February 1966:

> The following resolution was passed by the Southern Unitarian Universalist Ministers' Association meeting in New Orleans, January 19, 1966:
>
> "'We are encouraged by the recent intensification of efforts by the United Nations, the United States and other individual governments to bring about a negotiated peace in Vietnam. In furtherance of this objective, we would urge that our government seek an indefinite extension of the present cease-fire, that the bombing of North Vietnam not be resumed, and that our government seek to involve the United Nations in further negotiations on the basis of the Geneva Accord."
>
> I support it.
>
> — GWC

https://www.britannica.com/event/Vietnam-War

Unfortunately, it would be another seven long years before the U.S. withdrew combat units on the ground in 1973, and the U.S. was still involved in the conflict for two more years. In 1975, South Vietnam fell to North Vietnam's communist regime which had been heavily funded by China and the Soviet Union. Approximately 58,200 American lives were lost. Overall, millions of civilians and military personnel were killed in the war. Many others were seriously injured and/or emotionally traumatized. Thousands of returning soldiers never fully recovered from the horrors abroad or the harassment and shaming upon their return home. I'm sure that Greta had many more reflections on this tragic war, and I have no doubt that I'll find further commentary when I anthologize her collection.

A Big Change for the Crosbys

In late 1966, a big change came up for Bob and Greta and their young son Paul. Bob found a job opportunity as a Biomedical Research Engineer at the Southwest Research Institute in San Antonio, Texas. Here is the historical record of the UU Church of Roanoke:

> The church was saddened in late fall of 1966 to hear that Greta Crosby would be leaving because her husband had accepted a position in Texas. She had endeared herself to the membership and would be greatly missed. The years of her ministry were pleasant and exciting ones for the church. On December 11, 1966, she gave her last sermon. She began:
>
> > Goodnight church on a hill,
> > Goodnight locomotive bell,

Ch 11 - The Rest of the 1960s

> Goodnight high, wide windows and sweet green walls,
> Goodnight songs, upstairs and down,
> Goodnight flowers put with love,
> Goodnight people, each one very much you,
> yet part of me,
> Goodnight.

The First Unitarian Church of Lynchburg held a picnic and gave her a beautiful artisan-quality silver bowl. The inscription reads: "Greta W. Crosby — This is a token of our appreciation for your ministry of patience, guidance and love. First Unitarian Church, Lynchburg — 1966."

We still have this bowl in our home. Just the other day I was polishing it and I placed it on display on a shelf with our winter 'Let it Snow' decor, which includes shades of blue, teal, white and *silver*.

Then while doing research for this era, I found a newspaper article that describes the Lynchburg church gifting the silver bowl to Mom — so I picked it up and read the inscription on the back. It was then that I realized this silver bowl has been in our family for all my life and I had no idea what it was and what it meant. I'm so grateful to know this now, and I extend gratitude to both the Roanoke and Lynchburg congregations for the Love and the lessons that were grown there.

The move away from Greta's beloved churches was genuinely bittersweet. To be relieved of 'Old Dominion' domination must have been refreshing. But, there were the people she dearly loved in both of her churches, and leaving those friendships, nay, those kinships must have been unfathomably hard. Similar to some of the members from the Church of the Reconciliation, Greta did keep in touch with a number of the members from her Virginia congregations.

One of those families from the Lynchburg congregation was Russell and Ruth Ball and their children. Russell was active, enjoying good health for many years, until he passed away in 2014. We were delighted to learn that Ruth has just turned 98. Ruth smiled brightly when their daughter Sarah told her I had been in touch — and Greta smiled brightly when I told her about Ruth and Sarah. Ruth remarked how "Greta was very important to the life and the direction of the church."

Sarah shares, "I was only six years old when your family moved from the area, so my memories are vague, but I do remember your parents and your brother Paul Jeff and going to their house out in the county. I remember talk of how your mother spoke out about racial injustice, in particular the Wansley case, and how my parents so respected her and defended her."

Russell and Ruth were our godparents. I remember them sending beautiful, colorful presents on gift-giving occasions. Sarah also reminisces, "I remember your mother wrote the loveliest Christmas letters and sent my parents Advent calendars, which I always enjoyed."

So, though separated by many miles, the invisible heart-strings from both congregations were still connected and still reverberate with the gentle melody of friendship and fellowship.

Helotes Home

The Crosbys settled into their Texas home in 1967. It was a little buff-brick ranch house on a hill, on two treed acres in Helotes, which was a quiet spot near San Antonio. Once there, 36-year-old Greta had nesting to do, for she was expecting her second baby. On Labor Day, Monday, September 4, 1967, Bob, Greta and Paul expanded their family when little Lara was born. During the time of raising young children, Greta did not apply for positions at churches in the area, though she did travel as a guest speaker to various UU congregations.

Motherhood offered something completely different for Greta in those years. As with most who are raising children, she experienced fantastically sublime moments, combined with ongoing frustrations and overwhelmingly low points. When I was a young mom of three energetic offspring, I commented that I love our kids so much, but it can be so hard. Mom replied, "With everything I've done in my life, raising two children was by far the hardest thing I ever accomplished." The thing is, I didn't really understand then how many hard things Mom had done in her life!

The Late 1960s

Returning to the timeline of the 1960s, more tragic losses and also significant legislative gains were on the horizon, particularly in 1968. On April 4, 1968, Dr. Martin Luther King, Jr. was assassinated, spawning violent riots across the nation and casting another shadow of profound grief across the U.S. and around the world. A few days later, Congress passed the Fair Housing Act, an important Civil Rights bill, which President Johnson signed into law on April 11, 1968.

Martin Luther King Jr. Assassination — Facts, Reaction & Impact | HISTORY

> https://history.com/topics/black-history/
> martin-luther-king-jr-assassination

Then on June 5, 1968, Robert F. Kennedy was assassinated after winning California's Democratic primary. This was another significant disappointment because it was hoped that Robert would be able to bring balance to the polarized country.

Robert F. Kennedy is fatally shot | June 5, 1968 | HISTORY

https://www.history.com/this-day-in-history/
bobby-kennedy-is-assassinated

Two months later, in August 1968, President Johnson signed the Housing and Urban Development Act, another historic Civil Rights bill that Congress had passed. This was not a perfect solution, but it paved the way for the development of affordable housing and other gradual improvements in support of Civil Rights in our country.

The Conclusion of Thomas Wansley's Story

Circling back to Thomas Wansley, he was not executed, but unbelievably his case continued to drag on for years. In 1966, his case went to the Virginia Supreme Court of Appeals, and his convictions were reversed due to the severe mishandling of the trial. Yet the case was not dismissed, there was to be a new trial. I believe it was at this point that a defense attorney from New York, William Kunstler, came in to represent Thomas Wansley on a pro bono basis. The first thing the Lynchburg press did was to cast false accusations of communist ties onto Kunstler when he took on the case. Upon studying the case, Wansley's new attorneys identified 89 procedural errors in his original trial. Kunstler's work proved to be beneficial, though navigating the ongoing legal corruption was still mind-blowingly treacherous.

First and foremost, the 1967 retrial should have been moved to a more neutral location, but that was blocked. As Brumfield explains:

All 61 prospective jurors who had filed into the packed courtroom past a mural that depicted enslaved Black people planting tobacco, claimed they had heard of the trial and read the articles about the 'rapist' Wansley and Kunstler's alleged involvement with communist activities. Wansley's frustrated attorneys again asked for the trial to be moved out of Lynchburg. Again, the court refused. They finally chose 12 jurors and one alternate.

Consequently, the possibility of neutrality and a fair trial was systematically shut down before it started. Additionally, in December 1962, when Thomas was first apprehended, Annie Carter could not pick him out of a line-up. In the first trial, Annie Carter testified that she was "not too sure" that Thomas Wansley was her assailant. But this time, four years later, she testified that she was sure that he was the assailant. From Brumfield's book:

When asked how both statements could be factual, she replied, "Well, naturally, I've seen his pictures in the newspapers, and I've seen him in court since then."

...(Wansley's attorneys also) tried to find Kyoko Fleshman, who had identified Wansley as her rapist, to put her on the stand and admit that she had fabricated the charges. As soon as she heard that Wansley's lawyers were looking for her, she left Lynchburg. They tracked her to the West Coast, then to Hawaii. When they located her there, she fled to Japan, where she was still a citizen and could not be extradited. And there she remained, refusing to respond to pleas to tell the truth and save Wansley's life.

Through the machinations of the corrupt Lynchburg court system, Thomas Wansley was again found guilty. This time, however, instead of being sentenced to death, he was sentenced to life imprisonment plus 20 years.

While incarcerated, Thomas had become a prisoner's rights advocate. Despite being a well-behaved prisoner, because he was working to improve prison conditions, he experienced cruel retaliation from prison officials. For example, Brumfield tells of how Thomas was sometimes shackled to his cot and he "remained locked in his cell, 24 hours a day, from July 19, 1968, through April 1, 1969."

For years there were more gains and losses in the case, then finally in late 1977, due to William Kunstler's dedication, as well as continued public outcry, Thomas Wansley was finally fully re-leased from prison. He could have left the commonwealth of Virginia, but he decided to stay in Harrisonburg where he went to work driving a truck. Sadly, he became an alcoholic due to the damaging psychological effects of his unjust incarceration. He was in his late 50's when he died on August 24, 2003.

Overall Systemic Improvements

There is something important to note about Thomas Wansley's story. As a direct result of some of the corrupt actions taken in this case, significant counter-gains were made. Thomas was illiterate because as a child he had an embarrassing scalp condition that caused him to miss so much school he couldn't keep up. He had dropped out of school in sixth grade. When Dr. Martin Luther King, Jr. visited Thomas in jail, Dr. King counselled Thomas to learn to read and write, and to do what he could from where he was to initiate changes for the highest good of all concerned.

Thomas Wansley followed Dr. King's advice. While incarcerated, he became literate, which opened the way for him to achieve system-wide improvements for prisoners. Additionally, due to the horrible injustices enacted in his case, laws were changed to ensure more fair and equitable trials in the future.

For example, as noted in the backstory for "Justice Without a Blindfold," there was no court reporter present at Thomas Wansley's first trial in February 1963. Though his attorney requested a continuance, Judge Cundiff denied the motion. Consequently, there was no transcript of the trial. Then on March 23, 1963, Thomas Wansley's attorney mysteriously died. Brumfield explains:

> This unexpected death created a nightmare scenario in that since no court reporter had transcribed the first trial, no defense attorney had heard the testimony. The law stated that in the event of an appeal, where there was no transcript of the original trial, the defense and the prosecutor had to agree on what was said. With Lawson deceased, this agreement was impossible.

But here is the impressive thing that Brumfield shares that came about as a result of that appalling injustice: "...In response to this fiasco, in June 1964, the General Assembly passed a law prohibiting the trials of persons charged with a felony if there was not a court reporter present." This is just *one* example of changes to the justice system that are directly related to Thomas Wansley's story. Imagine the ripple-effects — how many people has that one law protected since 1964?

Likewise, Thomas Wansley's case played a significant role in the establishment of the twenty-year moratorium on executions in the commonwealth. Subsequently, Virginia had many gains and losses with regard to this primitive practice. However, in March 2021, the Virginia General Assembly made history when both the Senate and the House passed a bill that *abolished* the death penalty in the commonwealth.

On March 24, 2021, Governor Ralph Northam signed the bill into law, making Virginia the first southern state to ban capital punishment. With these overall improvements in mind, I am reminded of Dr. Martin Luther King, Jr.'s prophetic words, "The arc of the moral universe is long, but it bends toward justice."

> ## Section III
> ## *The 1970s*

From *73 Voices:
An Anthology of Aspirations, Meditations, and Prayers*
published in 1971

Prayer — Meditation

Lord,

We are hidden in ourselves. We live, and move, and have our being in deep mystery. But this is not enough for us. We play hide and seek with ourselves, a desperate game that is not play. We hide even what we know because we are afraid; we seek even what is not there because we are afraid. The last thing in the world we want is to be known as we are. We are masters of masquerade to protect us from detection.

And yet, O Lord, we ache to be understood. Grant us the courage to face the fear of betrayal and the fear of unworthiness that blind our eyes and bind our hands. We would grow in freedom and reach out in love and trust.

— Greta Worstell Crosby

CHAPTER 12

The Early 1970s

Going into 1970, my brother Paul would have just turned six and I was three. We were having a wonderful time growing up in Texas hill country. My brother warmly remembers how we were raised as free-range children. He notes that "we grew up in a house with a library, but no television."

Greta was an amazing mom; she loved us so much and she took excellent care of us. Though I've heard she didn't cook that well, I don't recall that being a problem. One of my favorite dishes was Mom's chicken curry. The aroma of yellow curry wafting through the house made my mouth water. She learned the recipe when she in France at the age of sixteen.

She stayed at home with us most of the time, though she was a member of social justice organizations such as the ACLU. She was also an active member of the First UU Church of San Antonio, even delivering Spoken Essays on occasion, as well as guest speaking at UU churches in surrounding areas.

I warmly remember going to a preschool called Discovery School at the UU Church of San Antonio. I was extremely shy as a child and I never wanted Mom to leave when she dropped me off. Gradually I would acclimate and by the time she came back to pick me up, I didn't want to leave my activities. She would say,

"Okay, La-La, it's time to go." Preschool was critically important for me to learn to socialize and to develop coping skills. It takes a village to raise a child and I feel so fortunate to have been raised in a UU village.

An Unexpected Loss

In November 1973, Greta experienced a significant loss. I remember I was in kindergarten and I had crawled into my mom's side of the bed in the early morning. We were all dozing when we were awakened by a phone call. It was Aunt Nancy, mom's sister, she was terribly upset and somehow disconnected the call. A moment later she called back and through sobs and tears, she gave Mom the news that their father had passed away from a sudden heart attack.

This was a difficult loss for my mom as well as for her whole family. She adored her father and she cherished their relationship so very much. She corresponded with him regularly and in return her father would send reel-to-reel tape recordings, updating her on their lives. Eventually, as technology improved, he converted to recorded cassette tapes. I think after his passing, she even received a tape that he had mailed which was in-transit when he passed.

More details about Greta's relationship with her father will be discussed in her last Commentary, "Fathers and Farewell." For now, it's helpful to understand the timing in late 1973 of the loss of her father who was her biggest fan.

Another Move

Since moving to Helotes in 1967, my father had been doing biomedical research at the Southwest Research Institute in San Antonio. Among other projects, he helped develop methods of tracking ovum within the fallopian tubes of rabbits, which paved the way to improve birth control methods. He also assisted with the transplantation of a mechanical heart into a goat, which was a milestone on the road to transplantation of mechanical heart valves, and eventually mechanical hearts, into humans.

Yet Bob's depression was exacerbated by the politics of research funding. He was truly brilliant; he saw simple solutions to complex problems, but he lacked anger management skills — so he was not the most diplomatic employee. I am not sure exactly what happened, but he lost his job maybe sometime in 1974. He applied for other jobs, but he did not get hired and there was no money coming in. Mom did her best to generate income with speaking engagements, but that wasn't going to be viable in the long term.

With no income, and while still grieving her father's loss, Mom had to make the difficult choice to go back to work as a UU minister. Even more problematic was the fact that finding placement at a UU church meant we had to move. She applied at locations all over the country, and in 1975 she was called to the First Unitarian Universalist Church of Wichita, Kansas. Though her placement at First UU was fortuitous, it was a difficult time for the Crosby family. I was 7 when we moved and I was devastated. Texans don't transplant well — I hated everything about it, and I was sure to broadcast this whenever the opportunity arose. I now realize that this move and life change was so much harder for Mom than it was for me.

My dad's clinical depression was so disabling that he never held another job again. He applied for jobs in Wichita, but the refrain from potential employers was often that Bob was 'over-qualified.' Additionally, I'm not sure if his anger management issues would have allowed him to maintain employment. That meant the financial burden of supporting the family on a minister's minimal salary fell on Mom's shoulders. A few years later, Dad's depression deepened so severely that he was admitted to Wesley Medical Center for suicidal behaviors. He then spent several months at another facility for psychological therapies, but his depression continued. Eventually, Dad was able to obtain disability payments, which helped some, but it was not even close to what was needed to support the household.

Mom once commented that living with Dad was like living with Dr. Jekyll and Mr. Hyde, we never knew which mood we were going to get. She couldn't depend on him for emotional support — to the contrary, he could be emotionally abusive.

To be fair, Bob was not awful all the time. As many scientists tend to be, Bob was also a talented artist. He worked with a wide range of modalities including pottery, wood-working, metalwork, gemstones, jewelry, and photography. He truly was artistically gifted and I'm grateful for the photos he took of our family over the years.

Additionally, Bob was the sound technician for First UU for thirty years. When Greta was installed as their minister in 1975, Bob installed a sound system so she could be properly heard and so her sermons could be recorded. Nearly every Sunday until 2006 or so, Bob was sitting at the electronics cabinet in the meeting house, getting the sound and recordings ready.

For years I perceived him as a scary monster because of his angry outbursts — and others did, too. But later I began to understand that he was actually extremely sensitive. In his last days, he described his sound & recording duties, and other tasks he did for the church as 'acts of love.' He genuinely wanted to help the world to be a better place, he just didn't go about it in a healthy way.

In May 1975, Greta, who had mothered Paul and me so beautifully, was now 'mother' to an entire congregation. Despite the difficulties at home, she did her job well. She dedicated herself to the work, not just for the paycheck — that may have been the initial need, but that's only what got her in the door. In my opinion, she was a minister's minister.

In addition to her normal office hours during the week, she spent many evenings attending meetings. She attended First UU's Board and Committee meetings. She performed numerous ceremonies for UU members and friends. Additionally, she provided kind-hearted pastoral care, with hospital and nursing home visitations and individual sessions for people in need.

One of Greta's first actions as minister of First UU was to memorialize the Reverend James Reeb because he was born and raised in Wichita, Kansas. As described in the section on the 1960s, James Reeb was the UU minister who was killed in Selma, Alabama in 1965, as a result of his participation in the March from Selma to Mongomery. She brought awareness of his dedication to Civil Rights to the congregation of First UU.

From 1975 to 1987, Greta was also active in a number of denominational and community organizations, though not all at the same time. She was the Scribe for the Berry Street Conference; a Board member for the Prairie Star UU District; a KAIROS Board of Governors member; a Board member for the Starr King School for the Ministry; a Board member for the South Central Kansas Civil Liberties Union; she was on the Organizing and Steering Committee for the Religious Caucus for Human Rights; she was on the advisory staff of the Work Options for Women; a Board member for the Religious Coalition for Social Action; she was a Board member, then Executive Committee member, then Vice-Chair of KPTS-Channel 8 (Public Television); and she was a Forum Board member, then a Board member for Wichita's Inter-Faith Ministries.

She also taught "Women and the Law," at Wichita State University in the Spring semesters of 1976 and 1977. And in 1978, she was awarded the Doctor of Sacred Theology, an honorary degree from the Starr King School for the Ministry, located in Berkeley, California. I'm impressed with how Greta managed all this and her ministerial duties, while still composing high quality Commentaries for the congregation on Sundays!

Yellow Legal Notepads & Elaine Bulatkin

I want to take a moment here to note something about Greta's writing and creative process. For most of her career, she hand-wrote her sermons on big yellow legal notepads. She would compose, and scratch-out, then rewrite on those canary yellow pages. I recall that Saturdays and sometimes even Sunday mornings were big days for writing and finalizing in preparation for the Sunday service. At the time, I thought it was a bit last minute, why couldn't she finish them during the week? Since serving on First UU's Worship Committee, I can empathize with the pressure on a minister to produce original sermons each week — once one is done, you've got to get on to the next one. Now I am positively awed at how brilliantly she composed her elegant masterpieces each Sunday.

One more fun fact about Greta's yellow notepad sermons; during the week after each service, Elaine Bulatkin, First UU's amazing office administrator, transcribed them into neatly-typed pages for Greta's files. Elaine was First UU's office administrator from 1975 to approximately 2002, and she was vital to the functioning of the church. At the end of the next four sermons you'll see "GWC:ebb" with the corresponding date. I've included them here in recognition of Elaine's incredible work in support of Greta's ministry.

Introduction to "Beautiful Dreamers"

I'm delighted to say that I was able to source the next four Commentaries from a notebook that Greta compiled of her own favorite sermons. These include: "Beautiful Dreamers," "A Celebration of Crows," "Lighting One Light with Another" and "Shadows."

"Beautiful Dreamers," which Greta shared at First UU on May 30, 1976, explains the many benefits of dream exploration. She was 45 years old when she delivered this sermon. In it she describes the traditional dream practices of the Senoi tribe, an indigenous population on Peninsular Malaysia. She appreciates their custom of listening to and honoring each member of the family, from the youngest to the eldest, particularly when sharing their dreams together.

At the church service, she read the entire 19-page section from a book published in 1972 called *Sources: An anthology of contemporary material useful for preserving personal sanity while braving the great technological wilderness*. The section was written about Kilton Stewart's research in dream interpretation. I'll be taking time to summarize Stewart's section from *Sources* in order to build a foundation for Greta's insightful messages in her sermon. For those who are particularly interested, the used book can be ordered from Amazon for a nominal price.

One thing to note about the Senoi tribe, however, is that Kilton Stewart studied them in 1935, and prior to that, his colleague H.D. Doone had spent seven years studying them. They both accumulated insights into the practices of the tribe before World War II. Since WW II, there have been changes to tribal practices based on the influx of other controlling influences. Apparently the tribe no longer uses these traditional dream interpretation processes. However, even if the tribe no longer practices communal dreamwork as they did in the past, I believe there is great wisdom in the concepts.

In reference to the subtitle of *Sources* — *"An anthology of contemporary material useful for preserving personal sanity while braving the great technological wilderness,"* Greta has her own method of preserving her sanity while braving the great technological wilderness — she avoids it almost entirely. She mentions in this Commentary how the overuse of television limits our interactions with each other on a human level. Fun factoid, Greta has never owned a television. She hasn't watched TV for more than a few minutes in passing, and to this day, she doesn't have a TV in her living quarters.

So with those little details all tucked-in, we are now ready to explore "Beautiful Dreamers."

Chapter 13

"Beautiful Dreamers"

Greta W. Crosby
First Unitarian Church of Wichita
Wichita, Kansas
May 30, 1976

[In the service, Greta read a section of the book *Sources* which was entitled "Dream Exploration Among the Senoi." The following is an overview of the section found in *Sources*, which begins with an excerpt from Kilton Stewart's 1960 essay "Creative Psychology and Dream Education."]

To "know thyself," said Socrates, is the whole meaning of philosophy. But the self most of us knows is no more than the wide-awake, sharply-focused, daylight fraction of our identity. Every morning, as soon as the alarm clock marshalls us to job or school, each of us undertakes a psychically obliterating discipline. Systematically, ruthlessly, but subliminally, we erase our dream life, until no more than faded images remain. And by day's end, even these are lost to us. How much of ourselves is thus roughly discarded with our sleep and dream experiences? How much of our essential identity, or our personal destiny, do we daily amputate in this way so that we might put on the orthodox consciousness society requires of us?

In the Hindu and Buddhist traditions, dream-mind and sleep-mind share equally with waking-mind in the composition of human identity. Thus the mantric seed-syllable AUM (OM) synthesizes the three modes of consciousness: A, being wakefulness (*jagarat*), U, being the dream (*svapna*), and M, being deep sleep (*susupti*). Finally "OM as a whole represents the all-encompassing cosmic consciousness (*turiya*) on the fourth plane, beyond words and consciousness..." (Lama Govinda). How tissue-thin our conventional western psychology seems by comparison. It is largely a mapping of the articulate surface, of the outer cerebral shell.

One need not go to these rich oriental traditions, however, to find sophisticated appreciation of the role played by the dream- and sleep-minds in shaping the person. Many primitive groups have fashioned oneirologies (studies of dreams) that far surpass even those of Freud and Jung. Jungians like Kilton Stewart have, however, been willing to learn from the primitives.

The entry goes on to describe Kilton Stewart's experiences on a 1935 expedition to Peninsular Mayalsia to study the Senoi, an indigenous highland tribe. The tribal leadership roles consisted primarily of "primitive psychologists" called *halaks*, as well as *Tohats*, which are like doctors, healers and educators. The tribe was peaceful, democratic and highly socially cooperative due to their practices of integrating the selves of the wakeful, dreaming and sleeping mind.

A government ethnologist, H.D. Doone had studied this tribe for seven years. He told Stewart about the Senoi and their cooperative society. According to the section in *Sources*, Stewart spent a year studying the Senoi and another year integrating Doone's years of study on the tribe. He then spent fifteen years experimenting with the Senoi techniques, and he believed that they could be beneficial to anyone who practiced them.

Kilton explains that were two parts to the Senoi dream theories: dream interpretation and dream expression. Dream expression is described as a "cooperative reverie" that is practiced at adolescence, marking the transition into adulthood.

The rest of the section focuses on the practice of dream interpretation, which was performed every morning by the male adults of each family. Breakfast was spent sharing and discussing the dreams of each of the children. Then, the older brothers and the father would join with the other males of the tribe to report these dreams and collaboratively interpret them. According to Stewart, the interpretive psychology of the Senoi was as follows:

> Man creates features or images of the outside world in his own mind as part of the adaptive process. Some of those features are in conflict with him and with each other. Once internalized, these hostile images turn man against himself and against his fellows. In dreams, man has the power to see these facets of his psyche, which have been disguised in external forms, associated with his own fearful emotions, and turned against him and the internal images of other people. If the individual does not receive aid through education and therapy, these hostile images...get tied together and associated with one another in a way which makes him physically, socially and psychologically abnormal.

These conflicted configurations tend to remain suppressed in the unconscious, but they still influence us, even though we don't know why we are triggered by them. The Senoi believe that, with help from others in the community, anyone can deal with these mental-emotional blocks by facing them, communicating with them, and learning from them.

The Senoi used specific approaches to accomplish this by co-operating with people in waking life, and by achieving lucid dreaming capabilities. Importantly, these abilities were fostered from childhood and onward. Each Senoi learned to control their inner-dreamworld, which helped resolve problems within those dreams, as well as in waking life. The Senoi not only believed that anyone could do this, it was believed that everyone should do this, as a personal responsibility to the community.

Stewart collected different Senoi dream accounts of all age groups and compared them with the collected dream content of other cultures. Stewart found differences in the Senoi approach, particularly regarding their belief in retrieving creative contributions from the Senoi dreamers.

He used an example of an anxiety-provoking dream of falling. When the Senoi child reports a falling dream, the adult encourages them to see it as an auspicious opportunity to learn important things from it. The Senoi believed that everything that happens in a dream has a purpose and a message. They encouraged dreamers to relax and enjoy themselves while falling in a dream. They explained that it was kind of like entering a wormhole, falling would get you to a new realm of insights faster because you are attracted to the vibration there, that's why you're falling into it. Similar analogies would be made for climbing, traveling, flying, or soaring dreams.

Stewart explains that working with the children from an early age to see their dreams differently and to exert control over their dreams helped them grow up with life skills to manage both waking-life and dream-life challenges.

> That which was an indwelling fear of anxiety, becomes an indwelling joy or act of will; that which was ill esteem toward forces which caused the child to fall in his dream, becomes good will toward the denizens of the dream world, because he relaxes in his dream and finds pleasurable adventures, rather than waking up with a clammy skin and crawling scalp.

The section goes on to explain that Senoi are expected to go forward and attack when they face danger in a dream. They may ask for help from friends, but they are to fight until help arrives. They have a specific belief about friends, which is that friends themselves would never attack the dreamer, so if one appears to attack then it is not their friend but something wearing a mask, appearing to be his friend. The Senoi believed that dream personas only seem hostile if the dreamer is running from them. Often, when the dreamer stops and faces them, they will transform into a friend.

One of the most interesting concepts that I've learned here is that when the dreamer is in an enjoyable dream, they should seek to receive a dream-gift of some kind. If they travel to another realm, they should acquire a new song, dance, poem, design, or unique knowledge to take back to the Senoi community.

Another fascinating concept deals with friends in waking life. If the dreamer dreams of harming one of their friends, they should be especially kind to their friend in waking life. If a friend seems to harm the dreamer in a dream, the dreamer should communicate this with their friend in order to address whatever might be causing dissonance between them. The Senoi worked proactively to communicate concerns while they were minor, rather than repressing and suppressing them, which only makes the unspoken conflict fester and intensify.

Stewart then listed seven steps the Senoi utilized in their dream interpretation for their children.

1. The child is heard and encouraged to share his innermost experiences. He is particularly praised when he reveals something related to anxiety, showing him the wonderful healing opportunities that are available to him.

2. The child is assured that he is doing good work, and that looking at what is coming up for him and doing his self-work is like doing homework.

3. Through adult interpretations of the child's dreams, the child learns to control his dreams by relaxing and practicing certain actions in his dreams. If there is a force that is difficult to control, he works with it until he can establish control and learn to manipulate as he wishes.

4. The child is guided to understand that the presence of anxiety provides opportunities to train him to direct his dreams. And he is made aware that the persistence of anxiety will block ability to retrieve creative and productive gifts from his dreams.

5. The child is raised with the understanding that he is responsible not only for his decisions in waking life, but also his eventual mastery of his dream-life. It will be important for him to manage his emotional and mental reactions as well as those things that seem to happen to him, whether in waking or dream lives.

6. It will be reinforced in different ways that it is so much better to look at his mental/emotional reactions than to try to hide them by suppressing them.

7. These principles provide a foundational upbringing and practice that will evolve throughout his lifetime. And it "assumes

that a human being who retains good will for his fellows and communicates his psychic reactions to them for approval and criticism, is the supreme ruler of all the individual forces of the spirit..."

Senoi adults modeled for their children the spreading of genuine goodwill to others in their communities. They were taught that what they saw in others mirrored their own beliefs. If what they saw in others was upsetting, they were trained to look within themselves, for there was something that needed healing work.

Another component was for the children to learn to ask for and expect to receive creative and constructive insights from the dreamworld. Stewart explains how a child's assertive behavior is expected to be channeled into a beneficial action for the community.

It's important to note, however, that the creative content that is brought through will be expected to be shared by the individual with the group and then the members of council will provide feedback, positive or critical, on the contributed content.

> Thus, accumulating social experience supports the organizing wisdom of the body in the dream, making the dreamer first unafraid of the negative image and its accompanying tension state, and later enabling him to break up that tension state and transmute the accumulated energy from anxiety into a poem, a song, a dance, a new type of trap, or some other creative product, to which an individual or the whole group will react with approval (or a critique) the following day.

He goes on to observe that with all the details of the Senoi practices, Stewart believes that "dreaming can and does become the deepest type of creative thought."

Stewart then expressed his belief that our modern civilization, with all its conflict and duality, may have gotten the way it is, in large part, due to our systematic suppression of mental/emotional conflict. We're blocking the normal communication pathways which would allow us to express and release our reactions to a whole range of problems.

Stewart shares another interesting observation, that nonsense dreams, scary dreams, anxious dreams, etc., tended to ebb by the time a Senoi became an adolescent. As their minds became trained and disciplined, their dreams became significantly more productive.

> From puberty on, the dream life becomes less and less fantastic and irrational, and more and more like reflective thinking, problem solving, exploration of unknown things or people, emotionally satisfying social intercourse, and the acquiring of knowledge from a dream teacher or spirit guide.

Greta's Commentary: "Beautiful Dreamers"

In Mexico, there is a way of bidding goodnight to children that goes like this: *"Que sueñes con los Angelitos"* — "May you dream with the little angels." This beautiful saying reminds me of dreaming with the Senoi.

This morning I am sharing an enthusiasm with you, the Senoi. Ever since I read Kilton Stewart's article on "Dream Exploration Among the Senoi" several years ago, I have been spreading the gospel according to the Senoi or at least announcing their good news and celebrating the expanded life they have developed via exploration of their inner world and imaginative, constructive, loving model for church life and community life.

I am not advocating the wholesale adoption of their unique

pattern of cultures centered on dream interpretation, but to our being open to stimulation by their ideas and patterns and perhaps the same values: individual creativity keyed into a community of support in a continuing process of constructive transformation. That, of course, is my ulterior motive this morning, but mainly I just want to share my enthusiasm for the Senoi and comment on my experience of their experience.

First of all, I rejoice in the Senoi as a dramatic vindication of the value of diversity in the human experiment. Here is a little tribe off in the Highlands of Malaysia that has developed attitudes and techniques to which the most sophisticated Western scientists and ordinary people throughout the world can go to school.

Perhaps the single most important thing that attracts me to the Senoi is that they have provided in their society for cradle-to-grave love in the powerful form of focused attention. Every Senoi has a constructive way of attracting attention; every Senoi's most private experience is regarded as valuable; every Senoi is trained both in deepening an inner experience and in relating in creative, positive ways to others. What would happen in our society if instead of rewarding violent acts with attention and even glorification, we began to reward the sharing of inner experiences and artistic and practical works with that same intensity of focused attention, beginning with earliest childhood?

I admire the Senoi breakfast gathering: Children being listened to, their inner experiences, even scary ones, received with warmth, enthusiasm, and competent guidance. I like the feeling of a child being cherished in this way; his or her ideas and feelings being welcomed, having a moment right in the sun of parental and peer attention; being encouraged in paths of creativity and cooperation. I like the feeling of a genuine adult, sharing his or her warmth and competence, concerned for children and peers, using knowledge and personal power for guidance of the young, for the good of others and oneself, and for sheer enjoyment.

I've even tried out experimentally the basic Senoi approach to dream control. I am not a very good subject myself — as yet — but our eight-year-old daughter Lara seems attuned to the far-off Senoi drummer. Not long ago, Lara was complaining to me about how hard it was to wake up from a bad dream. Apparently, she had spoken to Bob about a dream in which she was chased by monsters and he, in his matter-of-fact way, had replied, "If you don't like your dream, wake up."

And so in her next dream, she told the monsters to let her lay down and rest and she lay down in the dream, which is apparently her way of waking up from the dream — and it worked, only she complained to me, it is so hard to wake up from a dream. There you are with a little girl with this fantastic power to wake up voluntarily from a bad dream, only it's hard, and she comes to you and asks for your help. You, who do not even have the power as yet to wake up voluntarily from bad dreams.

What's a mother to do? Well, this one decided that she had a little Senoi on her hands and decided to proceed with the training. "Lara, the next time the monsters are chasing you," I said, prompted by the Senoi, "instead of asking the monsters to let you rest, turn around and make friends with them and ask them for a present, a song, or a design." The next morning came the report: "I did what you said, and Dracula and Frankenstein gave me a design for an Easter egg and took me to a place where there are lots of treasures." I was delighted to realize the possibility that the Senoi techniques are translatable to our own culture and useful at least in helping children transform their nightmares.

There is better evidence than my personal anecdote for this in *Creative Dreaming*, by a psychology student of dream control, Patricia Garfield. This is a well-based how-to book for those of us who might be interested in exploring our dreams and exerting dream control of certain kinds.

Dr. Garfield, among other things, interviewed the Senoi and has distilled their method into sets of rules to which I refer you. She summarized what we can learn from the Senoi as follows: "You can eliminate nightmares, produce creative products, and integrate your personality by applying the Senoi rules of dream control: confront and conquer dream danger, advance toward dream pleasure, and achieve positive outcomes in your dreams."

Without pursing other matters in Creative Dreaming too far from the Senoi—my major quarry today—I might mention that Dr. Garfield's research has led her to believe that not only is dream control productive of dream pleasure — a drugless trip, so to speak — but that there is a beneficial carryover into waking life of the self-confidence and exuberance achieved by dream experiences of mastery and pleasure. And I would add that certain personal dream experiences of my own tend to corroborate her assertion.

Back to my commentary on my experience of the Senoi. I admire the institutionalization among the Senoi of love and personal worth in the form of focused attention given to each person's inner experiences. I think we can learn from them in this matter, regardless of whether we adopt their dream interpretation techniques.

What other things of value do I perceive in the Senoi way?

It occurs to me that dream training could well be important to our culture or to ourselves as a "Plan B" in case of various kinds of technological or personal disasters.

I have in mind, for example, the advantages to our culture that might ensue if we were gradually and quietly to replace television's entertainment and sociability functions with personal dream production in conjunction with dream conferences in the family and in peer groups. Instead of telling each other what we saw on television last night — even "Saturday Night" — we could tell each other what we saw on 'introvision.' I think it would be an improvement. Just think — no electronics, no commercials, all that energy conserved, no eyestrain, a happy night's sleep, and a legitimate basis for personally focused communication.

While I'm at it, I think I will replace the current drug culture, alcohol in the lead, with a Senoi-like dream culture — a genuine possibility when you recall that well-invited dreams constitute good trips, while even bad dream-trips do not inflict the chemical bodily harm of alcohol or other drugs.

So much for dreams of glory, but I am quite serious about "Plan B" as a matter of personal, if not culture-wide choice, and as a matter of having extra strings to our bow and arrows in certain kinds of personal disasters. Have you ever thought what you would do if you were hospitalized or imprisoned or immobilized or isolated for a long time? It occurs to me that dream culture would remain among the human possibilities in many states of outer deprivation. I like to keep such ideas tucked away in the back of my head, in case of need, since one of the basic religious realizations of our life is that we can't count on any status quo. You know, one of the reasons we gather together in this place is to outfit our psychic survival kits.

Stewart, in the readings this morning, expressed the root value of dream culture among the Senoi. It is a way to self-understanding, to the integration within a self of its disparate parts, and to the integration of people into a caring, competent community.

I embrace the Senoi for discovering a way to help people welcome all the parts of themselves into an inner and outer commonwealth, an improvement over our own popular Freudian psychology that in some mysterious backward flip instead of relieving us of untoward guilt and fear, manages to encourage us to fear our dreams and feel guilty about them.

And I am delighted with the Senoi for solving the dilemma of self-expression versus communication and the good of the community in their intriguing way, sacrificing neither personal creativity nor public good.

I wonder how we could begin to implement a Senoi-like Vision in our church life and in our community life? Besides the practice of focused attention, I think I will begin next year with developing a short religious education unit on dreams and visiting the church school with it on my off-Sundays.

Let's practice a little now. I invite you to the exercise of silence for reflection on a dream of our choice, whether it is a night dream or a daydream. And then in a moment, I will invite you to turn to a neighbor, if you are willing, and share in turn some portion of your dream or reflection.

SILENCE
CONGREGATIONAL SHARING
GWC: ebb 6/3/76

Chapter 14

The Mid 1970s

Follow-up on "Beautiful Dreamers"

As mentioned in the introduction to "Beautiful Dreamers," the Senoi tribe may no longer use these practices. However, a consistent observation that several dream researchers have made is: Whether or not the tribe currently practices them, the Senoi dream theories work.

I know this because they worked for eight-year-old me. I remember when Mom explained how to reverse my bad dreams. I specifically remember her telling me to stop running from whatever is chasing me and ask it for a gift of some kind. This helped me change my thinking to the idea that whatever is chasing me is just trying to catch up to me so it can give me a gift. I don't remember the Easter egg design specifically, but I do vividly remember being in a boat with Dracula and Frankenstein — we were floating on a river to a shimmering place with 'lots of treasures.' Additionally, I passed this dream-advice down to each of my children to help them reverse their bad dreams.

I also agree with Greta's comment contrasting the Senoi's communicative approach with Freud's, which tends to trigger guilt and fear. Based on my research on dream journaling, I believe our deep subconscious is conveying healing messages into our conscious mind. It is wise to listen to what our Inner Self is trying to tell us. The pure messages are sometimes distorted because of our tendency to fear what we don't understand. This is why it's helpful to take time to reflect on our dream symbols. A part of us will understand what the subconscious is telling us, but the message won't get through if we ignore our dream content.

I personally recommend the fantastic dream-author extraordinaire, Robert Moss. He's a wonderful master-teacher of dream exploration with many books on dreaming, as well as numerous interviews that can be accessed on YouTube.

Civil Unions

As mentioned before, Greta's ministry included performing various ceremonies for members and friends of First UU. She also performed a certain type of ceremony that was unique for Wichita at that time. At some point in her ministry, she began performing Civil Unions for same-sex couples. Because same-sex marriages were not allowed, Civil Unions between people of the same gender were a way to observe the bond of a marriage ceremony, even if it was not recognized by most churches or the federal government.

Similar to the Civil Rights Movement in the 1960s, the 1970's brought an awareness of discrimination against people who are homosexual in their sexual orientation. And once again, Greta, who would prefer *not* to be at the center of controversy, felt compelled to be a voice of reason in this matter — please note that the terminology of the time was "Gay Rights."

In 1977, conflicting views were emerging across the country regarding clauses in city, county and state ordinances that protected the rights of homosexuals from discrimination. A few cities had repealed existing ordinances. Other cities had added ordinances. In Wichita, an ordinance protecting gay rights had passed the city commission 3-2. This ordinance upset a lot of people and it attracted national attention. There was a concerted national and local effort to repeal the ordinance in Wichita, as well as attempts to recall the commissioners who voted for it. In a letter to the editor, Greta perfectly expressed the importance of respecting every person's basic Constitutional survival rights.

September 22, 1977 — Wichita *Eagle-Beacon* — Letter to the Editor — "Support for Gay Ordinance"

I support City Commissioners Connie Peters, Garry Porter and Jack Shanahan in their vote in favor of the amendment prohibiting discrimination in housing, employment and public accommodations on the basis of sexual or affectional preferences.

I commend them on their sense of justice and on their understanding of our democracy. American fair play requires that people respect the basic human rights of others, regardless of who is in the majority, and it should be clear by now that the opportunity to eat, to work, and to have a roof over one's head is a basic human right.　　—Greta W. Crosby, Wichita

You cannot get more logical than that, yet Greta's activism in support of gay rights generated vitriolic pushback. Nevertheless, she persisted in her compassionate and logical arguments supporting the most basic human survival rights of all people regardless of sexual or affectional preferences.

As the controversy swept the nation, her enlightened messages of equanimity were quoted on TV news reports and in newspapers around the country, including, St. Louis, Missouri; Rutland, Vermont; Greenland, Mississippi; West Palm Beach, Florida; Brunswick, Maine; Longview, Texas; and Seattle, Washington.

Here is an example from a May 6, 1978 article that appeared in Longview, Texas in the Longview *News-Journal*:

> ... the Rev. Greta Crosby, dismissed as dangerous one of the more emotional arguments used by an anti-gay group called Concerned Citizens for Community Standards. Crosby said trying to prevent homosexuals from being school teachers, positions in which they would allegedly 'infect' young children, could not be based on facts.
>
> "The protection of children requires a society in which each child can develop into leading productive lives," said Crosby, minister of the First Unitarian Church. "This applies to the 5 to 10 percent of children of age 3 or 4 who will have homosexual orientation in their sexuality. This applies to the children of Concerned Citizens; this applies to my children.
>
> I want to protect *all* our children, and the way to that is to give all of them access to what it takes to be a civilized human being and a good American citizen — a live person — and that means access to survival."

The ordinance was so contested in Wichita that it was added to the ballot as a referendum on May 9, 1978. The Gay Rights ordinance was overwhelmingly repealed by Wichita voters, with 47,246 votes in favor and 10,005 votes against repealing the ordinance protecting gay rights. The Wichita *Eagle-Beacon* followed up with an article on May 10th, and Greta's gracious words were among those quoted in the article:

> "I believe that every 'no' vote cast against the repeal of the

ordinance was a victory of love and enlightenment," said the Rev. Greta Crosby, a member of the Religious Caucus for Human Rights. "I am thankful to all who have come forward to support the survival rights of fellow human beings. We have found ourselves in good company, if not in the majority."

Sowing Seeds of Compassion

It is not easy to stand up for what is equitable and reasonable. I know when I have done this, I have felt all alone. I feel hurt when I am treated with disdain, and I wonder if my efforts are making any difference at all. Have you experienced this, too?

Most social justice issues can be distilled into one prevailing ability, that of being able to step out of our current situation to see the problem from many other viewpoints. When Greta was in the middle of controversy, encouraging people to think outside of egocentric viewpoints, it must have been difficult for her to know that her voice was making a difference. It's like planting a seed, it seems invisible at first — it takes time to germinate and push through the soil.

But there *is* growth! We can't gauge our success by whether Point A took us directly to Point B in that moment. However, when we look back at where we were sixty years ago to now, it is astounding to see the improvements that have flourished. Many societal norms we now take for granted were causes that Greta was among the first to step-up and say, "No, it is not Okay to deny people their basic human rights." Gradually, very incrementally, those seeds of compassion did germinate — not all of them, but some of them. It's encouraging to know that as each of us sows the seeds of compassion, some of those invisible seeds will eventually result in growth and in viable, visible signs of progress!

It is important, however, to communicate these truths from a peaceful place. I had a recent experience where I responded to an injustice, but not in a peaceful way. I met the aggressive action with an equally aggressive reaction. I lashed out in anger and as soon as I did, I discerned that I was not handling the situation appropriately. The feelings generated from that interaction provided a learning tool for me to understand how to respond to injustices more effectively in the future.

I now see the profound importance of communicating my "No" to injustice as Greta did, in a centered, grounded, peaceful and Loving way whenever possible. This approach begins with a powerful Inner-Vision of a better way for our society to work together. Then our strength comes from holding onto that Vision with unwavering faith, knowing that, despite pushback and setbacks, changes will surface eventually.

As we sow the seeds of compassion, it may be helpful to remember these words of wisdom attributed to Arthur Schopenhauer: "All Truth must pass through three stages. First, it is ridiculed. Second, it is violently opposed. Third, it is accepted as being self-evident." It may take a while for humanity to reach the acceptance stage where universal equality has become self-evident. In the meantime, we endeavor to persevere.

Introduction to "A Celebration of Crows"

The next Commentary, "A Celebration of Crows," was presented at First UU on February 26, 1978, when Greta was 46 years old. Current First UU members who were present at the time still recall this service with fondness.

In preparing this collection of Greta's Commentaries, I've tried to include a variety of sermon topics, representing many facets of her skill set. This sermon demonstrates a wonderful collaboration between her and numerous members who contributed relevant material for the service. Because so many elements of the service were crow-related, and were supported by First UU members, the whole service has been included.

One of the features of the service was a tape recording of various crow calls, each call having a different meaning. Below is a YouTube link that demonstrates most of the calls that were played at First UU's Celebration of Crows.

11 Crow Sounds & Calls
https://youtu.be/s1gxWM_E_D8?si=xLVXC3ZFa7kwLSWx

Chapter 15

"A Celebration of Crows"

Greta W. Crosby
First Unitarian Universalist Church of Wichita
Wichita, Kansas
February 26, 1978

> Why?
> 'Twas a warm gentle snow.
> Crows winged across the whiteness.
> I wonder why.
> -- Jesse Bing, First UU Member

PRELUDE
OPENING WORDS: "The Poets" by Loren Eiseley

The mockingbird in the bush cries caw and caw again,
hesitant, tentative in the evening light,
he sits up close quite unafraid as though to try
that old coarse word from the high air
trails off uncertainly — caw again — his voice box failing.
"Yes, I hear it," I reassure him in the bush.
"A trifle faint, but then
you're not so large, you haven't got the beak,

the body for that word, you're made to sing."
"Caw," he says timidly and cocks his head,
caw in the bush, caw from a small bird.
A faint defiance. Then he flies away,
typical poet trying a new meter, trying all sound
he can't avoid, born to listen and repeat
harsh notes and beautiful, whatever the wind brings.
These birds are sound-devourers, for what purpose
no one knows, or if there is a purpose, but there he is collecting
old sheet music from the wind.
Perhaps he's kept
notes from some vanished species not his own—
How do I know? His line is very old, a dim phylogeny
much linked with wind and sound. "Come back," I whisper
to the bush,
"I'll sing something for you, you can keep it,
something about girls and leaves, more beautiful than caw."
But "caw," he says, and still trying from another bush.
It's in the wind now, harsh, repellent, he must speak
what's in the wind, from the wind only.
"Caw," he says,
won't listen, I'm a groundling, caw has his attention now.
It's from the wind, like crows.
A mockingbird will tell you only what's upon the wind.
Tonight it's crows, with poets it's tomorrow,
a dissonance no poet can encompass.
"Caw," we all say, our throats grown hoarse.

SONG #266: "Morning Has Broken"
SOUND OF CROWS: [Joe Brewer, First UU Member, playing a tape recording]
CHILDREN'S STORY: "Crow Boy" by Taro Yashima, selected and read by Millie Mastin, First UU Member

YouTube link to Crow Boy:
https://youtu.be/KHSkaaLNz7Q?si=q6fLhdO4NsxQiDXn

CHOIR PRESENTATION: "The Happy Wanderer" by Ridge and Moller

READING: "The Many-Winter'd Crow" by George Neavoll (printed in the Wichita *Eagle-Beacon* January 8, 1978)

    Crows and Kansas go together.
    Scudding across the redding skies of late afternoon in long, scraggly rows, the ebony birds resemble so many commuters rushing home to their spouses and dinner; avian counterparts of the human motorists on the freeways below.
    The wary cottontail emerging from its daytime thicket along the little Arkansas notes their passage, cocking an anxious eye upward at any movement suggesting a hawk or owl.
    The starlings, preening themselves in the lengthening rays of the sun atop some mottle-barked sycamore in Riverside Park, nod as though in greeting at the sight of their wilder cousins.
    Around many a Kansas farmstead, the evening flight of crows may be the most activity that has been seen in the natural world all day. Somehow the birds' passage lightens the workload just a little, and takes the edge off the winter's chill.
    The sere rolling prairies of the Flint Hills, once alive with

blossoms and green things growing, are reborn momentarily when the crows come by. The calling flocks are a reminder that all things are transitory, and that the sleeping earth, come another springtime, again will be an amphitheater of life.

The great crow-flights are a reminder, too, of the Kansas heritage; of the time when the same winter spectacle must have aroused a similar sense of wonderment among the Kansa, the Osage, the Pawnee and the Wichita.

The wavering lines continue to rise and fall above the Osage Plains, until the sun's burning orb sinks into the smooth edge of the prairie horizon.

Somewhere the roosting flocks are settling for the night. Somewhere the commuter is sitting down to dinner. Somewhere — far to the west — another day is beginning, and the caw of the crow again is heard in the land.

OFFERING AND CHOIR PRESENTATION:
  "Blackbird" John Lennon and Paul McCartney
CONCERNS OF THE CHURCH
LEARNING SONG TUNE NO. 301: (New words selected by
  Helen Brewer, First UU Member)

The Dust of Snow
by Robert Frost

The way a crow
Shook down on me
The dust of snow
From a hemlock tree.
Has given my heart

A change of mood
And saved some part
Of a day I had rued.

READING: "The Crows" by Margaret Joseph, First UU Member

Suddenly this fall there are crows
gathering in the graveyard each night
at dusk unfurling across the sky
a flag of darkness on darkening air
murky caws jumbling together
sound blackening with sight.
Coalescing in flocks astonishingly large
they transmogrify an otherwise very
ordinary suburban cemetery
nestled in the gracious green
of old money lawns.
Draping the trees funereally
as if in preparation for
especially elaborate obsequies
with living wreaths of bone and feather.
Gathering in quarrelsome covens
only waiting for night, perhaps,
to transmute feather and bone
to black silk and broomsticks.
The crow phenomenon
has brought people out
whose houses border the cemetery
at dusk spilling onto our lawns
in little puddles of uneasy humanity.

Only our property lines consent
to meet and touch—
We are strangers.
We watch and mutter and
are amazed, amused, and outraged
according to our various temperaments
night after night.
There is something unnervingly indefinite
about it — downright spooky.
So it's not entirely a surprise when
those of us least willing to tolerate anything
as inchoate as a visitation of crows,
eventually bring out shotguns
and proceed to settle matters
with death.
As if the crows' gathering there
were somehow an affront;
As if there weren't already enough death,
even in a graveyard, to satisfy.
For the next few nights, here and there,
a tree drips with blood from its leaf tips.
Only a few dozen crows are actually killed.
Most eventually recognize inhospitality
when it's spelled out in buckshot.
Gradually the flock retreats
deeper and deeper into the wood
until it is no longer anything
to do with us,
until it is invisible.
We, too, withdraw

Into stolid houses
A little sorry now
That the excitement is over
A little relieved
To find ourselves
released from the crows'
Dark flights.

WORDS AND MUSIC: Composed by Gerald Burns for this service (The opening words are from "The Painted Bird" by Jerry Kosinski; the other word images are Gerry's own.)
Clarinet: Gerald Burns, First UU Member
Readings: John Millet, First UU Member

READINGS AND COMMENTARY — **Greta's Commentary: "Something to Crow About"**

This is one service where it's hard to get a word in edgewise. As I said in the newsletter, I seem to have discovered your secret religion: crow-watching. All I said was "caw" and I was inundated with all this marvelous material for our celebration, too much for one day. And this is the first time I can remember that Betty Welsbacher actually asked to do a third song with the choir.

Helen Brewer (First UU Member) gave me a most interesting article entitled, "The Crow, Bird Citizen of Every Land" by E.R. Kalmbach from the April 1920 issue of *The National Geographic.* Kalmbach reported the work of scientists so devoted to truth that they studied the contents of crows' stomachs to see what they really ate and established their great value to humankind as devourers of insects harmful to crops. Consider for a moment then, the daily grasshopper consumption of a family of six crows, two old and four young, located, we will say, at Onaga, Kansas, where in 1913, crows were found subsisting on grasshoppers to the extent of about 42% of their food.

(According to our calculations) we find that such a corvine household under normal conditions would destroy over 1,827 of these pests every day the young were in the nest, and for the entire nestling period of about three weeks, the surprising total of 38,367 hoppers would have been cared for!

Of course, everything is relative. As a grasshopper, I would not care to be cared for by a crow.

I refer you to the article itself for other scientific word-pictures and will share now only two brief things that struck my fancy. First, the full subtitle of the article, "A Feathered Rogue Who Has Many Fascinating Traits and Many Admirable Qualities Despite His Marauding Propensities." And then the final paragraphs which were captioned: "The Human Attributes of the Robin Hoods of the Bird World."

Aside from any economic considerations which are sufficient in themselves, the passing of the crow would leave a distinct void in our attractive bird life. Its crimes are many, but its virtues must not be overlooked...

Who can deny that our Robin Hoods and other adventurous spirits have left us in the story of their lives, though checkered, much that is good and much to be admired? The world would have been poorer without them. To one whose association with the crow has been at all intimate there comes a bit of the same feeling.

There is much of human character—fear and boldness, affection and hate, ingenuity, perseverance, and revenge—to be found in the life habits of this interesting bird. Let those who would actually exterminate it pause long enough in their efforts to learn more of the crow's real and potential powers in the control of certain pests. Then, and only then, will the general attitude toward the bird become an intellectual one.

Janet Thompson (First UU Member) brought me the story of the crow Silverspot, as told by the naturalist Ernest Thompson Seton in the late 1890's. Seton tells the tale of this magnificent individual while at the same time telling the summer story of migrating crows.

Old Silverspot was the leader of a large band of crows that made their headquarters near Toronto, Canada. In Castle Frank, which is a pine-clad hill on the northeast edge of the city. This band numbered about two hundred...in mild winters they stayed along the Niagara River; in cold winters, they went much farther south.

But each year in the last week of February, Old Silverspot would muster his followers and boldly cross the forty miles of open water that lies between Toronto and Niagara; not, however, in a straight line would he go, but always in a curve to the west, whereby he kept in sight of the familiar landmark of Dundas Mountain, until the pine-clad hill itself came into view. Each year he came with his troop, and for about six weeks took up his abode on the hill. Each morning thereafter the crows set out in three bands to forage. One band went southeast to Ashbridge's Bay. One went north up to the Don, and one, the largest, went northwestward up the ravine. The last, Silverspot led in person...

Seton, like Crow Boy, learned the crow calls, which he gives in musical notation — though I understand that crows of other countries have different crow song languages: I use Seton's English translation. Steve will play the notes.

"All's well, come right along!"
"Be on your guard"
"Danger"
"Great danger—a gun"
"Great danger—a gun, a gun; scatter for your lives"
"Hawk, hawk"
"Wheel around"
"Good day"
"Attention"

(Seton goes on to explain that) early in April there began to be great doing among the crows. Some new cause of excitement seemed to have come on them. They spent half the day among the pines, instead of foraging from dawn till dark. Pairs and trios might be seen chasing each other, and from time to time they showed off in various feats of flight. A favorite sport was to dart down suddenly from a great height toward some perching crow, and just before touching it, to turn at a hairbreadth and rebound in the air so fast that the wings of the swooper whirred with a sound like distant thunder. Sometimes one crow would lower his head, raise every feather, and coming close to another would gurgle out a long note like "CRRRRAW."

What did it all mean? I soon learned. They were making love and pairing off. The males were showing off their wing powers and their voices to the lady crows. And they must have been highly appreciated, for by the middle of April, all had mated and scattered over the country for their honeymoon, leaving the somber old pines of Castle Frank deserted and silent.

One May, Seton discovered Silverspot's home — a deserted hawk's nest that looked utterly abandoned from below, in which the young were carefully cared for. Crows are good parents. Seton describes then the reassembling of the crows in June, young and old alike, and the schooling given the young crows in crowlore and, every morning, company drill.

> When at length September comes we find a great change. The rabble of silly little crows have begun to learn more sense. The delicate blue iris of their eyes, the sign of a fool-crow, has given place to the dark brown eye of the old stager. They know their drill now and have learned sentry duty.
>
> ...September sees great change in old crows, too. Their moulting is over. They are now in full feather again and proud of their handsome coats. Their health is again good, and with it their tempers are improved. Even Old Silverspot, the strict teacher, becomes quite jolly, and the youngsters, who have long ago learned to respect him, begin to really love him.
>
> He has hammered away at drill, teaching them all the signals and words of command in use, and now it is a pleasure to see them in the early morning.
>
> Finally, each November sees the troop sail away southward to learn new modes of life, new landmarks and new kinds of food, under the guidance of the everwise Silverspot.

There are many stories of Silverspot — how he hoarded shells and other white shiny things, and how he hid the hoard when Seton found it; how he once dropped a piece of bread in a stream, and when the bread disappeared on the current into a tunnel, flew straight to the other end, waited, and retrieved it. The saddest is when Seton found Silverspot dead, victim of the crows' nighttime nemesis: the horned owl. Crows have reason to be afraid of the dark. It was 1893. He had flown for almost thirty years.

For my own word in edgewise, I simply want to share what was on my mind in centering on crows this morning, what my religious intents and purposes were. I don't want to go on and on. I want to leave time for your sharing — I know that several of you have had crow experiences that will brighten or enlighten our day.

The first element in my centering on crows today is a personal fascination with the suchness of a crow. I have never before lived among them; crows have never before been a conscious part of my world. Many of you know how Wichita has given me wheatfields for the first time in my life, and it has given me the crow, too. If I were to design a totem pole for my Wichita life, I would have a good start with wheat and crow.

It's hard to describe or analyze a fascination with a suchness because by definition a fascination *is* rather than does. An experience of fascination combining both attraction and repulsion is one of the fundamental religious experiences — and in a miniature way, I sometimes have that kind of experience with crows.

When I encounter or focus upon a single crow on the ground, as I did yesterday from that church window, I am conscious of its size, its blackness, its eye, and its sheer presence. I sense intelligence. I also sense strangeness. I remember the biblical phrase: "My ways are not your ways." And finally, I sense a kind of kinship. For some reason, crows remind me of human beings without losing their unbridgeable strangeness.

If this were only a private aberration, it would be questionable whether I should intrude my crow feelings upon your Sunday morning. But it turns out that my personal reactions to crows are shared by a great many people, living and dead. By the thread of these feelings I am linked to the American Indians and others who made divinities, images, myths, legends and stories centering on Crow, the intelligent trickster, sometimes divinity, sometimes companion of divinities and humankind. And by the thread of these feelings I am linked to some of you.

It is important to know that we share the feelings, the experiences, the raw material of religion and art, now and in the past. But something else is at work here, too, besides knowing.

One process of importance here, I believe, is the process I call "becoming native." This is true in my case more obviously because I came to Wichita from elsewhere nearly three years ago now. To become linked to a common phenomenon in interest and attraction and pleasure together with a queasy feeling mild enough to give zest to the encounters is a help in becoming native to a locality. In a larger sense, it helps us to feel at home in the whole world. This process of becoming native is a mitigation of our loneliness on the earth. Nomads that many of us are, we cannot count on the particular things, fauna and flora, to be everywhere we go — though crows and their cousins are close to being ubiquitous — everywhere except South America — but we can count on the *process* of becoming native once we get the hang of it.

Another important thing at work with crows — and I will touch just lightly upon it — is that in their presence, we cannot deny death. It is not only that they perform the ancient and honorable ecological task of the scavenger; not only their color that is the absence of color, that evokes night and the long night; not only their common habitat among graves; but something about crows that remind us of the trickster death. At least, I feel uncanny around crows — but I love that mild uncanny feeling, the way a child loves the slight seasickness of a carnival ride.

My last edgewise word is the haiku I wrote the first November I was with you. It was the Thanksgiving it snowed. You had all left the church after our shared Thanksgiving dinner. I was the last one out of the church house door, standing by a tree in the churchyard:

From the naked tree,
> Crows in a band suddenly
>> Rise — sound of dark wings.

SILENCE: Let us join in the exercise of silence for reflection, meditation, or prayer. In a moment I will ask if anyone wishes to share a crowing experience.
CONGREGATIONAL SHARING: Is anyone ready to share a crowing experience?
CLOSING SONG: Bye-Bye Blackbird
POSTLUDE
FELLOWSHIP

GWC: ebb 3/7/78

CHAPTER 16

The Late 1970s

Follow-up on "A Celebration of Crows"

I REMEMBER when Greta was preparing for this service and she told me how intelligent crows were, particularly how their crow calls had different meanings. I was surprised to hear of her fascination with crows, but then again, I wasn't that surprised. It's just so fitting for her to highlight the under-appreciated qualities in something many dismiss as a marauding nuisance.

About a year later, on March 3, 1979, Greta presented "A Celebration of Crows" in Oklahoma City. It was sponsored by the Women's Alliance at the OKC First Unitarian Church. I wonder if they loved it as much as our Wichita congregation did.

May 7, 1979 — *The Roanoke Times*
"Woman Minister Likes New Area Attitudes"

My research of *The Roanoke Times* shows that Greta returned a few times as a guest speaker to the UU Church of Roanoke. I found guest speaking dates published in 1970, 1979, and 1986.

In May 1979, she had the honor of returning to Roanoke, Virginia, as the UU Church of Roanoke celebrated the 25th anniversary of its founding. She had the honor of delivering the morning sermon at the celebration. A May 7th article in *The Roanoke*

Times focused on the role of women in the pulpit:

> For Unitarians, Mrs. Crosby points out, the female clergy issue has not had the theological overtones that have plagued some more traditional denominations. To her, it's clearly a question of justice on a human level... To her it is more important to be a pastor of a "real church where people care for each other" than to be a symbol of liberation.
>
> "But the principle remains important," she noted. She is proud that the Unitarian Church — an American-born denomination standing for intellectual inquiry and individual freedom of belief, was the first to ordain a woman 100 years ago.
>
> ...When she was minister of the fledgling Roanoke Valley congregation in the 1960s, Mrs. Crosby lived in Lynchburg with her husband... She drove to Roanoke once a month and performed pastoral duties on a part-time basis.
>
> ...It was a number of years later, after she gave up her duties at Roanoke...that the congregation was able to progress to employment of a full-time minister. But Greta Crosby was a warm memory to those who have remained part of the church since those days.

First UU Member Letters

To this day, I still have people tell me how much they appreciate my mom's sermons and social justice work in Wichita in the 1970's and 1980's. Additionally, several First UU members have told me they started attending because my mom helped welcome them into our First UU congregation.

The following are letters or recollections from people who were members of the Wichita congregation when Greta was their minister. Four will be shared here and two more will appear in the section on her post-retirement years. The first letter is from Ned Lakin, who was recently president of the First UU congregation:

> I first met your mom sometime around 1986. I got acquainted with her after a friend and co-worker of mine told me about First UU. As I remember it, I was intrigued enough about what my friend told me that I called the Church and they set up an appointment to come down from Newton to Wichita and visit with your mom.
>
> At any rate, I think we spent about an hour talking, and it was my first real exposure to liberal religion. I remember Greta as calm, steady, thoughtful, and kind. She was also obviously extremely bright! The end result, though, was that after our visit, I started attending First UU, became increasingly involved in it, and have never looked back since. Being invited to craft my own religion was an extremely freeing experience for me!

The next observation is from Charles Merrifield, another long-time member who has been active in First UU leadership roles as well.

> ...I was an intermittent visitor, less than once a year from 1970, so I did see your mother lead a few services. I was impressed with the skills of your mother. Clearly she was an extremely bright and articulate speaker who could convey a deep understanding of her subject matter...

The next letter is from Bonnie Till, a dear friend who was also active at First UU until she and her husband moved to Kansas City in 2020. The move has allowed them to live near one of their daughters, their son-in-law and their beloved grandchildren.

Bonnie shares:

A little background:

In 1979, my husband Bob had retired from the Air Force after 20 years of service. We had two young children: Jennifer age 7 and Kate age 3. I had discovered a UU Fellowship in Plattsburgh, NY (Bob's last duty station before he retired). From the moment I walked into the Plattsburgh Fellowship, I knew I had found kindred spirits. How we ended up in Wichita is a whole other story for another time.

As soon as we got settled in Wichita, I hunted up the UU church and discovered Greta Crosby and Elaine Bulatkin. I'm happy to report that upon entering First UU of Wichita I experienced that same wonderful feeling of coming home to kindred spirits.

What I remember most about Greta are her sermons. Every Sunday, she challenged me to explore and think deeply about the subjects she presented in her sermons. I always left church feeling a little intellectually intimidated, but inspired to think more deeply about the issues raised.

I do remember one particular conversation with Greta. It occurred after church one Sunday as the Thanksgiving/Christmas holidays were approaching. I shared my excitement and good memories of Christmases of old and how I was looking forward to the holidays and spending time with my family. Greta gently mentioned that the holidays could also be a time when some people experienced sad feelings or depression because they did not have good memories of those times.

It was a lightbulb moment for me. Having been blessed with loving, kind parents and a family that lived a safe and secure existence, I was reminded of how fortunate I was/am.

Again, Greta challenged me to look beyond my very stable life and observe what was happening around me. I remember that conversation (see it and hear it) very often. I believe that conversation and the teachings of my parents made me a less self-centered person. 'To those whom much is given, much is expected.' There are some great prose and poetry in the Bible.

Postscript: A little of my end-of-life beliefs that really aren't relevant to your request. Well, yes they do have to do with the subject, because your mom helped me be a more caring person.

I have come to have great regard for Jesus or the purported entity of such as he/she/it. I feel very strongly that Jesus = Love. That's where he/she/it should begin and end. The rest of the bull that we humans have made up about he/she/it is just a means of gaining power and order in the community (and, all of that usually ends in war). Can you imagine if we REALLY followed what Jesus said about LOVE. We could spend all of our time making others happy and in turn making ourselves happy.

[NOTE: Yes, Bonnie, I agree.]

Longtime member LaRilla Combs recently shared a significant memory she had of Greta as minister all those years ago. She recalled that at a certain time during Greta's ministry, First UU was home to a number of people with abundant artistic talents. There were musicians, artists, dancers, writers and poets, and they received high praise at First UU. It was wonderful that they found a place where they could be supported in their self-expression.

However, what if a person was not gifted with a creative talent? LaRilla was one who felt she didn't have those kinds of abilities. She felt maybe she should discontinue her attendance at First UU, because she didn't feel like she fit in. She wasn't harboring resentment toward the artists, it was more just a sense of being unable to contribute anything of value to the First UU culture, so she had decided she was going to leave the church.

Then, in some kind of serendipitous alignment of the stars, Greta shared a Commentary on exactly what LaRilla was sensing inside herself. Greta reflected on recognizing the extraordinary within the ordinary. This Commentary helped LaRilla realize the importance of each person in the congregation — how every individual contributes a highly valuable presence to the First UU community. LaRilla was so deeply moved by Greta's Commentary, she decided to continue attending First UU.

I was surprised by LaRilla's story. I had no idea how close we came to losing our dear LaRilla as a vital member of our community. There are so many wonderful things she has done for the church, especially with her participation on the Caring Committee. She's been supporting the church quietly yet consistently for all these years and her selfless acts of Love are genuinely appreciated! This appreciation extends to all who have supported First UU by contributing time, talent and treasure to our church community.

My heart is full of gratitude to Ned, Charles, Bonnie and LaRilla for sharing their memories, and to everyone who has told me over the years, "Your mom really made a difference in my life and in this community."

> Section IV
> *The 1980s*

(Posted on uua.org's worship web digital resource)

May We Trust in the Spirit

Let us join in the exercise of silence for reflection, repose, meditation, or prayer.

(Silence)

In reflecting upon the dispiriting time in which we live, I have come to believe that the basic religious response is to refuse to be dispirited for long.

May we seek grounding wherever it may be found: perhaps in the buds blooming; in the grace of a touch, a smile, a word, a helping hand, a decision or an election that goes well, a discovery that enlightens or encourages us.

May we trust that the spirit will not be quelled forever, the spirit that rises up in people from some mysterious source, energy that comes again to affirm that people matter, their needs and aspirations matter, and that the condition of people's flourishing is the cultivation of truth and love.

— Greta W. Crosby

Chapter 17

The Early 1980s

THE 1980s were a complex time for Greta both personally and professionally. There were crushing disappointments as well as career high points and great successes. I cannot give the exact chronological timeline of what occurred, because I don't know some information. I've made inquiries and attempted research, but I haven't been able to come up with complete answers. So, I'll share what I do know.

Separation and Sabbatical

Over their twenty-year marriage, Bob had struggled with mental illness which deeply affected the whole family, but primarily Greta. She encouraged him to get professional help, and to his credit he tried many approaches such as medications, psychological therapies and even group psycho-drama sessions — but nothing helped. The following notes are drawn from a composition that she wrote in 1992 called "Spiritual Odyssey." She recounts:

> My hope that my husband's accepting help would help him recover was not fulfilled. He did not respond to treatment, but his condition was verified as: disabling chronic depression and phobic behaviors. It became clear that we differed in irreconcilable ways about what it means to be married. I lost hope that our marriage would ever be in any way reciprocal.

I left to live alone instead of in perpetual heaviness and pain.

Immediately after the break in late 1980, I lived with a variety of church families for a few months. Then in early 1981, I went on a previously-planned sabbatical to Harvard Divinity School, as the recipient of the Merrill Fellowship.

The sabbatical helped me embark richly on life alone after twenty years of marriage. It also gave me time to live through the worst of the inner-hell involved in reversing that life commitment. I had never unloved anyone before; I had never dis-committed. There was time for the inner-theater of the absurd — anger and pain played out in vivid remembered scenarios, as well as fear from imagined future outcomes.

I intentionally focused as much as I could on the good I had known in that long, hard marriage, and on what remained. Where else would I ever have gotten those wonderful children?

Upon my return to Wichita, I took an apartment I had once seen while walking along the Arkansas river. And that river became a support to me for years afterward, endlessly fascinating in all lights and seasons, inviting me to walk with it regularly.

When my mom separated from my dad in late 1980, it was decided that my brother Paul and I would stay with him, because Mom's hours were so unpredictable. Since my dad wasn't working, the thought was that he would be available to take care of us. After a time, however, I was having emotional problems dealing with their separation and from living with my dad's dysfunctional patterns. He just didn't think and function normally.

For example, the house became infested with mice. I would

lie in bed at night hearing them scratching and chewing things around me. I had such extreme anxiety I wanted to crawl out of my skin. A normal adult would do something to get the mice out of the house, but Dad did nothing about it. And so I lay awake every night terrified that the mice would invade my bed.

Eventually I became severely emotionally unstable and it was evident that I needed to go live with Mom. She got a two-bedroom apartment with a balcony that directly faced the Arkansas river. I moved in with her, and my life got a lot better after that. She did everything she could to take care of me and I really needed that support. A little later my brother came and stayed on the sofa-bed until he graduated high school and went to college.

Controversy At First UU

Unfortunately, there was another ugly problem that surfaced around this same timeframe. At some point, maybe around 1982, there was a small group of First UU members who wanted to oust Greta. My mom kept me insulated from this, so I knew nothing about it at the time. The only thing I ever heard from her on the subject was that there's a saying in seminary, "If seven or more people are against a minister, they'll probably succeed in ousting the minister."

I've asked many First UU members what happened and most of them do not know who the people were or why they wanted her to go. However, I finally got in touch with one First UU member who knew the main person who tried to make her leave the church. She told me that the disgruntled man was a psychologist and he complained about the way Greta delivered sermons. He did not like that she wrote them ahead of time and read them during the services. Because this man wanted her to leave, he nitpicked everything she did, and his criticisms were harsh and hurtful. Then he recruited a few more members who wanted Greta to step down as minister. Their undermining actions caused a great deal of stress for my mom who needed to support our family on her meager minister's income.

The purse string should not be mistaken for a marionette string

I found out twenty years later that one of the women who wanted Greta to leave was a major contributor to the church and for this reason this woman's efforts to get rid of her likely gained traction. Yet, regardless of their financial status, I believe it is inappropriate to allow a minister to be harassed by church members.

In "The Care of Ministers," a sermon that Greta wrote for a different congregation one month before she retired, she touched on this issue:

>...I am asking you to preserve your minister-to-be from obedience to you.
>
> I pass over lightly one of the most noxious and obnoxious forms of the demand for obedience. This congregation has never shown signs of it, I mention it only because it is the source of such secret tyranny in our culture at large. It is a tyranny that will exist as long as people put up with it. The basic fallacy is this: The purse string is mistaken for a marionette string.
>
> I don't think that you would ever want a marionette for a minister in this pulpit or in the community. I believe that you are committed to the free pulpit, willing to take its risks for the sake of catching someone alive in the pulpit and of hearing something she really believes is true and important.

I experienced this noxious tyranny first-hand when First UU went through a similar situation in 2013. Triangulation and undermining are unethical, yet disgruntled people held super-secret meetings to try to get the minister ousted. However, the efforts were averted through open communication with the congregation about what was happening. Unfortunately, in the 1980's this was not the case for Greta. Also from her sermon on "The Care of Ministers," she warns:

> If the minister's visibility and accessibility sometimes makes her a handy model for veneration, the same things, visibility and accessibility — and vulnerability — also make her a dandy target. Some aspects of the minister's vocation easily lead to misunderstanding. Most of her work is invisible to most of the people most of the time, which leads some to think that it is non-existent. I remember one man grumbling to me as though he meant it: "Ministers sure have an easy life, working just an hour a week!"

I suspect that passive-aggressive remark came from the disgruntled man who was trying to get rid of her. And because the maneuvers to oust her remained under-the-radar, other members at First UU did not understand what was going on. Greta, being the ultimate confidentiality-keeper, didn't divulge the issues. I feel the leadership should have informed the congregation of the complaints and who was making them. Then the people of the church would have a say in how to proceed. The ongoing abuse of a minister should not be tolerated, and one way to prevent this is total transparency.

I think one reason that Greta did her best to stay at First UU, despite a hostile work environment, is because she knew how badly I was affected when we moved from Texas. Over the years

I had formed a network of friendships and connections in Kansas. If she left First UU, we would have to leave Wichita, so I think she endured the mistreatment in order to maintain continuity for my brother Paul and me.

I also want to clarify that there were many at First UU who loved her and supported her ministry, and for that I am grateful.

Tree and Jubilee

On a wonderful high note, in 1982 the UUA's Beacon Press published *Tree and Jubilee*, a book of meditations composed and compiled by Greta. The volume offers several different forms of daily meditations during the time of Lent or Springtime observances. Some of the entries are written by other authors, and several are her original writings.

The Beacon Press was the same publishing company that declined to publish her sermons in 1972, so this was a lovely bookend to that disappointment. I don't have any memories of Greta preparing the book for publication, so I'm relying on her reflections within the book to describe its origins. Here is an excerpt from her Foreword:

> I approached the making of this book of meditations with special delight. As a child in the first church I chose, I took home booklets of the daily readings... I loved the surprise, something new each day.
>
> This book was not so much made as grown. Its ground is the earthly season of dearth and greening, the human season of withdrawal and renewal. Its background is the religious season developed in many ways in celebrating communities: Tu Bishvat and Passover, Lent and Easter, and many more...
>
> ... In growing this book, I have followed the Golden Rule:

"So always treat others as you would like them to treat you; that is the meaning of the Law and the Prophets" (Mathew 7:12 JB). I give you the book I would have enjoyed receiving. I give you what in fact I have joyfully received from the hands of others and from my own heart. — Greta W. Crosby

---

Though *Tree and Jubilee* is not currently in print, there are often used copies available on Amazon. Alternatively, feel free to contact me through *larapollock.com* and I may be able to provide one for you.

I have several favorite entries written by Greta in *Tree and Jubilee* and here is one of them:

Odyssey

Paul, at six picked up the book I was reading, Rouse's translation of the Odyssey. He attached himself like a barnacle to a tiny line drawing of Odysseus clinging to a raft. "Who is that man?" he asked. I shivered. Rouse's Homer so often called Odysseus "that man." And I felt Christian references of "ecce homo," "Behold the man" on a saving cross. I answered Paul: "That man is Odysseus trying to get home after a war." "Read me," said Paul. I was dubious. He insisted. I began, thinking he would soon tire of the story too long and too old for him. Day after day, Paul brought me the book until I had read the whole epic aloud to him. I grit my teeth but read it all when Odysseus and his men poked out the eye of the Cyclops to avoid being eaten for supper. This act led to Poseidon's opposition to Odysseus' homecoming (the Cyclops was the son of the sea god), forming one of the many recurring motifs of revenge in the story.

It was not until I had read the Odyssey aloud that its religious significance became clear to me. At the end of the story, Odysseus is to leave home again with an oar over his shoulder as a missionary to establish the cult of the sea god where it has never been heard before. The meaning of the task is the reconciliation of Poseidon and Odysseus.

The final message of the Odyssey is reconciliation of a man with the powers of nature, and of men enmeshed in hostilities, with each other. After the homecoming, Odysseus killed the suitors of his wife and wasters of his substance. The relatives of the suitors gather to take their revenge in turn. As Odysseus and the relatives prepare for the slaughter, the goddess Athena appears. She "lifted her voice and stayed them all: 'Stay your hands from battle, men of Ithica, be reconciled and let bloodshed cease.'"

Some days after I had finished reading the story to Paul, he came to me. "Is there a good kind of revenge?" he asked.

"Do you mean a revenge that just hurts the one who had hurt you and only as much as you have been hurt?"

"No," said Paul, "I mean is there a good kind of revenge when someone does something good to you and you do something good back?"

My son, my teacher.

— GWC

May 1983 — Paul's Graduation

In 1983, my brother Paul graduated high school. He went to Bethel College, then to the University of Kansas to study Psychology.

Introduction to "Lighting One Light with Another"

Another high point in Greta's career occurred in June 1984. Many of her early Spoken Essays mention 'May Meetings,' which then evolved into the UUA's General Assembly (GA), which now occurs in late June. This is the annual meeting of hundreds of UU's in the U.S., and even from other countries. It is held in a different host city each year. They have workshops on all kinds of subjects, such as social justice causes, compassionate care for elders, and singing new UU songs.

In 1984, Greta, who was 53 at the time, was invited to give the address at GA's Service of the Living Tradition, which was a gathering of approximately 1,500 people. By a remarkable synchronicity, that year the UUA's GA was held in Greta's childhood hometown of Columbus, Ohio. Her illuminating Commentary, delivered on June 28, 1984 was entitled, "Lighting One Light with Another."

CHAPTER 18

"Lighting One Light with Another"

A sermon by
The Reverend Greta W. Crosby
Offered at the Service of the Living Tradition
General Assembly of the Unitarian Universalist Association
Mershon Auditorium
Ohio State University
Columbus, Ohio
June 28, 1984

Note from the Order of Service:

The speaker for the service is the Reverend Greta W. Crosby, minister of the First Unitarian Church of Wichita, Kansas since 1975. She holds a Bachelor of Arts degree from Ohio Wesleyan and a Doctor of laws degree from Harvard. In 1959, she earned a Bachelor of Divinity at Meadville/Lombard Theological School and in 1978 was awarded an honorary Doctorate by Starr King School for the Ministry. She served our congregations in Utica, New York; Roanoke & Lynchburg, Virginia; prior to her Wichita ministry, and is the author of *Tree and Jubilee*, a book of meditations composed and compiled for publication by the Unitarian Universalist Association in 1982.

Greta's Spoken Essay: "Lighting One Light with Another"

For our general assembling, I offer these words of Maxwell Anderson from *Lost in the Stars*:

> Each lives alone
> In a world of dark,
> Crossing the skies
> In a lonely arc,
> Save when love leaps out like a leaping spark
> Over thousands and thousands of miles.

I seek to encompass this space, this number. But even as I look about me, I realize that no matter how wide the space, how many the number, the inside of each and all is infinitely larger than this room, this multitude. But to keep from dizziness, I remember, too, that I only speak with *one* person, however multiplied. One times one times one times one is still one.

My friend, the one person I address that is each of us, this is a strange and wonderful service. It is something like a graduation, a commemoration, and a worship service combined. It is a celebration of ministry, extensive and intensive. It is the celebration of the kindred. Welcome to the service of the Living tradition.

We have come together, first in General Assembly, and now here at this service, from across thousands and thousands of miles. Those thousands are for some, geographical. Across the continent — and some from farther shores — we have journeyed. We have made a pilgrimage, the annual movable pilgrimage of free religious spirits.

For many, those thousands of miles are inward. We cross inner spaces. Some pilgrim through fatigue and pain and loneliness in

Ch 18 - "Lighting One Light with Another" 195

hopes of renewal. Some come in hope of sparkling experience. (The recent fulfilment of that hope here may add a verse to our denominational anthem: This little *laser* light of mine, I'm going to let it shine!) Some come in joy of reunion. And we float up and down in memory, remembering here especially: "Days of comrades gone before, Lives that speak and deeds that beckon..." from our hymn, "Rank by Rank Again We Stand."

For me, this is a double pilgrimage: in space and in time. I am full of overflowing memory. I grew up in Columbus — "C'lumbus" — as we said. I lived in a wooded ravine called Walhalla in a nest of streets named from Norse mythology. I read under a favorite oak tree, now blown down. Traveling downtown, I watched for the tower of the A.I.U. building, grey in overcast, yellow in sunlight, alight at night. Now known as the LeVeque Tower, from 1927 to 1973, it was the tallest building in the city. Now it has been surpassed in height by an even taller building.

A few blocks north of our meeting place this evening, in what is now Ramseyer Hall, I attended University High School, since abolished by the state legislature.

At fourteen, through a high school friend, I first found the Unitarians. My parents had raised me as a Unitarian Universalist without their knowing it. Imagine my astonishment at finding a church like me! I have never lost that astonishment.

I attended First Unitarian at Hillel Foundation near the University and then in the church's own building on Eleventh, a few blocks south of this place. At the Universalist Church on Sixteenth, I practiced leading responsive readings and other parts of the service. I was a young lawyer at Battelle Memorial Institute with the — to others — very odd idea of entering the ministry.

Two of my ministers from that finding time are here: Jack

Hayward and Sid Peterman. This is not quite apostolic succession — but almost. The first person I told of my decision to enter the ministry was Beach Miller, minister at First Parish in Cambridge. The year was 1954. Maine slowness has been alluded to in our Assembly, but Beach Miller's response was instantaneous. He warmly replied, "Wonderful, Gretter."

At fourteen, I found a church, and the whole course of my life was changed. The tree is gone, the school is gone, the tower has been surpassed, but the church endures and flourishes.

Let us celebrate the ministry that conduces to enduring and flourishing in life. I offer the familiar words from Matthew 5:13 [slightly adapted]:

> You are the salt of the earth: but if the salt has lost
> Its savor, wherewith shall it be salted?...
> You are the light of the world. A city that is
> Set on a hill cannot be hid.
> Neither do we light a candle, and put it under a
> bushel, but on a candlestick; and it gives light
> to all that are in the house.

And from a Japanese poet of the eighteenth century, Buson, I offer my entitling text:

> Lighting one light
>   With another—
>   Spring evening

In one breath: The linkage of the generations; the mystery and mutuality of igniting; and the light, one and many. "Lighting one light with another" is, for me, the central image of ministry — not only the ministry of ministers who walk in black-robed Batman costumes on solemn and joyous occasions, but of all our ministries, the ministry of all of us. It is my deep conviction that all are called to minister in different ways and that our ministry is mutual.

This is not to deny but to affirm the importance of ministry as my *calling*, the calling we celebrate tonight, one to which many of us dedicate "our lives, our fortunes, and our sacred honor." Following our calling, we have sought education, experience, denominational recognition, and the answering call of a body of people. We celebrate here the *living* tradition of the ministry, the underlying ministry of us *all*, and the intensified ministry of those called to preach and teach and serve and grow and celebrate communities under the name of minister.

Being asked to speak on this occasion passed anew for me the question: What does the offer of a free pulpit mean, whether for part of an hour or for the duration of a ministry. What am I asked to do? What is within my power to do?

I am not asked, nor would I agree, simply to please or to entertain. As neither proclaimer nor entertainer, what am I? I think of myself as a *sharer*, as one who is asked and who agrees to seek, and to find, something within my power to offer within the time available — "pursued by Sundays," as Charles Merrill Smith observed — something worthy of consideration and resonance in the minds and hearts of the hearers. Sharer: One who lights one light with another light, like the helper candle in the Hanukkah's menorah. I choose to be a sharer, person to person, equal to equal, receiving light and offering light reciprocally.

Lighting one light with another — itself a picture and a feeling. It is the story of our own conception and connection with all the generations and all the eons. It is the image of celebration of our birthdays, holidays and holy days, including the shrine of our own heart. It is the symbol of all education that is not molding into a form but an enlightenment and an igniting of sense in many senses: sensibility, sensitivity, making sense, enjoying the senses, and developing good sense. Lighting one light with another. It is the sign and hope of heritage, fellowship and ministry.

In theological school, I found in the library, an entry in a notebook, "A Theological Common-place Book with a Copious Index." The notebook itself had been printed in Cambridge in 1832. At some unknown subsequent date, the anonymous minister had written within the copious index under "M." :

Minister

"Whatever else he does or omits to do, he must *preach well*...

1st — A minister must show people their condition and wants.

2nd — How to improve the one & supply the other..."

To which I added in my own notebook in 1957, "Merely!"

To whatever else she does or omits to do, she must *preach well*. To hear that across a century required of me that I get over being allergic to the word "preach." It is an old word meaning simply "to make known, to tell, to assert publicly." But in everyday parlance, a certain connotation has become attached to it. It imposes an echo of hypocrisy, as in "not practicing what one preaches." Or one is said "to preach" when one offers many empty words or speaks from on high, looking down on the people and sitting in judgment upon them.

To preach well means none of these things. To preach *well* means many things, and I have not yet experienced them all, nor have I found the words to tell all I know. But preaching well in the context of a service has something to do with respecting the gathering and the occasion, knowing that in the economy of group life, a service is the one thing offered equally to all comers.

CH 18 - "LIGHTING ONE LIGHT WITH ANOTHER" 199

Preaching well has something to do with taking pains. And preaching well has a great deal to do with finding one's own authority, not an authority over another, but speaking and acting out of one's own center, reaching toward another without self-consciousness or consciousness of self. Mary Caroline Richards said, "We must mean what we say, from our innermost heart to the outermost galaxy...we carry the light within us. ...Others carry light within them. These lights must wake each other..."

Preaching well *means* dealing with people's conditions and wants, "how to improve the one and supply the other." And it means considering how our own light has been kindled by others and by our encounters with the world and with the depths of the mystery from which all spring. Preaching well means speaking out of our gratitude for what we have received of light and life: for sometimes "we have reaped where we have *not* sown." Preaching well means an urgence and an excitement in seeking to share something of value. And the most important preaching, as we all know, is done without words in how we conduct our lives and in what we are, all of us together, and in what we imagine and hope and love and work to bring into being and into our life in common. Have I not been speaking of teaching and serving and celebrating and gathering as well as of preaching?

Light one light with another. I spoke earlier of a few memories of my Columbus childhood. I now share recent discoveries as a minister residing in the Great Plains. Since being called as minister of the First Unitarian Church of Wichita, Kansas, over nine years ago, I have seen much more of the skyline than I would have thought possible. My eye trained by artists such as Turner and Monet, I have become a devotee of the vast free light when the sun is on the horizon. I have grown to love the literal light of day, its light and lights, its play of changing colors. A square of window, framing only sky, only the golden lavender perhaps that comes and goes after certain sunsets, fills me with joy, gratitude, a kind of love. I feel expanded, both more myself and less full of myself. I want to cry, "Light! Light!'

As I have come to love the literal light greeted by eye and mind in welcome encounter, my sense of my inner world has changed. It, too, seems more alight — less like a whispered life carried on in the dark. Of this inner world illuminated, at times I want to cry, "Light! Light!" Even my sense of dying has changed from going into the dark — to becoming Light.

My friend, You, the One with whom I have been speaking, I share with you "The Depths," a poem by Denise Levertov:

>When the white fog burns off
>The abyss of everlasting light
>Is revealed. The last cobwebs
>Of fog in the
>Black fir trees are flakes
>Of white ash in the world's hearth.
>Cold of the sea is counterpart
>To the great fire. Plunging
>Out of the burning cold of ocean
>We enter an ocean of intense
>Noon. Sacred salt
>Sparkles on our bodies.
>After the mist has wrapped us again
>In fine wool, may the taste of salt
>Recall us to the great depths about us.

My kindred, may we be lights unto ourselves, light one light with another, and not hide our light under a bushel. May one life light another, life without end! I echo the song: Life that makes all things new... the seekers [and the sharers] of the light are one.

GWC: ebb 7/28/84

Chapter 19

The Mid 1980s

Follow-up on "Lighting One Light With Another"

I AM FASCINATED with a number synchronicities related to G.A.'s selection of Columbus in June 1984, and Greta's career path that brought her to the Service of the Living Tradition that evening.

In Greta's 1956 letter to Dr. Robbins, she describes her religious pilgrimage that began in Columbus. She recalled how the bishop had asked the children what is the meaning of "not hiding your light under a bushel," which he demonstrated with a candle under a bushel basket. The bishop's encouragement to not hide her light under a bushel made a life-long impression on Greta. Coming full circle, she even included that exact quote from Mathew in her sermon at G.A.

More insights from Greta's childhood emerge in this sermon. I now see how the street names in her childhood neighborhood contributed to her love of Norse mythology. Additionally, she grew up in a wooded area, and subsequently, wherever she moved to, she tried to find a quiet location with green-space.

Perhaps you noticed the title of this book embedded in Greta's sermon: "And the most important preaching, as we all know, is done without words in how we conduct our lives and in what we are, *all of us together*, and in what we imagine and hope and love and work to bring into being and into our life in common."

Her reference to being unintentionally raised as a UU also made me smile. "My parents had raised me as a Unitarian Universalist without their knowing it. Imagine my astonishment at finding a church like me! I have never lost that astonishment."

The astonishment that I personally feel is that UU's continue to exist together at all. There are so many diverging opinions in a UU Church — often quite vocal ones. Sometimes there are irreconcilable differences within UU congregations, but for the most part, we've managed to find more common ground together than differences.

When shared ideas ignite ideas in others, no light is lost, it is only gained. This is demonstrated in one of my favorite lines of her sermon, "At fourteen, I found a church, and the whole course of my life was changed. The tree is gone, the school is gone, the tower has been surpassed, but the church endures and flourishes."

Finally, here is my very favorite line of all her sermons: "Even my sense of dying has changed from going into the dark — to becoming *Light*."

Paper Trail

In doing research for *All of Us Together*, I had hoped to find some newspaper articles about Greta to fill in a few blanks in my timeline. I used *newspapers.com* and cross-referenced the relevant data. It took some super-sleuthing to target the correct parameters. I also know that I haven't found all of them — for example, Washington's Yakima *Herald-Republic* is not available in digital format — and I'm sure there are other newspapers she's appeared in that aren't digitized or that aren't registered with *newspapers.com*.

Once I established my process of tagging and downloading relevant articles, I was amazed with how many I was able to locate. To date I've accessed well over 230 entries with Greta Worstell or Greta W. Crosby's name on the page. Though I can't include every article, I've included several examples which provide excellent insights into her dedicated ministry over the years.

Some of the clippings are simply postings from UU churches announcing the title of her upcoming sermons, wedding ceremonies or memorial services. However, a large proportion of the newspaper articles relay Greta's Visionary insights on human rights, discussing the related issues with compassion and equanimity. Those collected articles could make a book of their own!

Once the newspaper articles were copied and organized into chronological order, I cross-referenced and tallied several of the humanitarian subjects that were important to her. The following is a list of the topics she frequently spoke out about during her tenure as a UU minister and even after her retirement:

- Supporting civil rights & preventing hate crimes — 21
- Abolishing the death penalty & encouraging prison reform — 11
- Supporting the separation of church & state — 16
- Affirming the role of women in the pulpit - 23 & UU religion — 8
- Supporting reproductive freedom — 12
- Supporting gay rights — 19
- Resisting government censorship — 9

Though often in the minority, Greta modeled the practice of mindfully considering controversial subjects. In this process, she would first seek common ground for all sides. She would view the concerns from different perspectives before arriving at an opinion.

Most importantly, she carefully considered the highest good of all concerned, not just her own best interests. While reviewing these articles, I am reminded of Edward Everett Hale's poem, "I Am Only One."

I am only one,
But still I am one.

I cannot do everything,
But still I can do something;

And because I cannot do everything,
I will not refuse to do the something that I can do.

Introduction to "Shadows"

The next Commentary representing the decade of the 1980's is entitled "Shadows." It includes many observations on the nature of shadows, covering both their dire as well as more whimsical aspects. Greta touches on shadow-themes with some frequency in her Commentaries.

We saw several references in her 1960s Spoken Essays on Civil Rights. Let's not forget the symbolism of Carl Sandburg's eerie parade of Sand Flat Shadows. She also occasionally refers to Jung's shadow-work, which I feel is important work, in order to release patterns and beliefs that do not serve us. And in her final Commentary, she'll share her fascination with the dappled light-and-shady patterns found in nature.

It is certainly fitting that Greta would compose a service around the theme of shadows. Before going to her Commentary, however, I'd like to describe two events that transpired around the time of her October 21, 1984 Commentary entitled "Shadows."

Critical Thinking Skills

An incident occurred in the Soviet Union about one year beforehand. Stanislav Petrov was the duty officer attending the Soviet monitoring systems intended to warn of a U.S. nuclear missile attack. On the morning of September 26, 1983, the Soviet monitoring system's computer was registering repeated 'confirmed' alerts that multiple U.S. missiles were on their way to Russia. Stanislav Petrov's sworn duty was to report the detection of airborne missiles to his superiors. His superiors very likely would have initiated a retaliatory armed missile launch. That was protocol.

Stanislav was agonizingly torn between his sworn duty to follow protocol and what he knew would transpire if he did — the probable annihilation of life as we know it on this planet. He tried other methods to confirm that the missiles were on their way, and the other data did not indicate missiles in the air. He had no way to be certain which information was accurate, and his orders were to act directly from the computer read-out. However, following his inner voice of conscience, he decided to suspend the report rather than to follow protocol. He knew it was a huge gamble, but he took it.

As it turns out, it was a false alarm due to serious malfunctions in the monitoring system. Not long afterwards Petrov was reprimanded and moved to a different position. The whole incident was kept quiet for about ten years, but after the Soviet Union collapsed, Stanislav's story made it to the press. There are several resources that describe the incident and this is a link to the BBC's version:

https://www.bbc.com /news/world-europe-24280831

At the end of this article, Stanislav shares a profound observation that resonates with me at a deep level: "He says he was the only officer in his team who had received a civilian education. 'My colleagues were all professional soldiers, they were taught to give and obey orders,' he told us.

"So, he believes, if somebody else had been on shift, the alarm would have been raised."

One aspect of shadows that Greta discusses in her October 21, 1984 Commentary relates to the potential shadow-effects of a nuclear disaster and what it could do to the earth's inhabitants. She is wise to voice her concerns about the threat of a nuclear event unfolding. I remember growing up in the tense Cold War era with both sides stockpiling evermore deadly weapons of mass destruction in their arsenals — capable of destroying life on this planet many times over. The political tensions were palpable, as was the weight of worry whether 'today' would be the day that 'the button' would be pushed.

Little did Greta know how close the world came to that devastating outcome just one year before she delivered this Commentary. It also makes a person wonder how many other close calls have occurred that have not been reported.

With the Cold War ending in the 1990's, this threat may now seem to be reduced. However, researching the current nuclear armament of numerous countries reveals there is still potential for a nuclear event to occur on this planet. What I choose to do in response to this risk is to go within, envisioning cooperative peace for all life on earth, and doing my best to respect the interdependent web of all existence of which we are a part. In addition, I have hope that the people making those decisions will not just 'obey orders,' but will rely on their critical thinking skills, as Stanislav Petrov did on September 26, 1983.

Overshadowed by a Personal Decision

On a personal level, there was another shadow hanging over Greta at the time she delivered this Commentary. Two days after her "Shadows" sermon, on October 23, 1984, she finalized her divorce from Bob. She had separated from him four years prior, but due to Reagan economic policies, the disability payments he had been receiving were discontinued for a time. Once they were reinstated, she was able to finalize their divorce.

It was an emotional time because she never wanted to divorce, she wanted to love and be with a partner for life. However, I believe that finalizing their divorce in 1984 is one of the best things that Greta ever did for her own mental health. I mention this now because when I read "Shadows" I can pick up on some subtle foreshadowing of her own release from that shadowed time in her life.

The Lighter Side of "Shadows"

Within "Shadows," 53-year-old Greta also enlightens us with a number of light-hearted shadow observations. Shadows are such a basic yin to the yang of everything, it seems we scarcely pay attention to them — but I have noticed them more often since exploring this insightful Commentary. I especially love her recollections of shadow-fun from her childhood, it makes me giggle to imagine the precocious young Greta 'throwing shade' on her little shadow.

Chapter 20

"Shadows"

Greta W. Crosby
First Unitarian Universalist Church of Wichita
Wichita, Kansas
October 21, 1984

[The following 'thought experiment' was read earlier in the service, then Greta referred back to it within her Commentary.]

Excerpts from "The Allegory of the Cave" from *The Republic* by Plato, Book VII, translated by Benjamin Jowett (slightly modified):

SOCRATES: And now, let me show in a story how far our nature is enlightened or unenlightened: Behold! Human beings living in an underground den, which has a mouth open towards the light and reaching all along the den; here they have been from their childhood, and have their legs and necks chained so that they cannot move, and can only see before them, being prevented by the chains from turning round their heads. Above and behind them a fire is blazing at a distance, and between the fire and the prisoners there is a raised way; and you will see, if you look, a low wall built along the way, like the screen which marionette players have in front of them, over which they show the puppets.

GLAUSON: I see.

SOCRATES: And do you see men passing along the wall carrying all sorts of vessels, and statues and figures of animals made of wood and stone and various materials, which appear over the wall? Some of them are talking, others silent.

GLAUCON: You have shown me a strange image, and they are strange prisoners.

SOCRATES: They are like ourselves, and they see only their own shadows, or the shadows of one another, which the fire throws on the opposite wall of the cave.

GLAUCON: True, how could they see anything but the shadows if they were never allowed to move their heads?

SOCRATES: And of the objects which are being carried in like manner, they would only see their shadows?

GLAUCON: Yes.

SOCRATES: And if they were able to converse with one another, would they not suppose that they were naming what was actually before them?

GLAUCON: Very true.

SOCRATES: And suppose further that the prison had an echo which came from the other side, would they not be sure to fancy when one of the passers-by spoke that the voice which they heard came from the passing shadow?

GLAUCON: No question.

SOCRATES: To them the truth would be literally nothing but the shadows of the images.

GLAUCON: That is certain.

SOCRATES: And now look again, and see what will naturally follow if the prisoners are released and disabused of their error. At first, when any of them is liberated and compelled suddenly to stand up and turn his neck round and walk and look towards the light, he will suffer sharp pains; the glare will distress him, and he will be unable to see the realities of which in his former state he had seen the shadows; and then conceive someone saying to him, that what he saw before was an illusion, but that now, when he is approaching nearer to being and his eye is turned towards more real existence, he has a clearer vision — what will be his reply? And you may further imagine that his instructor is pointing to the objects as they pass and requiring him to name them — will he not be perplexed? Will he not fancy that the shadows which he formerly saw are truer than the objects which are now shown to him?

GLAUCON: Far truer.

SOCRATES: And if he is compelled to look straight at the light, will he not have a pain in his eyes which will make him turn away to take refuge in the objects of vision which he can see, and which he will conceive to be in reality clearer than the things which are now being shown to him?

GLAUCON: True.

SOCRATES: And suppose once more, that he is reluctantly dragged up a steep and rugged ascent, and held fast until he is forced into the presence of the sun himself, is he not likely to be pained and irritated? When he approaches the light his eyes will be dazzled, and he will not be able to see anything at all of what are now called realities.

GLAUCON: Not all in a moment.

SOCRATES: He will require to grow accustomed to the sight of the upper world. And first he will see the shadows best, next the reflections of men and other objects in the water, and then the objects themselves; then he will gaze upon the light of the moon and the stars and the spangled heaven; and he will see the sky and the stars by night better than the sun or the light of the sun by day?

GLAUCON: Certainly.

SOCRATES: Last of all he will be able to see the sun, and not mere reflections of it in the water, but he will see it in his own proper place, and not in another; and he will contemplate it as it is.

GLAUCON: Certainly.

SOCRATES: He will then proceed to argue that the sun is he who gives the season and the years, and is the guardian of all that is in the visible world, and in a certain way the cause of all things which he and his fellows have been accustomed to behold?

GLAUCON: Clearly, he would first see the sun and then he would see reason about him...

Greta's Commentary: "Shadows"

This service began for me in fascination; fascination with what happens when something gets in the way of the light, fascination with the side of things that are less well-illuminated; in short, with shadows. Later I will ask you to share, if you are willing, your own encounters with shadows, the shady side of the street, of life, of anything that speaks to you as a shadow story.

From my collection of childhood memories, I remember most of all learning about my own shadow, the long and the short of it. Playing in the afternoon sun, I, too, tried to step on the head of my shadow. Walking in the evening, in the company of my father, I watched our shadows shrink and stretch as we approached, passed, and left behind each streetlight. I am told that when I first discovered my shadow I exclaimed and named it, "More Greta!" We are not always so pleased to own and to welcome the appearance of our shadows, even though such recognition marks an advance in our depth perception, our capacity to perceive the depths of things.

In the history of art, too, there was such a moment. Art, to me, is basically the endeavor to represent surfaces in such a way as to convey depth. The record of one such discovery in art is found in the 15th century illuminated manuscript, *The Very Rich Book of Hours of the Duke of Berry*. The painting for the month of October in the book's calendar reveals the first time known in western art that a painter portrayed shadows of people and objects. This indicated an advance in the observation of light as well as of shadow, and in the pictorial language available to artists to indicate the volume of things, the sense of their 3-dimensional shape, weight, and density — their suchness. "That object really is there," said the painters in their own chosen language: "Look, it gets in the way of light and casts a shadow." (Sometimes *people* feel that way, too, that the only way they can convey their presence and value is... to cast a shadow)

Since I discovered that October painting, shadows in an illuminated manuscript, I knew that one day I must celebrate shadows. And why not in October? In memory of the artist pioneers and in honor of the radiance of light in October that elongates the shadows we cast.

I am grown now, if not exactly grown up, which would imply a completion of growing, a sureness and perhaps a grimness I cannot quite claim. My literal shadow still amuses and, on occasion, amazes me. Walking a bridge in early morning, long shadows cast onto the river, I watch my shadow cross its shadow bridge, backlit by the newly risen sun, there is a shimmer around the walking shadow. It's the closest I might come to having a halo and walking on water.

Last summer I saw something in the way of shadows that I had never seen before: Morning sun, dewy, grassy river-bank; my shadow lightly cast against the bank. A trick of the light unfamiliar to me, doubled my shadow, not overlapping it, but forming two distinct shadows, one above the other, moving along the bank. No wonder thoughtful ancient peoples have projected more than one mind, soul, self, or spirit per person! They have only believed their own eyes!

I am not the only grown person fascinated with shadows. Besides artists, there are, among my acquaintances, poets, philosophers, psychologists, scientists, and others who take the fate of the earth seriously. Here are some examples of each:

Poets: The Japanese poet, Kobayashi Issa (1763 - 1828 C.E.), expressing his pleasure at somehow having survived another winter of poverty, trouble and loneliness:

> Even my shadow
> Is safe and sound and in the best of health,
> This first morning of spring

Another poet, Masaoka Shiki (1867 - 1902 C.E.), observes while taking out the family dolls for the Japanese doll festival:

> Lighting of the Light,
> The shadows of the dolls,
> One for each.

Philosophers: Plato's images of the cave were very useful to me once in explaining something about myself to my daughter, so that she could hear and understand it, remember it, and be a bit intrigued by it. How rare when you are nearly two generations away from your own daughter! I was explaining why I seldom watched television, though I realized it could be a window on the world and that much of value could be seen with its help. I was trying to tell her how I valued my sense of reality, my response to color 'out there,' the feeling of the air, the real presence of people, my coming and going personally through space.

I know that what I see is also a projection of the world, but I prefer my productions to those of television. I told how reduced in complexity things must be to qualify for placement on television — how when I appear on a discussion panel, for example, I must reduce everything I hope to convey almost to slogans — no nuances, no play of words and meaning, no shades of meaning or subtle balancing of the scales of judgement — and not much data. Finally, I remembered Plato's Allegory of the Cave, and borrowed the image. I said, "I get restless when I watch television for long — for me it's like watching shadows in a cave." The next day Lara said, "I liked the story about the cave." This is not to deny that upon occasion I have become as hypnotized as anyone else by those shadows — I, who can become hypnotized even by a sugar-formed Easter egg with a view.

Shadows of the dolls, one for each.

Shiki's shadows emphasize the solidity and uniqueness of each doll — and at the same time, their communality, their unity, citizens in the democracy of things that cast shadows.

"One for each" — not only shadows of our bodily forms moving on the ground when we walk in the light's way, but shadows of our mental forms cast across our lives and those of other people. There are many ways of looking at the configurations of our minds and our accustomed ways of functioning in the common world. In last year's services, I returned several times to different aspects of the Myer's-Briggs Personality Types, according to which we have preferred orientations and functions, ways of perceiving, making decisions, and dealing with the world.

One day, after the revolving fund for workshops has been restored to our somewhat overshadowed budget, when more of us who so desire have had an opportunity to identify our preferred ways of seeing and choosing, I will return to the question of what Jung called 'the shadow' the less preferred, less practiced functions of our personalities. Those who find this model useful tell us that it is from the less practiced side, our 'shadow side' that we can expect the unexpected and the — to us — uncanny. Here lies the potential for disproportionate trouble and joy. If one is particularly out of touch with one's other side, the shadow side of one's own moon, the isolated shadow can emerge with the force, and sometimes with the face, of a demon. Surprised, we say, "I don't know why I did it, I don't know what made me do it." Or in some circles, 'the devil made me do it.'

My favored Myers-Briggs functions are intuition and feeling, the perceiving of things as wholes and in systems of relationship and the making of choices on the basis of values, on what seems to be important and to whom it matters. My shadow side is thinking and sensing. My thinking has been fairly well-developed by our educational system. But my deep shadow is sensing, that perceiving of data through the reports of my senses.

From my relative lack of practice in gathering and building data through my senses instead of my sense, comes my characteristic stressors — finding my car in a parking lot, or dealing with cars at all, for that matter, or filing and finding things, keeping track of things, noticing and remembering exact data.

We are much more welcoming of our shadow when we are surprised by joy. And from my shadow, my sensing function, come my unexpected joys—the surprise of things that break through my constitutional inattention. The particular play one day of a pattern of sound; my son's laughter; rain on a window; the touch of my cat's paw on my cheek; the texture of a chosen fabric; the good smell of popcorn, coffee or carnations; the particular play one day of light and shadow: such are the shadows of my life that compelled this service.

I have spoken little of the great shadows on the earth: the shadows of the clouds, the eclipsing of the sun. Do you remember, not long ago, the eeriness of our dimmed sun when the moon got in its way? And let us not forget, our dependable night exists in the earth's shadow as we rotate away from our sun.

I scarcely remember my childhood fear of the dark, so pleasant did I find the nightly, spangled darkness. I practice prudence now, unwillingly though, not in fear of the night, but of those who, for various reasons, some valid, do not feel included in the same human circle with others.

There is one shadow I would not be eager to enter, the dark night and bleak 'winter' nights that would follow a nuclear war. We learned of the threat of nuclear winter by chance. The US Mariner 9 spacecraft arrived at Mars in late 1971 in time to probe its atmosphere and surface while they were shadowed by a global dust storm. This gave information that both American and Russian scientists used to calculate the level and duration of the darkness, the coldness, and the radioactive fallout from one 5,000 megaton nuclear weapon of modest yield. The darkness, coldness, and radioactivity of a nuclear attack and retaliation occurring on our planet would be much longer and deeper and greater in quantity than was imagined before our spacecraft studied the shadow-effects of a dust storm on another planet. Lasting for many months or years, a nuclear winter could end the story of life on our planet, or return it to Genesis by mass extinction.

Our safety does not lie in denying scope to explorations and extensions of our perception and our power in technology, but to a turn of human fascination with death to life, from developing powers to destroy to developing powers to create, particularly alternative energy sources.

I close with a story of fascination. Ruth Tasch [a member at the time] told me of something she had seen on television (ha, TV is redeemed!) A man blind from birth, was enabled by electronic means to create within his mind pictures of objects. With help, he literally could see in his mind's eye. He was enabled, within his dark, fireless cave, to see the shapes and shadows of things. Shown a lighted candle by this special means, he exclaimed: "I never knew a flame had a shape."

More and more I have come to believe that we cannot lift the shadow that democratically falls on all the world by staving off destruction alone, though that is essential, but by turning efforts away from pre-occupations and preparations for death-dealing and channeling it into ways of supporting life and improving its quality.

"Yea, though I walk through the valley of the shadow of death, I will fear no evil; for thou art with me, thy rod and thy staff, they comfort me." Psalm 23:4

Accompanying presence, support, comfort — this is much, and we help each other by being these things for each other, making the inner images of God come true in the common world shared by people. But presence and comfort are not enough. We must learn to turn and to walk out of the shadow, remove, where possible, what casts the shadow of death, and make something *better* happen. One way to keep bad things from happening is to use the same energy to make better things happen — such as utilizing the sun's blinding light or healing the blind. These are connected. Where, on the balance, will we put our resources in the coming years?

We are not all-powerful, but let us learn to use the power we have to develop in the service of life. Let us use our light to lift the shadow of death.

Congregational sharing: Shadow Stories

GWC: ebb 10/30/84

Chapter 21

The Late 1980s

Follow-up on "Shadows"

As I mentioned in the introduction for "Shadows," I've noticed shadows more frequently since reading Greta's Commentary. What I've particularly paid attention to is a variation on Carl Sanburg's "Sand Flat Shadows." A wooded area stands to the east of our house and as the morning sunlight streams through bare winter branches, I've been communing with my own version of Sand Flat Shadows.

First, the backlighting on the obtuse angles of the tree branches themselves delineates odd-looking practice shapes. Then I find myself gazing at the menagerie of long shadows cast on the ground as the glowing sun hovers on the horizon. If a breeze blows, the long ground-crawling shadows come alive with eerie animated movement. And on certain early-morning walks, purple-gray clouds aggregate at the skyline, and I imagine the slow parade of practice shapes making their way across the hippodrome. Though not true Sand Flat Shadows, Kansas Flat Shadows lend an inkling of understanding to this fireborn Heartland resident.

March 15, 1985 — *UU World* Magazine — "Confrontation"
[Last Nov 13 (1984), a week after the US Federal elections, the Rev. Greta W. Crosby encountered Jerry Falwell at an

appearance by the latter at a local university. Here is her account of the event, excerpted from a sermon to the congregation of the First Unitarian Universalist Church of Wichita, of which she has been a minister since 1975.]

I went to hear Falwell at Wichita State University last Tuesday. I had not intended to go as I had so many other things to do. But finally I decided to go and hear what his agenda is for our country, to hear it directly from him and not refracted through the media.

No surprises there: abortion is murder and the greatest sin of our country; we must save Central America from the threat of communism; we must preserve our economic system from socialism which is mutually shared poverty; we must preserve the family which begins when a man marries a woman, in that order.

I was a little surprised at his definition of education in view of his personal pride in his children, sons studying law and theology, a daughter studying to become a surgeon. He asked the students present whether they hadn't come to learn to compete and win, wasn't that what an education was for?

What I was totally unprepared for was his treatment of his questioners during the question period following the talk. I sat in the overflow room, listening to question after question, good questions, not heckling ones, questions designed to indicate the complexity of the issues, and the differing views of morally concerned people.

His response to question after question was to hold the questioner up to scorn as a member of a category assigned by appearance or subject of the question, a category to be discounted: woman, black, homosexual, peacemaker, even bearded young male.

I reached a point when I could no longer witness that abuse of power without underlining it, naming it, calling attention to it. I could not have planned what followed. I made my way through the cluster of people standing in the doorway of the auditorium. Because of the way the auditorium is built I found myself on a level with Jerry Falwell, on stage, so to speak. I raised my hand and advanced, made known somehow my determination to speak.

Falwell looked at me and said: "Are you a professor?" "No, I am a minister of religion." "What is your name?" I told him. "What is your church?" I hesitated not wishing to involve others, but then I realized it would be worse to withhold the name. "Unitarian Universalist," I said. Falwell turned his back to me and said, "I thought so, you're not one of us," handing me over to the scorn of his admirers, who laughed loudly.

My answer, "I share it with Thomas Jefferson," was swallowed in the laughter of the crowd. "Well, what's your question?" he asked. "I don't have a question. I am here in protest..." "What's your protest?" he interrupted. "I protest your mockery of your questioners," I said slowly, my heart pounding. The room exploded in applause and boos, for I had named what Falwell had just acted out. I felt supported as well as scorned.

I am grateful for the support of others that sometimes makes itself felt at such times. And I am most grateful that even a master of crowds such as Jerry Falwell cannot help revealing himself. I am grateful for life, despite threat, pain, limitation, and the things to which I must say "thanks anyway."

Ch 21 - The Late 1980s

Interestingly, Jerry Falwell was born and raised in Lynchburg, Virginia. He co-founded Liberty University in Lynchburg, which still has an influence in the city, though there has been much integrative progress since the 1960s.

Notice Greta's reference to not wanting to say the name of her church because she didn't want to drag them into this. In part, this harkens back to 1963, when some Lynchburg UU's were really angry for her actions defending Thomas Wansley. She learned that what she did in protest could reflect on the members of her church. Fortunately, I'm confident that members of First UU were proud of her for having the courage to step up in protest of Falwell's bullying tactics. As I think about it, the event coordinators at WSU never should have permitted the degradation of the people asking questions. To do nothing, to tolerate those inappropriate behaviors, tacitly approves of them, which allows them to permeate society.

Greta was moved from a knowing place inside of her that Jerry Falwell's mocking insults were absolutely inappropriate. Rather than being swept away in the sea of acquiescence, she refused to be dragged down in its undertow. She anchored herself deep down and stood up, creating an island of "No." She named the injustice, and made her "No" visible, both seen and heard.

The master of crowds is a master of crowds because he stacks the deck with his supporters in the front rows and then he counts on acquiescence from the rest. And that is often how it goes — unless someone stands up and points out the abuse of power, which often results in the 'master' revealing himself to be much less powerful than he wants us to believe.

Then, to Greta's surprise, her "No" was reported on the TV news, in several newspapers, and in the UUA's *UU World* magazine article. I feel her refusal to tolerate his intimidating tactics planted seeds in the minds of the people who were there, in those who heard about it later, and even now as this account is being read by you. They are unseen seeds that gently germinate and push through the soil in their own way, in their own time, eventually blossoming for the highest good of all concerned.

August 1985 — China Travels

In August 1985, The Friendship Force of Kansas traveled to China to spread goodwill and to learn of Chinese customs. Greta was among over twenty people to visit China for several weeks. She thoroughly enjoyed the food, the rich culture, and getting to know the people there. A short article in the Wichita *Eagle-Beacon* on October 6, 1985, touches on a few details of the adventure.

First China, then Newton — Traveling members of The Friendship Force of Kansas met in Newton recently for a reunion in the home of Nellie Mae and Virgil Borger, where they reminisced about their adventures in the People's Republic of China. After a buffet, complete with sweet and sour pork, slides from the trip were shown...

...(one traveler explains that) those who went to China landed in Toyko four times trying to get to Shanghai. "The pilot kept trying to get it right...finally we stayed overnight in a hotel at the Tokyo airport, and they brought a new plane the next day from Honolulu. I was certainly glad about that."

I was in high school at the time so I stayed at our apartment while my mom was traveling in China. What stands out in my mind about her travels is that a Boeing 747 crashed in Japan on August 12, 1985, and I wondered whether she was on that flight.

I made some phone calls and after a time I was able to confirm that she was not on that flight, but there were certainly moments of anxiety in the process.

I'm so pleased that she enjoyed safe travels and a beautifully enriching international experience with the Friendship Force of Kansas.

February 1986 — A Complicating Physical Illness

In February of 1986, at the age of 54, Greta came down with a virus that triggered what I would describe as an autoimmune reaction that affected her health for years to come. From this point forward, her energy reserves were unreliable and she had to plan her activities carefully to ensure that she could complete her tasks. Greta explains in "Spiritual Odessey," her 1992 composition reflecting on her life experiences:

> In 1986 a strange interlude began — a virus in February — then prolonged weakness, and then something else that was, months later, diagnosed as endogenous depression, now called dysthymic disorder.
>
> It was as though the force of gravity had been doubled, literally. In every other crisis of my life, I had been able to call upon reserves of energy. In every other bad time of my life, I had not been cut off continually from the spirit of life — there was always the sense of being alive; there were always moments of joy possible.
>
> In my life I had lost much, but I had always been able to count on myself when I was in deepest need. There I was, without a mark on me, and yet I did not have myself at my disposal. I had help from medical and psychological professionals, though I remember my young doctor saying at

first, "Well, Greta, you have to realize that it's natural not to have as much energy as you used to have."

I was fortunate to have had a sudden and remembered onset. I could answer, at least to myself, "That may be so, but I didn't suddenly get old between February and March of one year."

Later the condition was diagnosed, and I had appropriate help, but there were still lingering problems with unreliable energy. The most significant help I had, however, came from an unusual source. I often walked on a nature trail next to our local zoo. It was a little more than a mile through a tiny marsh, woodland, prairie and then around a lake.

Toward the end of May, without warning, as I explored a patch of the dry towering reeds called Arundo by the side of the canal, I came upon a swan sitting on her nest. The unexpected sight took my breath away. The swan simply sat on her nest, alert and serene. She moved her head slowly from side to side, alert for danger, serene in strength.

When I finally caught my breath, I wanted to climb into that nest and nestle under her wing. Since that was not a possibility, I yearned to be like her, alert and serene. Even one of those — alert *or* serene. Finally, I had to settle for letting her tame me. And thus began my journey of wonder and healing.

I returned almost daily. Seeing 'my' swan — possessive-affectionate, not possessive-possessive — became the joy of my life. One day she stood. Yes, there were eggs — huge. The zoo people told me no swan eggs had ever hatched there. I began the sort of awkward body English, mental 'pulling-for' that some UU's go through to avoid admitting we're doing something like praying.

On a later day, from a distance respectful of the beak-range of the swan-mate, who was doing his job of encouraging me to keep a respectful distance, I watched while the swan stood in her nest and raised her wing, as if, *as if* she were showing off their offspring: six or seven fluffy cygnets — though within days, the cygnets were down to two.

I saw in the four-swan family, my own four-person family when the children were small. One day I happened to be present for 'moving day' from the canal to an earthen embankment by the lake. The swans were slipping and sliding, with the cygnets rolling head-over-webfoot. They looked so fragile!

The zookeepers eventually called me the Swan Lady due to my daily visits. And the two cygnets grew, day by day, to adult swan-hood. I felt sustained in the company of these swans who had inadvertently tamed me by being themselves.

I was saved by swans long before I learned of Marija Gimbutas' speculations about waterbirds as the earliest known image of Divinity.

May 1986 — Lara's Graduation & Greta's Corresponding Preparations for Resignation

While Greta was still recovering from her health crisis, I graduated high school in May 1986. Then I went to Bethel College in North Newton, Kansas, majoring in English for Secondary Education and minoring in Psychology. I got settled-in on campus in the fall of 1986. This marked the moment where Greta had successfully raised her own pair of cygnets. And it was exactly at that point, after serving First UU for nearly twelve years, that she began preparations to resign as their minister.

At the end of 1986, she was still recovering from the illness that had begun in February 1986. From her 1992 notes on her "Spiritual Odyssey" she shares, "I struggled through without disgrace, but hardly gracefully to bring my church into its centennial year, I resigned in January 1987, and then took a year's personal sabbatical."

One of the final acts she performed before stepping down as minister of First UU was to establish a memorial foundation in the name of the Reverend James Reeb. Here is the formal letter she wrote from her church office letterhead:

In honor of the centennial year of First Unitarian Church of Wichita, and in memory of James Joseph Reeb, Unitarian minister born in Wichita, January 1, 1927, who answered the call of Dr. Martin Luther King, Jr., to Selma, Alabama, and whose death in Birmingham, Alabama, on March 11, 1965, as a result of injuries inflicted at Selma, aided the passage of the Voting Rights Act of 1965, I make this first contribution to the JAMES JOSEPH REEB MEMORIAL FUND. I ask that the income of this fund be awarded annually by the Board of Trustees of First Unitarian Universalist Church of Wichita, or in accordance with a process established by the Board of Trustees to an organization or organizations active in Wichita in addressing basic human needs, including but not limited to: food, clothing, housing, utilities, transportation, employment, education, health care, child care, reproductive freedom, and shelter from domestic violence.

Greta Worstell Crosby
January 25, 1987

That act concluded the twelve-year odyssey of Greta's tenure at First UU. There is no doubt that leaving so many beloved and bonded people was bittersweet in the most poignant sense. It was time, but it was exceedingly difficult to pull away from the good people at First UU and then to move forward on her life journey alone — unencumbered, yet entirely alone.

May 1987 — Conscientious Objection

In 1987, a protest movement was growing in Wichita. McConnell, the local Air Force Base in Wichita, was scheduled to house 17 B-1 Bombers in early 1988. These Bombers were equipped to carry 4 to 8 nuclear warheads, but the plan was to eventually outfit them with as many as twenty-four per airplane. In the event of a nuclear attack, the armed warheads would be loaded and in the air within five minutes.

People from many religious and community organizations were concerned and they began speaking-out about the plan for the nuclear-capable B-1B's to be housed at McConnell. Greta was certainly among those concerned citizens.

A Welcoming Ceremony was planned for the B-1B's upon their arrival in February 1988. Though it was not formally announced until August 20, 1987, somehow Greta had heard about a B-1B Nose Cone Art Contest for school children, which she found deeply troubling. I feel confident that she wrote a letter to the editor concerning this, but I did not find one, so it may not have been published. This may be because there were many who wrote letters to the editor objecting to the contest.

The following excerpts are from a letter to the editor published in the Wichita *Eagle-Beacon* on August 26, 1987. The authors were Andrew and Kay Davis and though they were not members of

First UU at the time, they have been very active members for many years now. Their sentiments echo Greta's concern about the B-1B's coming to Wichita and the children's Nose Cone Art Contest:

> As parents of school-aged children and citizens of Wichita, we are deeply troubled by the article, 'Area Children to Help Adorn Bomber's Nose,' which appeared in the Aug. 20 *Eagle-Beacon*. We strenuously object to the contest for several reasons.
>
> The B-1B is a machine designed to destroy lives and property and presents a continuous threat to do so when not engaged in actual bombing missions. As such, it is an integral part of our government's longstanding policy of mutually assured destruction (MAD). There is no other purpose for this machine. It destroys or it threatens to destroy.
>
> It is true, as noted by State Rep. Elizabeth Baker of Derby, that McConnell Air Force Base provides a great deal of economic support to the Wichita area. It is also true that not all of Wichita's citizens value this support as appropriate. While we do not support a military establishment whose official policy is to maintain the capability to destroy the world several times over, we appreciate honesty on its part. MAD, while in our opinion an insane policy, is at least honest.
>
> The B-1B nose art contest blurs the lines between honesty and deceit by throwing children into the equation, implying innocence by association, hoping a cute picture can mask the ugly reality of a machine designed solely for the purpose of killing...
>
> ... In a Friday, Aug. 21 *Eagle-Beacon* article, Derby superintendent of schools, Charles Hubbard, compared the B-1B nose art contest to the Walk for Mankind, since they are both 'Civic projects.' The Walk for Mankind is designed to nurture

and improve the quality of life. The B-1B, as noted above, is designed to destroy life. While it is true that Mr. Hubbard can make such a comparison, it does not stand up to the test of logic. There is a qualitative and irrefutable difference between the intention to nurture and the intention to kill. To blur this distinction is to lose one's ability to judge between right and wrong, good and evil. This we hold to be an injustice perpetuated against the children of this community.

We ask that all parents of school-aged children and any other concerned citizens of the Wichita-Derby area who oppose this contest write to the principal(s) of the school(s) their children will attend, the school board in their community and McConnell Air Force Base asking for one of two things to happen:

That the B-1B nose art contest be cancelled. Then, if that is not deemed inappropriate,

That the schools give equal classroom time to groups opposed to such activities who would be willing to advocate positive peace — that is, peace independent of threat.

Andrew K. Davis
M. Kay Miller Davis
Wichita

Though not written by Greta, this letter to the editor reflects her profound conscientious objection to the issues at hand, particularly the nose cone art contest involving school-age children. With these troubling concerns in mind, and because she was not affiliated as a minister to any church at that time, she felt deeply compelled to make her "No" visible.

On Memorial Day, May 25, 1987, Greta attended a peaceful demonstration held at McConnell Air Force Base. Though she is not directly quoted in this article from the Wichita *Eagle-Beacon*, published on May 26, 1987, these excerpts describe what transpired:

A singing, chanting crowd of more than 100 people from at least five states converged on McConnell Air Force Base Monday for a peaceful protest that included the first recorded acts of civil disobedience in McConnell's history.

Sixty-eight demonstrators were detained for trespassing on military property during the largest peace demonstration ever at the base, a future home of the B-1B bomber.

"About 18 years ago, my husband was killed in Vietnam," Billie Knighton of Wichita said as she watched the protest unfold under warm, sunny skies. "I told myself it wouldn't be in vain if we learned from our mistakes. But I don't think we have... That's why I'm here. It seemed like the right thing to do on Memorial Day."

Air Force officials said 68 demonstrators were detained during the carefully orchestrated rally, which ended without violence or injuries.

"It went just exactly as we had scripted," said Lt. Col. Paul Muehring, chief of public affairs at McConnell.

Muehring said those who crossed the white boundary line that marked McConnell property were taken to the Kansas Air National Guard cafeteria. There, they were searched, fingerprinted, photographed and issued an official letter warning them to stay off McConnell grounds for the next two years.

The demonstration, which capped a three-day 'Prairie Peace Pilgrim Faith and Resistance Retreat' in Newton, was similar to rallies held the past two years at the Strategic Air Command headquarters in Omaha. Non-violent civil disobedience also has taken place recently in Nebraska, Missouri,

South Dakota, and Michigan.

"We believe in a different way of keeping peace," McPherson farmer David Stucky said. "Not with bombs and guns, but by mediation and talks with those that are involved in any conflict."

Led by marchers beating handheld drums and singing a Buddhist chant in Japanese, the protesters had a variety of reasons for being at the base that in February will receive a wing of 17 B-1B bombers, one of the most controversial components of the nation's nuclear weapons arsenal.

"I'm here to oppose the insanity of the nuclear arms race," Jean Ann Walton of Kansas City, Mo., said moments before she stepped across the white boundary line. "To do nothing is to do no good at all."

Demonstrators carried signs and banners proclaiming: 'They Shall Beat Swords Into Plowshares,' and 'We Want Bread, Not Bombs.'

"I've decided to accept my share of the responsibility for what the government is doing," said Mary Harren, president of the Wichita-based Kansans for Peace and Justice. "When I'm gone, I don't want to be thought of like the 'good Germans' and other people who did nothing when their government was doing things that were wrong."...

... As the protestors began crossing the line...the 30 Sedgwick County sheriff's officers standing by to assist 40 McConnell soldiers assigned to the demonstration had to do little more than watch...

..."I don't think a lot of people will notice," said WSU student Mary Green, whose father works at Boeing Military Airplane Co. in Wichita, where more than half of its business is connected to military contracts. "But a few of them will, and they'll see more things like this and start thinking about it and then start becoming more interested.

"It's a gradual change. And that's how we have to do it. I don't see any other way you can do it."

This was the first among several similar peaceful demonstrations to take place at McConnell ABF and Mary Green's concluding quote perfectly encapsulates the significance of these protests. I love her reference to a few people noticing these actions, then they would become more interested in what's going on here. She shares, "It's a gradual change. And that's how we have to do it. I don't see any other way you can do it." That is the peaceful planting of seeds of compassion. They seem invisible at the time. Some seeds grow, some don't, but those that do will push through the soil and will flourish.

Another significant presence at that Memorial Day protest was Billie Knighton, who was quoted in this article. Billie is a long-time member of First UU, as well as a longtime activist on many fronts of social justice.

I am also proud to say that my mom, Greta W. Crosby, the gentlest bad-ass I know, was among the 68 who were arrested for civil disobedience by crossing the white line and trespassing onto McConnell AFB. Her letter from the Department of the Air Force reads in part:

ORDER NOT TO REENTER MCCONNELL AIR FORCE BASE, KANSAS

1. You are hereby notified that, effective upon your receipt of this letter, you are ordered not to reenter or be found within the limits of the United States military reservation at McConnell AFB...

2. The reason for this action is your unlawful entry and refusal to depart McConnell Air Force Base, Kansas, a military installation, on May 25, 1987. Prior to your detention, you were informed that your entry onto McConnell Air Force Base was prohibited both by law and lawful regulation. Despite being so informed, asked to leave, and given the opportunity to leave, you refused to comply and entered McConnell Air Force Base in direct violation of 18 U.S.C. section 1382.

3. This order will remain in effect until May 25, 1989...

... 5. You are further informed that should you reenter or be found upon the limits of the United States military reservation at McConnell AFB, Kansas, in violation of this order, you will be subject to apprehension and detainment by the military for prompt delivery to appropriate civil authorities.

An Act 'In Defense of Creation'

For Greta, this was a deeply symbolic, deliberate action of conscientious objection to the madness of the of the Cold War's death-dealing weapons and our mutually assured destruction. She refused to acquiesce to the madness. In "Justice Without a Blindfold," Greta asks, "Well, what are the ways of refusing to acquiesce? How do I say the 'No' that ends acquiescence? There is no other way but simply to *begin* — to say or to do 'No.' (...Then...) I shall begin to find my way into more vigorous expressions of 'No' until it becomes a sturdy island in the sea of acquiescence."

In 1989, Greta referenced her experience at McConnell AFB when she was a guest speaker at the First UU Church of San Antonio. In her Commentary, she described the nature trail she visited every day during the summer of 1986, when she was recovering from her debilitating illness. The daily visits to her swan family were more healing for her than any prescription medication. And then I discovered this description of her powerful personal decision to cross the white line on Memorial Day 1987:

> All that summer I visited the trail, watching things grow, seeing more and more clearly much that I had never seen before, inside and out, adding living beads to my rosary of recognition, practicing contemplation and gratitude, finding worlds within worlds... I felt sustained in the company of these swans who had inadvertently tamed me by being themselves.
>
> And when on Memorial Day 1987, I was deciding for the first time in my life whether or not to commit an act of civil disobedience — very civilly and respectfully, in good company, toward opponents whom I respected — it was the Vision of the swans that weighed in the balance of decision *toward* an act 'in defense of creation."

CHAPTER 22

Installation at Yakima, Washington

Candidating for Placement in Another UU Church

GRETA was fifty-five years old when she resigned from First UU in January 1987. Along the same lines of when she first began as a woman UU minister in 1959, the UUA's Department of Ministry had a less than positive outlook on her prospects for being placed at another church. From her 1992 "Spiritual Odyssey" notes, she explains, "I again had to overcome the 'realism' of the Department of the Ministry's pronouncement: 'It is very difficult to be called to a church after the age of fifty-five.' The Department was, as usual, pessimistic but helpful."

Greta followed the protocols for applying to several UU churches around the country. She was asked to speak at UU churches in Florida and in Washington state. Not long afterward, she was called by the UU Church of Yakima, Washington. Gratefully, finding placement in another church also afforded her an opportunity to be paid a reasonably higher wage than what she had been paid at First UU.

I include portions of her installation service at the UU Church of Yakima, because it celebrates a time in her life when she finally found a balance in her life's calling. Though she still had to use her time and energy strategically, due to her dysthymic disorder, she was finally in a good place. She was not stuck in an emotionally abusive marriage. She was not hindered by the demands of raising a family. She was not harassed in a hostile work environment, she was loved and respected, and thankfully well-treated by her Yakima congregation.

May 22, 1988 — Greta's Installation Service
Yakima, Washington

Pat Ball, Chair of the Search Committee & the Committee on Ministry: "Our search led us to you, Greta. We called you and you answered our call with yes. Help us to cherish our dreams, nurture them, give them scope, power and life. Be with us in our time of need. Encourage us when we falter. Share our joys; enhance our delights. Help us to deepen and expand our awareness; to seek, to find and to give meaning; and to live our love and truth with grace."

Philip A. Lamb, President of the UUCY Congregation: Will the members of the Unitarian Universalist Church of Yakima please rise and say with me the following words:

"We lay no strict charge upon you — we ask only this: That with love you draw us toward love; with insight, toward understanding; with sensitivity, toward a sense of our own worth; with caring, toward commitment; with joy, toward fulfilment. Be with us and move with us in all these ways that together we may create a spirited community of inquiry, concern, action and celebration; that together we may live as a beloved community in active relationship with others in ever-widening circles."

The Rev. Greta W. Crosby: "With delight and zest; with thanksgiving and reverence, in trust, hope and love, I accept the call of the congregation and enter upon the ministry of the Unitarian Universalist Church of Yakima. I commit myself to this ministry and offer you the gifts of life that I have received in mind, heart, strength and spirit, knowing that these alone will not suffice. With your encouragement, with your shared gifts of life, with your endeavors in fellowship one with another, together we will nurture and challenge each other, our religious community, and our wider communities, that we may each and all grow in truth and love, wisdom and stature. Now let us enter upon our mutual ministry and walk together the way of life, inward to the wellsprings and outward to the galaxies. I ask the congregation to join me in these words of intent:

<u>Together</u>: We unite as congregation and minister in the joy, work, vision and challenge of living together a life in community, shaped by love and understanding.

Greta's Closing Blessing:
Bless this house, that herein be found
Good health,
Faithfulness,
Spiritual strength,
Perspective,
Good will and humor,
The fullness of life,
And thanksgiving to all givers:
And may this blessing remain on this house
And on all who gather herein.
So be it. Amen.

The following is among the first of many UUCY newsletter articles that Greta wrote for her Yakima congregation. Interestingly, her accumulated church newsletter articles could make a book of their own, too!

September 1988 — UUCY Newsletter Article

How did we get this way?
A panorama of American Unitarian History

I will be shaking one branch of our religious family tree in search of insight, inspiration, and just plain information. This will be a lecture romp through American Unitarian history from Puritan roots to consolidation with American Universalism. I vow equal time and attention to the Universalist branch next month.

On the brink of September, the river of time seems to flow faster and faster. The rhythm of life changes in measure — *andante* moves toward *allegro*. Do you, too, feel as though you are stepping into a whirlpool? As the tempo of church, school and work, of social and political life increases, do you, too, move from reluctance toward exhilaration?

I look forward to greeting you in person (in parson) from the pulpit again beginning September 11, and enjoying the Sunday offering of activities — seeing the children, visiting in fellowship time, brunching with those who wish to continue the conversation. This is the broadest and most visible part of church life, but it is supported by a less visible but indispensable network of people at work and at play, growing the life of the church in us. Everything counts: board, committees, teaching and staff workers; friendly and stimulating encounters with people inside and outside the church; study, reflection and conscientious endeavors in private and public life; sheer presence, sometimes, to signify that we stand by, and for, our people and our values of love and truth.

— Greta

November 1988 — Yakima *Herald-Republic*
Letter to the Editor

In the spirit of Thanksgiving, I share words that came to me when driving the Yakima River Canyon in this radiant autumn. It is a song of joy in response to the hand of creation that sculpts with the river continually over millions of years:

River ramparts, dark –
   Cutaway, winding, keeping
      Lava-layered time.

Cordially,
Greta W. Crosby

And so began Greta's ministry with the congregation of the UU Church of Yakima. As we shall see, it was a wonderful placement. She was well-treated and she provided well for her congregation. I'm grateful that she was called to the state of Washington by the good people of the Unitarian Universalist Church of Yakima.

February 1989 — A Letter from First UU

In a letter dated February 21, 1989, Dean Garner, who was the President of the First UU Congregation at that time, wrote to Greta with the following announcement:

... At our mid-year meeting on February 5, 1989, the congregation approved a board-sponsored resolution to confer upon you the title of Minister Emerita of First Unitarian Universalist Church of Wichita. This seems to me a small token of our appreciation for all that you have been and have done for us. We care more than is really within our capability to express.

We wish you the best and much joy in your new ministry.

The twist to this announcement was that Greta's best friend, Betty Welsbacher had flown to visit her in Yakima. Little did Greta know that Betty had traveled to Yakima to read Dean's letter during the Sunday service! Greta responded to Dean Garner's letter on March 29, 1989:

> What a wonderful surprise in the midst of the service here when Betty Welsbacher read your graceful letter with the news of the vote of the congregation naming me Minister Emerita of the First Unitarian Universalist Church of Wichita.
>
> I was touched by this outward and visible sign of the inward and abiding bond between us, the people of the church and myself.
>
> I thank you and Patt and the people of the church for all the love and care that has gone into this affirming act.
>
> Love, cheers, and thanks,
Greta W. Crosby
Minister Emerita

Section V
The 1990s to Current

Meditation at Camp Roganunda, Naches, Washington
Intergenerational Congregational Gathering
June 12, 1994

It has been a while since we have practiced a ladder of silence that leads from the outer world to the inner world. Let's try it now.

The first step is a <u>looking silence</u>. We keep very quiet, but we can look all around with attention and become aware of what is around us, trees, sky, other people. We do not talk or make noise, but we can nod or smile.

The second step is <u>a listening silence.</u> We close our eyes and listen, listen intently, and become aware of many surrounding sounds, the wind in the trees, birds, people and automobile sounds in the distance; the sound we make as we breathe gently and deeply.

The third step is <u>a feeling silence</u>. We feel how warm or cold the air is and how it changes; the hardness or softness of our seating or of the ground under our feet; the touch of our clothing. And then we move to our inner sense of our own body, its comforts and discomforts. And then we move into our present feelings, our mood.

The fourth step is <u>a thinking, reflective silence</u> in which we become aware of our thoughts and reflections, our memories and desires.

And finally we let go of the work and play of our minds and hearts and enter an inner silence, and rest there a while.

(Silent Pause)

And when we are ready, we slowly climb back up the ladder, one step at a time, to the light of day.

— Greta W. Crosby

CHAPTER 23

The Early 1990s

The 1991 War in the Persian Gulf

ON AUGUST 2, 1990, Iraq's leader, Saddam Hussein ordered the invasion of Kuwait, citing the siphoning of crude oil from Iraq's border and demanding the cancellation of 30 billion dollars of foreign debt to Saudi Arabia and Kuwait.

On August 8, 1990, Iraq formally annexed Kuwait, calling the country its 19th province. Two thirds of the Arab League turned to the U.S. and other N.A.T.O. members for support.

On November 29, 1990, the U.N. Security Council authorized the use of "all necessary means" to remove Iraqi forces from their occupation of Kuwait. Saddam Hussein had until January 15, 1991 to leave Kuwait.

On January 8th, in response to the increasing prospect of war with Iraq, Greta sent the following letter to the President of the United States.

4602 Tieton Drive, #N-70
Yakima, WA 98908
January 8, 1991

President George Bush
The White House
Washington, D.C. 20500

Dear President Bush:

I urge you to protect American interests without war. Continue to cooperate in international economic pressures on Iraq. Negotiate in good faith. Do not destroy Kuwait to "save" it. Do not bomb the people of Baghdad, a third of whom are under the age of fourteen.

Consider the long-term consequences of your actions. Avoid triggering religious war in the Middle East. Do not divert our resources needed for human concerns in our own country. Improve our health and education systems for all ages. Do not send us our children in body bags.

With deep concern,
Greta W. Crosby

On January 17, 1991, without further diplomatic negotiations, the U.S. led 'Operation Desert Storm,' a massive and devastating bombing of Iraq. Though Iraqi military facilities were targeted, they also destroyed critical infrastructure necessary for civilian survival in Iraq. The operation vastly 'overkilled' with its aggressive tactics.

https://www.washingtoninstitute.org/policy-analysis/infrastructure-targeting-and-postwar-iraq

Once the bombing began, Greta sent the following letters to President Bush, Washington state's Senator Brock Adams, and a letter to the editor of the Yakima *Herald-Republic*:

4602 Tieton Drive, #N-70
Yakima, WA 98908
January 17, 1991

President George Bush
The White House
Washington, D.C. 20500

Dear President Bush:

I protest your use of force in the Gulf Crisis. It was premature. You did not give economic and diplomatic sanctions time to work.

I protest your involving our country in the march of folly. You divert our resources from constructive to destructive ends.

I protest your involving me, an American, against my will in this ill-advised and massive violence. This is not the way to defend our country and human rights in the world. Your stated good ends are vitiated by your means.

Turn back from the path of war.

With deep concern,
Greta W. Crosby

4602 Tieton Drive, #N-70
Yakima, WA 98908
January 29, 1991

Senator Brock Adams
Senate Office Building
Washington, D.C. 20510

Dear Senator Adams:

I commend you on your good record on the Council for a Livable World 1990 voting record, Senate Nuclear Arms Race index.

I was glad of your vote against the granting of permission

for the use of force in the Gulf Crisis. I am sorry that you found it necessary to change your position after the use of force began in supporting the resolution commending President Bush for his conduct of the war. The use of force was premature, there having been no negotiations in good faith.

Now I urge you to use your influence to support measures to limit the scope of the war and to bring about genuine negotiations.

With deep concern,
Greta W. Crosby

To his credit, Senator Brock Adams responded with a three-page letter to her inquiry. He explained that he did not support the bombing, but once troops were to be deployed on the ground, he felt it was important to fund them, or risk making them vulnerable to attack.

February 8, 1991 — Yakima *Herald-Republic*
Letter to the Editor — "Rainbow Ribbon"

To the editor — I wear a rainbow ribbon. Seeing yellow ribbons, my heart goes out to our people in the Middle East, our people at risk, and to all the people of which they are a part: families, friends, lovers, children, newborn infants left behind.

But I cannot wear yellow alone because it does not include those others to whom my heart goes out: Kuwaitis, Saudis, others from the UN, Israelis, Iraqis, too and those at risk around the world from escalation and retaliation, and all their dear ones. And more. I include concern for the people who are ill without care with AIDS and other conditions, those who are poor, hungry, homeless, unemployed, underemployed, the aging who will outlive their resources — all those whose human condition might be bettered by attention and concentration of resources now diverted to war.

I grieve for all those hostages. They are not hostages to fate but to the decision-making of two men who imitate the storm and battle gods of old, George Bush and Saddam Hussein.

I wear a rainbow ribbon. It includes the yellow. I am with the wearers of the yellow who want their loved ones alive, well and home. But with the rainbow, I seek a more inclusive solidarity with all born of planet Earth. For people of the Book — Jew, Christian, Moslem — the rainbow is the sign of survival and reconciliation, peace after storm and annihilation, promise of ongoing life. For all people, the rainbow is a shimmering wonder and the sign of hope. I wear a rainbow ribbon for life, hope and peace.

Greta W. Crosby
Yakima

The Yakima *Herald-Republic* published her letter, and she also felt called to submit her beautiful rainbow ribbon letter to *Newsweek*, The Christian Science Publishing Society, *The New York Times*, a Canadian periodical called *Changes*, and UUA's *UU World*.

April 1992 — Los Angeles Riots

In the early 1990's, there was growing unrest in L.A. The Los Angeles police department had been systematically abusing black people for years. One man, Rodney King, had been brutally assaulted by four arresting officers in 1991, and they were put on trial in April 1992. The jury had ten white people, one Latina and one Asian-American person. Though the videotaped evidence was irrefutable, the four officers were acquitted of wrongdoing. Violent riots, fires and destruction of property ensued. Approximately sixty people were killed, many more were injured, and approximately one billion dollars' worth of damage occurred to areas of Los Angeles.

https://www.history.com/topics/1990s/the-los-angeles-riots

In Greta's files, I found the following letter to the editor published in response to these tragic events.

May 5, 1992 — Yakima *Herald-Republic* — Letter to the Editor: "Root Causes"

To the Editor — I am angry at the miscarriage of justice in the Rodney King case. Police have authority to detain, to investigate, and, if necessary, to subdue a resisting suspect. They have no authority to inflict pain and injury on one already made helpless.

I am anguished in the face of the violence and chaos that have erupted, but I am not entirely surprised. Violence begets violence; lawlessness and neglect on the part of people in power begets chaos.

I am heartened by the instances of courage that have emerged in the midst of devastation, as in the rescue of the beaten truck driver by four African Americans (reported in the Yakima *Herald-Republic*, May 1).

My hope is that now attention will be paid. But will attention be turned to what will help, to what will give all people a stake in a peaceful society? Only the creation of conditions and opportunities for full lives for those now denied them will quench the volcanic fires of rage and frustration.

Greta W. Crosby
Yakima

Introduction to "First Things First: Dignity and Worth"

Up to this point, for all of the Spoken Essays and Commentaries included in *All of Us Together,* I had the benefit of sourcing Greta's hand-selected sermons from her own collected favorites. Now it was up to me to select the last two Commentaries to be included in this book. But which ones?

As I pondered this difficult selection process, it occurred to me to include her last sermon before her retirement as a bookend to "Mobile Deity," which was her last sermon before graduating Meadville Theological School in 1959. That felt right, so I searched for her final Commentary. It took some digging, but, yes, I found it! It's entitled "Fathers and Farewell."

That solved one dilemma for what to include in Greta's Commentaries of the 1990's. This meant I had one remaining sermon to select for our collection — one of the approximately 200 that she delivered in the 1990's. How, oh how was I going to do it?

There were many excellent possibilities, yet "First Things First: Dignity and Worth" stood out to me as a beautiful encapsulation of Greta's lifelong philosophy of first and always viewing people with steady nonjudgment; of looking for the good in people — and finding it — even if they can't see it in themselves, and even if others refuse to see it in the people affected by war, bigotry and rioting.

Greta shared her Commentary "First Things First: Dignity and Worth" with the Yakima congregation on December 6, 1992, when she was 61 years old. Her title refers to the first principle listed in our Seven UU Principles:

1. We affirm and promote the inherent worth and dignity of every person.

This Commentary was delivered in early December, in preparation for the Christmas season. Greta touches on several significant insights in her sermon, and I especially appreciate her observations of inclusion within the traditional nativity scene.

There's one more detail to be aware of while we read the story of the birth of a child. At the time of her sermon in December 1992, I was pregnant with my first child, Miranda. So Greta was expecting her first grandchild to be born a just few months after this sermon, and within her Commentary, I can sense her excitement for this blessed event.

Chapter 24

"First Things First: Dignity and Worth"

Greta W. Crosby
Unitarian Universalist Church of Yakima
Yakima, Washington
December 6, 1992

[The following readings were incorporated into the church service before the sermon, then Greta referred back to them within her Commentary.]

Story for All Ages: Fly Away Home
This is a story about families who cannot afford to live in a home and so they subsist in an airport. The story can be searched by inputting *Fly Away Home* by Eve Bunting. Or it can be accessed from the following YouTube link:

https://youtu.be/xVISBMSIxZw?si=-gKCbtFNQu9bBjz8

———

Reading: "Broadway's Newest Feature: The Cornstalk" by Steven Lee Myers, *The New York Times,* August 13, 1991, p B12.

NEW YORK — Someone working with obvious devotion and care has raised a small crop of corn on Broadway at 153rd Street — 131 stalks, some nearly six feet tall, capped with tassels and sprouting cigar-sized ears. The question remains: Who?

Ch 24 - "First Things First: Dignity and Worth"

"I first noticed it a few weeks ago," Mildred Duran, the district manager of Community Board 9, said today. "I said, 'Oh, my God, corn on Upper Broadway!' I don't know who planted it, but it seems to be planted well. It just makes you curious."

Up and down Broadway, neighbors in the working-class community of Jamaicans, Dominicans and other immigrants seem a bit bewildered. Many unseemly things happen early in the morning and late at night in Washington Heights, they say, but farming, evidently, is not among them.

"That's corn?" Tina Forsythe, 17 years old, asked today, her eyes straining in the sun as she looked at the surreptitious crop across the street. "Yes, indeed," her mother, Sonia, interjected, "We know it in Jamaica. It's very pretty."

A group of young men at a fruit stand selling guavas, papayas and pineapple not more than 20 feet from the corn denied any knowledge of it. "What corn?" one said, declining to give his name.

In the shrub-filled median, straddled by lanes of heavy traffic, the corn looked a little weary. The sun was obviously exacting a toll, but the stalks, arranged in two neat rows beneath London plane trees, was well-tended. A few ears of blood-red corn had grown to five or six inches long.

Lenis A. Nelson, a professor of agronomy at the University of Nebraska in Lincoln, where they know a thing or two about corn, said that in spite of pollution, and other urban assaults there is "no reason not to expect" corn to grow well in Manhattan. "It's a pretty hardy plant," he said. "Soybeans are another matter."

Just who did plant the crop remains a mystery. While the

neighborhood is not exactly abuzz over the question, many people have taken note of the agricultural oddity, and a number of them offered possible motives.

"Someone might have done it on their own, like to feed the pigeons," said Gwenn Brown, a day-care worker at the gothic Church of the Intercession, which overlooks the crop.

"Somebody's going to make sour mash," said Norman (Skip) Garrett, a spokesman for the Department of Parks and Recreation, who added, "This is an old Ohio farmer talking."

But the best clues came from Jeannette Boyd, also with the Parks Department. Part of Ms. Boyd's job is to recruit volunteers to tend the many malls and medians in New York City. One morning last spring, driving down Broadway, she spotted a thin, gray-haired, Spanish-speaking man carefully cultivating the soil, picking up trash and pulling weeds at 153rd Street.

"I stopped to talk to him," Ms. Boyd said. "And he told me — he spoke only broken English — 'I plant; I take care.' He said he lived nearby. That's all he said."

Greta's Commentary
"First Things First: Dignity and Worth"

Our stories this morning can be understood on many levels. They can lead in many directions. Now they are a part of you, and you will do with them as you will.

I originally chose *Fly Away Home* to bring to mind in a contemporary way, age-old themes of the sacred December season. One of the calls of the holy days in balance with the holidays is to put oneself in the place of the other. We do this, for example, when we choose gifts for family and friends. We do this at another level when we reflect upon the blessings of our own lives and upon the things we take for granted that support our lives — and then reflect upon the situation of many others who live in lack and want. *Fly Away Home* reminds us of the people in our Valley who do not even have homes. For them, as in the Christian nativity story, there is "no room in the inn." To pursue this theme in a detailed way, attend our forum this morning at 11:00. Phoebe Nelson, director of the Yakima County Homeless Coalition will share information on housing conditions and needs.

Fly Away Home, however, and the news story of the corn growing on Broadway, are not primarily stories of want and deprivation. They are stories of human dignity and worth. In *Fly Away Home*, people manage to survive, to find shelter, to keep families together, to cooperate for survival and companionship, to live humanly and humanely while they seek the work and the space that will permit them to emerge from their shadow-world. In the story of the Broadway corn, we meet a man of simple skill and devotion who works a minor miracle in a median strip. His words ring in my ears: "I plant. I take care." They suggest to me a life motto that might well be adopted for a church as well as a person: "We plant. We take care."

What do we plant as a religious community? Of what do we take care? People and values. *People* and *values*.

The two stories converge in their affirmation of the dignity and worth of people. I chose them to embody and to remind us of one of the key values of our religious way. It is placed first in the most recent formulation of the principles of the Unitarian Universalist Association voted by its General Assemblies in 1984 and 1985. The list of seven affirmations of principles begins with:

"We affirm THE INHERENT WORTH AND DIGNITY OF EVERY PERSON."

In stories and in lives, of course, worth and dignity can be embodied, can be shown forth — or not. The "inherent" part is a matter of faith. It is what we must take on faith just as other religious bodies take certain things on faith, making certain assumptions about the world and about people. While we cannot prove inherent worth and dignity, we can show what happens when it is denied.

There is a wonderful passage in William Ellery Channing's Baltimore Sermon in 1819, "Unitarian Christianity," about the effects of belief in the Calvinist doctrine of the utter depravity of human nature and of God's choosing at will, not even on merit, of people for salvation and condemning the rest to eternal damnation. Channing in this sermon was the spokesperson chosen by his colleagues for the first phase of emerging Unitarianism in this country:

> That this religious system [the Calvinist] does not produce all the effects on character, which might be anticipated, we most joyfully admit. It is often, very often counteracted by nature, conscience, common sense, by the general strain of scripture, by the mild example and precepts of Christ, and by many positive declarations of God's universal kindness and perfect equity. But still we think that we see its unhappy influences. It tends to discourage the timid, to give excuses to the bad, to feed the vanity of the fanatical, and to offer shelter to the bad feelings of the malignant.
>
> By shocking, as it does, the fundamental principles of morality, and by exhibiting a severe and partial Deity, it tends strongly to pervert the moral faculty, to form a gloomy,

forbidding, and servile religion, and to lead men to substitute censoriousness, bitterness, and persecution, for a tender and impartial charity. We think, too, that this system, which begins with degrading human nature, may be expected to end in pride; for pride grows out of a consciousness of high distinction, however obtained, and no distinction is so great as that which is made between the elected and abandoned of God.

The Unitarian Christians in early 19th century Massachusetts separated from the Calvinist Congregational churches, or actually were extruded from them by the orthodox, because the Unitarians held a different view of human nature and of God. The Unitarians believed that Calvinist views of the utter depravity of humankind and the double election by God to heaven or hell misrepresented both the potential of human nature and the character of a loving, just God.

Here we find some of the roots of our first principle: the worth and dignity of every person. The early Unitarians could not believe that God would create an inherently depraved humanity or condemn before birth the majority of humanity to eternal suffering.

Other early roots lay in Universalism's emphasis on a loving God, so loving, so powerful, that God would find a way ultimately to reconcile, to save every soul. John Murray, one of the two founders of American Universalism in the 18th century, is remembered for these stirring words:

> Go out into the highways and by-ways for America, your new country. Give the people, blanketed with a decaying and crumbling Calvinism, something of your new vision. You may possess only a small light but uncover it, use it in order to bring more light and understanding to the hearts and minds

of men and women. Give them, not Hell, but hope and courage. Do not push them deeper into their theological despair, but preach the kindness and everlasting love of God.

In other words, people are created and called to hope and to love. People are worth it. We are of worth, we have the dignity of worth, we have the dignity of a worthy place in creation. We are called to act worthily, with the dignity of a loving creation.

Whether the inherent worth and dignity of every person comes from the loving Creator of tradition, or from the recognition of our mysterious participation in the interdependent life of our planet, whether from the realization of the potential for good in recognizing and supporting this dignity and worth, or from the potential for evil in denying it, or from some other source, this inherent worth and dignity of every person is our first affirmation as Unitarian Universalists. It is worthy of our reflection and careful, I say care-full, action.

As a seasonal exercise, I suggest, for example, considering the nativity story, the manger scene that is so much before our eyes now. What does a Unitarian Universalist do with it? We may, of course, reject it as false propaganda for an outmoded belief system. That's the bah-humbug approach, always freely available to Unitarian Universalists. Or we may enjoy it as a continually enhanced creation of people over a period of nearly two thousand years in which each detail may reveal something of the heart and mind of people across time and space. Or, as I suggest today, we may meditate upon it in light of our own religious principles, such as the inherent worth and dignity of every person.

I cannot do your reflection or meditation for you, but I share a few responses and thoughts stimulated by the manger scene in the light of our First Principle.

Taking the inherent worth and dignity of every person seriously, I could focus in turn on each person in the scene. But I'll start from the center: the newborn child. In traditional Christianity, this is a real infant and at the same time the incarnation of God taking on humanity to overcome an ancient universal separation between God and humanity, to heal the rift, to reconcile God and humanity, to establish a way for people to come to eternal bliss.

What is the child for this Unitarian Universalist, neither a bah-humbugger nor a traditional Christian? It is, of course, for me, the infant of the legend that grew up, about the birth of Jesus, a Jewish teacher, prophet, and rebel against the way of Rome. The man around whom the early Christians developed their church theology of a coming realm of God on earth and hope and of life eternal. But more importantly, it is the infant, the archetypal infant, the miraculous infant that is every infant born into the world, the tiny person of inherent worth and dignity. Sophia Fahs wrote: "Each night a child is born is a holy night."

Instead of denying the divinity of the child in the manger, as a Unitarian Universalist is free to do, I prefer to affirm that all children, all of us, are incarnations of the divine, temporary, limited, subject to distortion, but nevertheless embodiments and participators in a creative sustaining, renewing spirit.

What do I make of all those who peopled or converged upon the manger? In traditional Christianity, they came to pay homage to the "newborn king." My Unitarian Universalist eyes delight in each and every one as persons of inherent worth and dignity — and in the animals of legend prefiguring ecological sensitivity.

Traditional Christianity delights in their homage; I delight in their variety and inclusivity — and in each one's capacity to give a gift, no matter what their circumstances. Each one makes a gift of self, in presence and present. Variety and inclusivity: age, race, gender, economic and political status. The manger scene is an equal opportunity display with perhaps affirmative action for the slighted. In traditional Christianity, God is born of a woman soon to be married. This Unitarian Universalist gives Joseph his fair share in the incarnation. Shepherds and wise men, poor and rich, young and old, men and women from near and far. Over time the wise men became kings from three continents and races, young, middle-aged, and old.

The traditional Christian sees the spread of Christianity symbolized. This Unitarian Universalist sees the capacity of diverse people of many origins and perspectives to rejoice in the birth of a child and in the hope of worldwide peace and joy and to give their very own gift to sustain life and hope.

And now what of us? How will we recognize one another's inherent worth and dignity? How will we express our own? What gift do we ourselves bring to welcome and sustain hope, joy, and peace in this world?

Greta's Closing Words

These words appear in Greta's book *Tree and Jubilee* under the title, "Worth." Greta explains: I wrote these words long ago, but I share them again today because they express one of the most important gifts in the world:

> If I could give you one key, and one key only, to more abundant life, I would give you a sense of your own worth, an unshakable sense of your own dignity as one grounded in the source of the cosmic dance, as one who plays a unique part in the unfolding of the story of the world.

When you and I look at these trees, these flowers, anything at all, we are the universe looking at our own handiwork. You have perhaps seen the pattern of cross and yarn called the "eye of God" made first in our southwest, in homage to the sun. We, too, all of us together, all the eyes of the creatures, are the eye of God. That is why we need each other, our many ways of seeing, that together we may rejoice, and see clearly, and find the many keys to more abundant life.

Once we are sure of our own innate worth, something that cannot be taken from us, we no longer need to prove it in elaborate ways so often damaging to others and to ourselves. Once secure in our own dignity, we no longer need someone to hurt, whole classes of people to despise. Secure in the sense of our own worth, we can rejoice in the worth of others and love out of fulness instead of inner emptiness.

Let us affirm one another as unique, irreplaceable persons of dignity and worth.

CHAPTER 25

The Mid 1990s

Follow-up on "First Things First: Dignity and Worth"

THERE are many threads of inclusion and compassion in this Commentary that resonate with me. The story *Fly Away Home* was eye-opening and touching. The newspaper article on cornstalks gracefully growing on the NYC median brought a touch of serendipity to the service.

Greta reminds us that historically both Unitarianism and Universalism were grown from the foundational belief in the inherent worth and dignity of every person. And I especially appreciate her inclusive description of the nativity.

Greta's Closing Words, entitled "Worth," came from *Tree and Jubilee*, and this meditation happens to be my tippy-top favorite. I think of it as a gentle reminder that instead of trying to fill the void within us with external things or with demands we place on other people, it's important to do inner healing.

You may have also noticed that "Worth" also contains the title to this book: "We, too, all of us together, all the eyes of the creatures, are the eye of God. That is why we need each other, our many ways of seeing, that together we may rejoice, and see clearly, and find the many keys to more abundant life."

February 16, 1993 — Greta's First Grandchild

As mentioned in the Introduction for this Commentary, Greta's first grandchild was due in mid-March 1993. However, when I went in for a routine check on February 15th, the doctor explained that the placenta was not functioning properly and the baby needed to come out. He scheduled me to be induced the following morning. I was stunned by this unexpected turn of events and I called Mom to let her know. I was induced on February 16th, and though there were some complicating factors, Miranda was safely delivered in the afternoon.

About an hour later, I was gazing at my husband Danny holding baby Miranda in a rocking chair. Her little pink hat peeked out from the crook of his elbow. Imagine my absolute surprise when I realized my mom was standing in the doorway of our birthing room! I had no idea she was coming!

She had made arrangements to fly from Yakima that morning. Her dear friend Betty Welsbacher picked her up at the Wichita airport and drove her straight to the hospital. This was before mom used a cell phone, so she was completely unsure of the outcome until she walked into our room and saw Miranda's little pink hat nestled into the comforting fold of Danny's elbow.

Of course she wanted to meet Miranda, and she took a few steps toward Danny in the rocking chair. Then she stopped herself and said "Well, first things first." She came over to my hospital bed, hugged me and made sure I was doing well. Then she made a bee-line for baby Miranda.

When deciding what term of endearment she would like to be used when we referred to her, Greta selected 'Yaya,' a Greek name for grandmother. Miranda's Yaya came back a month later to watch her when I went back to work. Meanwhile, the members of the Yakima church had held a grandbaby shower for Greta and she brought us those items to share with us. We were so surprised and we loved all of their kind gifts.

In particular, a church member had sewn a small blanket with white polka-dotted cotton on one side, and pink flannel on the other side. This became Miranda's special blanket that followed her everywhere. As a self-soothing action, Miranda would pull up the little fuzzies on the flannel between her straightened fingers. Because of this blanket, homemade by a UUCY church member, to this day, Miranda is still a flannel-baby — even in her 30's she still self-soothes with her flannel fabrics that she always keeps on hand.

What's in a Name?

If you'll indulge me, here's one more note about how Greta's first grandchild got her name. Greta often christened the vehicles she drove with a name that was significant to her. There was Archy, a faded red 1950's VW beetle. His name was based on Don Marquis' humorous character from "Archy and Mehitabel," in *The New York Times*. Then there was Nero, a pale green 1960s VW van, named after the infamous Nero Claudius Caesar Augustus Germanicus. Beowulf was a sky blue 1972 VW beetle, named after the hero of the Old English epic poem. But there was also Miranda, a powder blue 1968 VW beetle — Miranda was the only female character in Shakespeare's last written play, *The Tempest*. Perhaps you see a pattern here of both VW's and names from history and literature?

I grew up with 'Miranda' being the car that my dad drove once my mom started driving Beowulf. I used to sit in the little blue beetle and pretend I was driving and changing gears. In my imagination, I 'drove' Miranda the VW beetle, many miles. I always loved the name, so in 1992, when an ultrasound revealed we were having a girl, we knew she would be called Miranda. And that is how Greta played a part in naming her first grandchild.

Letters from Members of the UU Church of Yakima

The people of the UU Church of Yakima truly appreciated Greta's thoughtful and gentle presence while she served at their church. Several were delighted to share their treasured memories of Greta as their minister. Longtime member Denise Edwards writes:

I was in my mid 30's looking for a spiritual community, around 1989. UUCY was about my 3rd tryout of Yakima options.

I entered a beautiful old church building. In the pulpit was a woman! She spoke eloquently, confidently, and made me think. Then she asked the congregation for comments at the end of the service. This was unfamiliar to me who was mostly familiar with scripted Catholic Mass. I was drawn to continue attending UUCY largely due to Greta's presence in the pulpit, as well as the tenor of the congregation. Over time, I witnessed her speaking her mind on humanitarian issues at church related events and bravely writing letters to the editor which were often published. She was always courteous while using the power of words and wisdom to clearly get the point across.

Greta conducted classes for new UU members, which I attended. She rotated through committee meetings so she could keep in touch with the workings of the church and help committees to work effectively together. She was not quick to judge but quick to respond with kindness and clarity when a situation called for it.

She visited people in the hospital regularly. This brought the opportunity for me to occasionally have lunch with her while I was employed at Yakima Valley Memorial hospital. In this way I got to know her in a broader context than church. She often talked to me about her granddaughter, Miranda, as she was close in age to my daughter. I had traveled to Russia in 1994 to adopt my daughter Oksana.

On Greta's last day in the pulpit at UUCY, she was in high demand and still managed to grant my request to have her include my daughter's naming ceremony. I was grateful to her for this and for being able to experience her personal kindness and professional excellence. After she moved away from Yakima, we occasionally wrote to each other or exchanged Christmas letters for many years, including comments about the girls.

Greta exemplified integrity and character. I miss her.

I recently attended a viewing of an online sermon by Rev. Michael Dowd titled "Being Calm in the Storm." He says what many of us are thinking. There is a truth I find apt for one of my age and difficult to digest when I think of our young ones. I wonder what Greta would have to say.

UUCY Member Mike Collins shares:

I felt Greta was humane and intelligent all at the same time. I felt inspired by her sermons.

The other thing I remember and appreciated about her was the way she read to the kids (and congregation) in the Story for All Ages. I was into reading to our kids at the time and I really appreciated Greta's style and choice of readings. Again simple and sophisticated at the same time.

Hannah King writes of her foundational childhood memories at UUCY:

> I grew up in UUCY when Greta was minister there. Here is a short memory from her time with us. She is missed!
>
> What I remember most from her time at UUCY is the Story for All Ages. I was just two years old when she arrived and 10 when she moved on, so as a kid, I was especially excited to be invited down to the front of the church. Sometimes we filled the first pew or overflowed onto the floor, cross-legged and wide-eyed at Greta's feet. From that vantage point, we had a great view of the illustrations and were even asked to join in sometimes with the storytelling. I always felt part of the service, the congregation, and the community. Undoubtedly, this ritual has had a lasting impact on my love of stories — especially picture books — and my strong belief that so-called children's books are for everyone!

Linda King warmly recalls several wonderful details of her time when Greta was in Yakima:

> Some things I remember about Greta's ministry at UUCY:
>
> 1. Her calm demeanor.
>
> 2. Her way with words.
>
> 3. Her ministry to me and my family when our daughter broke her leg.
>
> 4. Her compassion and kindness.
>
> 5. Her ability to remain steadfast whatever was going on.
>
> 6. The way she would pose this question on Sunday mornings: "What church is this, children?"
>
> 7. We began having year-round services during Greta's

time at UUCY. She was a believer in having a presence and being available.

8. How she ministered to me when my mother died, even though she had retired and moved on from UUCY.

9. The things she taught me:
- You must give people time to process and wait for their response without interrupting.
- In speaking of ministry, she let me know that she gave her message and it was up to people to then take what was useful for them and make it their own. The audience could also discard what didn't resonate with them.
- She taught me that the careful consideration of words was important in all correspondence.

10. Before we had our current Healthy Relations Covenant, she taught me what it looked like to speak with courage and humility.

Margaret Morris describes her memories of UUCY when Greta served as minister there:

After moving back from California (I grew up in lower Yakima Valley), in a few years I realized my son and daughter were finding religion in their friend's churches and questioning some of the practices and beliefs. Since I had worked in the Tacoma UU church while in college, I knew that church was consistent with my own beliefs and from my children's comments believed they might be interested. I enjoyed the first sermon by Greta and decided to join the very next week, in 1991.

Greta was supportive from the beginning. After a time, I did a reading for a service. I read something about Coyote and didn't allow time for her sermon. She handled the situation with grace and I didn't even know I'd erred (until later).

Many pleasant evenings were spent in Greta's company at Pat Ball's house with a group of women for good conversation and great food.

She also invited everyone in the congregation to join her at the local brewery once a month for sampling of the beer and good conversation.

When hospitalized, she brought me a small replica of 'She who watches' which is a favorite Native American symbol of mine.

In addition, Greta was very supportive when my mother passed away. It was much appreciated because life with mother had been difficult and I needed help.

Her sermons always left me with something to think about and thankful I'd made the effort to attend. She spoke using her fine, intellectual mind which I enjoyed. She was one of the most loving, kind, intelligent, supportive friends I've ever known.

Thank you Denise, Mike, Hannah, Linda, and Margaret for sharing your kind memories of Greta's ministry at UUCY. It warms my heart to hear of your treasured times together with my mom. She dearly loved and appreciated the members of UUCY.

Introduction to "Fathers & Farewell"

Greta turned 65 years old on April 19, 1996. It had been forty years since she entered Meadville Theological School. Her ministerial career of service to humanity had spanned five decades, and it was time for her to retire. It was certainly a difficult decision because she dearly loved her congregation. However, the lingering after-effects of the dysthymia that she had managed for ten years, provided the tipping point for her to step down and rest.

Greta's Commentary covers two subjects: Fathers and her Farewell. "Fathers" is included because her final sermon was shared on Father's Day, which is appropriate because her father is very near and dear to her heart. The second subject is Greta's farewell to the Yakima church and to her active ministry.

One thing you may notice about Greta's "Farewell" is that it will be somewhat brief. She doesn't delve too deeply into her memories of being a minister in this sermon. This is because on the Sundays leading up to her farewell, she shared numerous insights that she had gained throughout her career. Some of her introspective sermons included, "Ringing the Changes," "The Care of Ministers," and "Age Trek: Reflections on Retirement." By the time she reached her final sermon on June 16th, her farewell was relatively brief, though genuinely heartfelt. In fact, I wonder if she kept it fairly short because of how difficult her farewell must have been.

Additionally, Greta always invited members of the congregation to share their thoughts after her Commentaries at the end of the service. I imagine extra time was reserved on that day, allowing many members to describe their cherished memories of their time with Greta.

I have to say, every time I read this final Commentary, it is with a very full heart. Even though this transition meant Yaya was coming back to Kansas, land of the golden wheat fields, I still deeply feel the ache of it. Both the wistfulness of the Yakima church members letting go of her gentle presence, as well as the conclusion of Greta's entire life's work in the pulpit. I'm sure there were many times when she was eager to arrive at the point of retirement — to cross that finish line — but when it arrived, I can only imagine that the finality of her last Commentary had to be overwhelming.

CHAPTER 26

"Fathers and Farewell"

Greta W. Crosby
Unitarian Universalist Church of Yakima
Yakima, Washington
June 16, 1996

My first reading is the poem "Pied Beauty" written in 1877 by Gerald Manley Hopkins:
   Glory be to God for dappled things –
   For the skies of couple-colour as a brindled cow:
   For rose-moles all in stipple upon
   Trout that swim;
   Fresh-firecoal chestnut falls; finches' wings;
   Landscape plotted and pieced — fold,
   Fallow, and plough;
   And all trades, their gear and tackle and
   Trim.
   "All things counter, original, spare, strange;
   Whatever is fickle, freckled (who knows
   how?)
   with swift, slow; sweet, sour; adazzle, dim;
   he fathers-forth whose beauty is past change:
   Praise Him.
   This is one of my favorite poems. I usually turn to it for its

praise of the beauty of a checkered creation. It came to mind when I first saw pink-orange larch trees scattered among dark evergreens. I remember the poem whenever I see the M.C. Escher print of birds flying between night and day, birds formed out of chessboard countryside, white birds by night, black by day. It comes to heart when I look at my cat "Muse," a calico pied beauty. In summer when I walk under leafed-out trees in dapples of sunlight and shade, the poem calls to me. If I do not exactly praise "Him," I do praise the mystery from which all things flow.

From within a Christian tradition, Hopkins gives expression to the yin and yang of things: "Swift, slow; sweet, sour; adazzle, dim." No wonder I thought of the poem for today, this bittersweet day of farewell to this morning hour with you. But more of that later. Now let us honor fatherhood as we have so often honored motherhood.

Hopkins expresses the fatherhood of the Source of Creation in a wonderful way. He says of his God: "He Fathers-forth." Contrast this example, in Genesis where the God, separate from His Creation, either calls it forth — "Let there be" — or makes it — as Adam is formed out of earth before the God breathes life into him. Hopkin's "Fathering-forth" is in keeping, I believe with Jesus' own emphasis on loving Fatherhood. In Mathew's presentation of Jesus' teaching as the sermon on the mount, we are to love our enemies, do good to them, go beyond reciprocity in returning good for good by unilaterally initiating good. And what is our model in this? "That we may be the children of your Father which is in Heaven; for he maketh his sun to rise on the evil and the good, and sendeth rain on the just and the unjust." [Mathew 5:45 AV]

I have often wondered what Joseph, the father of Jesus, was

like that his son — childless himself so far as we know — had so fine a concept of fatherhood. Was Joseph a loving father and so rare an example of humanhood that he gave form to Jesus' experience of the divine? Or was he harsh or absent, perhaps early in death so that Jesus found a fatherhood in the divine that was missing from his life? Or was Joseph, like the rest of us, checkered in light and dark, a quilted creation?

"Father's-forth" to my mind and heart does not mean to me simply making or even simply fathering in the strictest sense the term so often carries. This term carries with it a sense of birthing and fostering and taking joy in what is fathered forth. And so I offer this word to you on this day of fathers. One of the things I have loved about this church is the prevalence of fathers who continue to father forth their children. Just as on the day of mothers I have noted that not all mothering is done by biological mothers or by women alone, so too today I note that not all fathering-forth is done by biological fathers or even by men. Some women have had to serve in some sense as fathers as well as mothers. And there is not only the fathering-forth of one's own children, but the fathering-forth of the children of the world in works of benefit to humankind.

I lighted two candles this morning, one in memory of my father, who died in 1973. He was my dear benevolent despot, accent on the benevolent, and my first model of the divine before my imagining evolved more toward the Tao of the East. His fathering was of both testaments — ethical and just, skillful as a surgeon, fine husband in a top-of-the-line, patriarchal kind of way, devoted to his children, interested and joying in them, lover of his country. He served in World War II because that was his way of protecting his family and country. He served not by killing but by healing. He was hard-headed and strangely soft-hearted. I loved him and know he loved me, a priceless heritage.

When I was twelve, a cousin committed suicide. My father took me into his den and quietly told me about the death and about the sorrow of my aunt in losing her daughter. He ended with the deep assurance that there was nothing, *nothing* I could ever do or be that would mean that I would ever lose his love or welcome, in my birth home. It was his way not only of suicide-proofing me, but of praying for my continued life. It was the human equivalent of Paul's affirmation that "neither death, nor life, nor angels, nor principalities, nor powers, nor things present, nor things to come, nor height, nor depth, nor any creature, shall be able to separate us from the love of God…" [Romans 8:38-39]

Not that he was always entirely happy with my life choices. He was understandably disappointed when I came home from law school announcing that I had decided to become a minister. But the night of my ordination and installation as minister of the Church of the Reconciliation some six years later, he came with my mother to the ceremony and told me afterwards that he was proud of me for fulfilling my intention — strange as the idea still must have seemed to him. After all, the idea still seems a little strange to me even after all these years. My one consolation after his death was that I no longer had to explain to him certain things about my life choices. In thinking for myself, as he taught me to do, my thoughts sometimes differed from his thoughts, and it was a little hard for him to understand how this could be.

I share with you part of a letter I wrote a few years ago to a colleague upon learning of the death of her father:

> I know nothing of the quality of your relationship [with

your father] except that you were able to be there for him and with him for some time before he died. It must have been hard but good to have warning and to be able to make that pilgrimage in time to see him and to say what was on your heart. Or better, perhaps, to begin to say. I know I continue to have internal conversations at times with my own father, who died years ago in the deep autumn of the year just before Thanksgiving.

I still feel the loss of one who knew me all the way back to the beginning and cared about me all the rest of his life. It leaves me feeling vulnerable still because he no longer stands between me and the edge of the world.

I hope you will take and make time for the inside work you have to do now — remembering, reliving, and reworking the fabric of your relationship with your father.

And finally, in this father's portion of the service, I share part of an answer I wrote to a beloved teacher who in his nineties asked me a hard question:

> Quite some time ago, you asked me two related questions, which I have since pondered but have not until now given you any sign that I have heard and cared and lived with them. I have not found answers — hardly an unusual state for a Unitarian Universalist.
>
> You asked: "Has the church any messages or consolation for the childless — the childless not by choice but by circumstances beyond control?" I am not aware of any churchly resources that specifically address those who are childless. I tend to think of attempts at consolation of anyone who feels a deep sense of loss or absence are perhaps presumptuous, though

the caring behind the attempts may well come through in love's fumbling way. I think that the church's message might be simply that there is a place and a body of people, complete with children, that at its best constitutes a larger family so that no one need be utterly cut off from on-going connection to the generations. At least, that was my own consolation when I thought I would be childless when I majored in unrequited love.

I realize that anticipating childlessness in one's youth is very different from experiencing it in later life. I share my own thoughts and consolations then as the only lived responses I can make to your question. I went into the ministry in part so that I might live and work in the circle of that larger family. I also felt keenly my kinship with one sister's growing family. The other sister is childless and finds real companionship with animals, presently a horse and three cats. It is with her that I 'talk cats and other creatures.'

I felt and feel strongly connections by the spirit line, especially the liberal spirit line, as well as by the blood line: friendship, attraction, attachment, kinship with people living and dead, known in person or by their traces left in writings and in images and in other creations such as churches. As to the implicit question in childlessness of 'immortality,' of on-goingness, I felt and feel deeply that a person's lived life continues to play a part in the story of humankind and of the Earth long after death and long after any memory of it has faded and that this 'immortality' is not at all dependent on having children of the body.

As to you and your wife, I believe this possibly even more because you are childless in that last sense, you cared and care for each other and for a myriad of students and friends in a special way, and so created a huge family by the spirit line. I know that by the way you both were with me and your students; you showed by example what 'the beloved community' could mean.

Your second question was a cry: "Is there no balm in Gilead?" I believe and want so much to say: "Yes, there is balm in Gilead!" But how can I truly say that for you or for any other person? I can *recognize* the heartfelt cry and ask in turn, because you are the one who has long lived that question: "Have you yet found balm in Gilead?"

As I move closer to my own farewell to this Sunday morning time with you "gathered here in the mystery of this hour," "Come, Sing a Song with Me" comes to mind. It is about gathering and sharing — and even about balm in Gilead [Jeremiah 8:22]. I know it is a favorite among many of you, as it is with me.

Singing Song #346 "Come Sing a Song with Me"
YouTube link —
https://youtu.be/oisrO48boDQ?si=maTz2dQADLKJwpgv

Part II

The second candle I lighted this morning was to light my farewell.

I feel a little like the Cheshire cat in Alice in Wonderland, slowly disappearing. Today is especially hard. It is my last Sunday morning in the pulpit as your minister, though I will see some of you individually from time to time and will be on-call for emergencies during my summer leave in July and August. Since I retire from full-time parish ministry on September 1, this is also my last service as a settled minister of any congregation. I know it, but I can hardly believe it or feel it yet in the roots of my being.

I share for the last time with you, favorite readings that have to do with friendship and the rituals of meeting, bonding, and parting of friends. From St. Augustine's Confessions [IV:8]:

> Other things there were in friends
> that did more take my mind:
> to talk and laugh together; to do kind offices by turns;
> to read together sweet-spoken books;
> to trifle and be serious together; to disagree at times, without offense,
> as...[one] might with...[one's] own self,
> and the very seldomness of disagreement to season many more agreements;
> sometimes to teach and sometimes to learn;
> to long for the absent with impatience, and to welcome the return with joy.
> These and the like tokens of attraction, given and requited from the heart,
> and expressed by looks, eyes, lips and a thousand pleasing gestures,
> were so much fuel to melt our souls together, and out
> of...[them] make but one.

From Antoine de St. Exupery's *The Little Prince*, I share passages on the rituals of friendship and the farewell of The Little Prince when the time comes for him to leave:

> "My life is very monotonous,"...said [the fox to The Little Prince]. "I hunt chickens; men hunt me...but if you tame me, it will be as if the sun came to shine on my life. I shall know the sound of a step that will be different from all others. Other

steps send me hurrying back beneath the ground. Yours will call me, like music, out of my burrow. And then look: you see the grain-fields down yonder? I do not eat bread. Wheat is of no use to me. The wheat fields have nothing to say to me! And that is sad. But you have hair that is the colour of gold. Think how wonderful that will be when you have tamed me! The grain, which is also golden, will bring me back the thought of you. And I shall love to listen to the wind in the wheat…"

"Please tame me!" he said. …

"What must I do, to tame you?" asked The Little Prince.

"You must first be very patient," replied the fox. "First you sit down at a little distance from me — like that — in the grass. I shall look at you out of the corner of my eye and you will say nothing…but you will sit a little closer to me every day…"

The next day The Little Prince came back.

"It would have been better to come back at the same hour," said the fox. "If, for example, you came at four o'clock in the afternoon, then at three o'clock I shall begin to be happy. I shall feel happier and happier as the hour advances. At four o'clock, I shall already be worrying and jumping about. I shall show you how happy I am! But if you come at just any time, I shall never know at what hour my heart is to be ready to greet you…one must observe the proper rituals…"

"What is a ritual?" asked The Little Prince.

"Those also are actions too often neglected," said the fox. "They are what make one day different from other days, one hour different from other hours. There is a ritual, for example, among hunters. Every Thursday they dance with the village girls. So Thursday is a wonderful day for me! I can take a walk as far as the vineyards. But if the hunters danced at just any time, every day would be like every other day..."

So The Little Prince tamed the fox. When the hour of his departure drew near —

"Ah,' said the fox. 'I shall cry."

"It is your own fault," said The Little Prince. "I never wished you any sort of harm; but you wanted me to tame you..."

"Yes, that is so," said the fox.

"But now you are going to cry!" said The Little Prince.

"Yes, that is so," said the fox.

"Then it has done you no good at all!"

"It has done me good," said the fox, "Because of the colour of the wheat fields."...

My friends, you know that I am not eager to leave you and this beautiful Valley. I do so because of a sense that it is time. Your settled minister must have reserves of energy upon which to call in responding to you, in providing a focus for the Sunday morning gathering, in voicing our values of truth and love in the larger community, and in keeping all the other promises of the parish ministry. I can no longer count indefinitely on those reserves. I also sense that it is time that I draw closer to my family in Kansas, to my children, and especially to my grandchild, Miranda. It is with her that I will be able to continue sharing for a while the stories for all ages that mean so much to me.

I will miss you as the living mosaic of unique, irreplaceable persons that I see now, in part before me, and which I inwardly enrich with the images of those with us in spirit. I think especially of your children and youth, many of whom I have watched develop over these past eight years—a great joy.

I will miss the Valley, this Garden of Eden, complete with river and fruit trees. I will not miss the serpent also present in our Valley and in ourselves who invites us to falls from full humanity in denying the full humanity of other human beings. That challenge to the exercise of our religion of inclusion can be encountered and — *countered* — everywhere.

I will miss so very many things — from Mount Adams, like a changing moon fixed on the horizon, hidden and revealed in turn by clouds, to the violet green swallows that acrobat over the talking river Yakima; from church picnics and potlucks and campouts, to the special moments that come as graces in church life, the moments when we lovingly reveal something of our inner depths to each other.

I will miss you.

I close with the benediction of the Golux in James Thurber's Thirteen Clocks: "Keep warm, ride close together, and remember laughter." To which I add the admonition of a dear nonagenarian: "And keep moving!"

SILENT TIME — Let us join in the mystery of silence for reflection, repose, meditation, or prayer.
SHARING — Congregation

SONG no. 106 "Who Would True Valor See"
YouTube link —
https://youtu.be/ydPn31WCkNs?si=GOZAoO2_GNSCNOX9

Closing Words / Extinguishing the Chalice

I give as my closing words my house blessing that I adapted from traditional sources, the blessing I gave when you installed me as your minister:

> Bless this house, that herein be found
> Good health,
> Faithfulness,
> Spiritual strength,
> Perspective,
> Good will and humor,
> The fullness of life,
> And thanksgiving to all givers:
> And may this blessing remain on this house
> And on all who gather herein.
> So be it. *Amen.*

CHAPTER 27

The Late 1990s

Follow-up on "Fathers & Farewell"

I REMEMBER my mom being quite taken with the story of *The Little Prince*. The 'taming' symbolism of the snippet she shared is significant. Ministers aren't meant to stay at a church for many decades. There is something to the idea of mixing it up, bringing in different backgrounds and experiences. Certainly there are reasons for ministers to move on, whether relocating or retiring — yet when the hour of farewell arrives, it is an exquisitely tenderhearted time:

>...The grain, which is also golden, will bring me back the thought of you. And I shall love to listen to the wind in the wheat...

It warms my heart to think of Yakima church members randomly noticing golden wheat, which inspires an image of their beloved Greta living with her family in Kansas.

The Rest of the 1990's — Post-Retirement Highlights

Here is how my mom made her way back to those amber waves of grain. Over the summer of 1996, she made arrangements for her relocation to Kansas. In late August, 1996, Danny, 2½-year-old Miranda and I flew to Yakima. We rented a big yellow moving truck with a car-towing trailer behind it. We loaded up her car and the contents of her apartment, and then we headed out for the heartland. On September 1, 1996, Mom said her last farewells, then she flew to Wichita with Muse, her calico Maine Coon cat.

At some point on our trek, we stopped at Burger King and got a kid's meal for Miranda. We spent an extra dollar on an Esmeralda puppet doll, as Disney's version of *The Hunchback of Notre Dame* had just come out. We had no idea how helpful that $1.00 investment would be. It became the source of *hours* of entertainment for little Mo-Mo on our scenic adventure. I also taught Miranda her letters and numbers while on the road, which provided a nice diversion from many miles of sitting in a car seat. The total road trip was 1,671 miles and we drove 350-ish miles per day from Washington, through Oregon, Idaho, Wyoming, Colorado, and finally Kansas.

In Wichita, Mom returned to the same apartment complex by the river where she had lived before moving to Washington. Once we arrived with the moving truck, we unloaded it and got everything situated in the apartment.

Greta Returns to First UU

After getting settled in, Greta began attending First UU as a regular church member. It was a little awkward at first because people knew her as First UU's minister, but she was no longer their minister. Out of respect for the current minister, she carefully observed the policies in place for retired UU ministers attending a UU church.

Leisurely Luncheons

Another regular routine my mom enjoyed in her retirement

was leisurely lunches with longtime friends. Nancy Milner was one such friend who was retired by the time Greta came back to Wichita, which allowed them to engage in quality conversations together. Greta enjoyed meeting Nancy at Cafe Bel Ami so she could order their Tilapia. Nancy had been attending First UU since 1978. Greta had even performed the marriage ceremony for Nancy and her husband Matt in 1985. They had many things in common and Nancy had a great appreciation for Greta's humanitarian view of the world.

Annie Welsbacher is the daughter of Betty Welsbacher, who was one of Greta's closest friends for many years. The Welsbacher family has been actively involved at First UU since the 1950's. Annie lived out of state while Greta was the minister at First UU in the 1970's and 1980's. However, Annie recalls that she was instrumental in establishing First UU as one of the first churches in Wichita to become a Welcoming Congregation. Annie also shared a heartwarming memory from Greta's post-retirement years:

The Exactitude of Greta's Friendship
by Annie Welsbacher

For years, my mother had a weekly lunch date with Greta. When I moved back to Wichita, they invited me to join them. Over the course of another 18 months or so, I dined with two women who always had something interesting to talk about, even though their routine had not changed in years — probably decades. I was honored to join their small circle, because Greta had demanding standards about the people she spent time with.

But the time came when my mother was confined to the place she lived for a short time at the end of her life, and then the time came, soon after, when my mother died. I was even more honored that Greta wanted to continue to meet, which we did for some time until she, too, was unable to go out much.

Greta has a deliberate way of living and speaking, elucidating with precision whatever details she believes necessary to communicate exactly what she wants to say, what she wants you to hear. This habit can be exasperating sometimes when the length of explanation runs long. But on one occasion, I was grateful for this habit.

A friend of mine saw us at the restaurant and stopped by to say hello. I introduced Greta and after a while my friend moved along and we returned to our lunch. For the next several minutes, Greta told me how much it meant to her that I had introduced her not as 'my mother's friend' — but as *my* friend.

From somebody else, the notion that by this time we had our own friendship would have been both trifling and understood. But having learned Greta's language, I knew that I had received a rare and lovely gift: her judiciously awarded affection.

Thursdays with Yaya

Though my mom had a consistent luncheon schedule with several friends, Thursdays were reserved for watching Miranda while I was at work. In "Fathers and Farewell," Greta shared that being able to spend time with Miranda was one of her reasons for retiring: "I also sense that it is time that I draw closer to my family in Kansas, to my children, and especially to my grandchild, Miranda."

And that was certainly a significant priority for Yaya, particularly before Miranda went to school. Miranda, now in her 30's, shared several of her fond memories, as well as the foundations that Yaya instilled that still influence her life today.

When I dropped Miranda off on Thursdays, Yaya found ways to keep her entertained. She had a shelf with toys for little Mo which included a set of Lion King toys and a miniature China tea set.

Miranda recalls with nostalgia eating strawberry-flavored applesauce and then going to the sink to wash the container and place it in the recycling bin. This was before we had single-stream recycling and I hadn't begun the habit yet, so Miranda was unfamiliar with this practice. Yaya's recycling routine made an impression on Miranda that continues today — she recycles regularly now and she wouldn't dream of not doing it.

Another cherished memory Miranda shares is how she and Yaya would go outside and walk to several different places. The reason for this is because my mom would not drive our kids anywhere. In her opinion, they were "precious cargo" and she didn't want to take a chance of something happening while she was driving them. So instead, they walked outside a lot.

Before heading outside, Mo recalls the scent-memory of Yaya putting sunscreen on her face and arms. They both had sunglasses and hats, too. Then they would walk by the river where Miranda had a favorite willow tree. In fact, Miranda and her husband later moved to apartments near Yaya's complex, and it made Miranda smile every time she went by the big magical tree from her childhood.

When Mo was little, sometimes she and Yaya would walk down to the apartment office to pay her rent. On certain days, they even walked a bit further to Braum's for lunch and ice cream treats. There was a Chinese buffet not too far, where Mo loved to get the sesame chicken. Whenever they went to eat at a restaurant, before they ate, Yaya would say, "Okay, it's time to wash our paws."

Miranda distinctly remembers how Yaya would adjust the water temperature whenever they washed their paws. She turned the faucet on and then tested the temperature with the back of her hand, not too hot or cold, setting the temperature just right for Miranda. This is one of those memories that has stayed in Miranda's mind. She is now a Speech Language Pathologist working with children with special needs, and when it's time to 'wash paws,' Miranda carefully tests the warm water with the back of her hand, not too hot or too cold.

Miranda also warmly recalls how Yaya was always kind and gentle. If any behavior needed correction, she did so very graciously. If Yaya didn't exactly agree with an idea Mo had, she would say, "Oh, I hadn't thought of it that way." Yaya had a way of complimenting Miranda that was not superficial, such as "You're so awesome." It was specific and meaningful, such as, "I like how you notice where the moon is in the sky." Or "Your hugs make me feel warm and fuzzy inside." On a daily basis, Miranda draws upon Yaya's example of being a supportive presence as she works with the children in her care — and those children dearly love Miranda.

Miranda's love of books was fostered by Yaya. Every gift-giving occasion provided an opportunity for Yaya to share another favorite book or series with Mo. One of our top-shelf favorite children's books is *Animalia* by Barbara Berger. Not to be confused with another book titled *Animalia* by Graeme Base, it's pretty good, too, but our favorite is Barbara Berger's *Animalia*.

It's a collection of wisdom stories from many cultures. The illustrations are beautiful and I highly recommend this book for any household.

Yaya also got Miranda started on the Harry Potter series. Mo has fond memories of me reading them to her when she was growing up. She recalls that whenever Yaya gifted her a book, it was inscribed with the date, a loving message and her signature in the book. Now Miranda enjoys gifting books, and just like Yaya, she takes time to inscribe the date, a meaningful message, and her signature in the book.

One more special memory of Yaya is the send-off she would give us when it was time to go home. Yaya's apartment was on the upper level, so we had to go down a set of stairs to get to the car. When we left, Yaya would stand on the landing and say goodbye as we went down the stairs. As we got in our car, a partition blocked Yaya's view of us, so she would bend over and keep waving as we got buckled up and drove away. It made Mo feel very loved to have Yaya watching and waving as we headed out of the parking lot.

The Power of the Pen — Greta's Social Justice Venue

Though she was retired, Greta still maintained methods of outreach for social justice concerns. Her primary means of expression were her letters to the editor. She submitted one or two letters per year and I'll include them here as they come up on the timeline.

August 12, 1997 — Wichita *Eagle* — Letter to the Editor
"Water Alert"

Thanks be to the Mothers of Munchkins. They alerted Wichita's citizens and City Hall to the risks to public health and trust posed by the proposal to add reclaimed water to the city water supply. They saved the city's livability quotient as well. Now we will be spared such lines in the national media as "Wichita: the city that injects dump water into its drinking water."

But now what? What risks does that landfill-tainted water still pose in its reclaiming and in its disposition? What ethical as well as technical and political questions are involved? Please keep your Eagle eye on these matters and keep us fully informed.

Greta W. Crosby
Wichita

November 28, 1997 — Wichita *Eagle* — Letter to the Editor
"Disney Boycott"

I could understand boycotting Disney products for hijacking history and maligning mythology. But I cannot understand Christian groups' boycotting Disney for being fair to its employees ("Baptist boycott of Disney moving ahead," Nov. 22 *Eagle*). It seems an odd way to follow the teachings of Jesus. A Christianity that ceases to be humane claims in vain faithfulness to its founder and loses moral authority in the world.

The article did state, however, that "many Christians, including some Baptists, agree with Disney."

Greta W. Crosby
Wichita

January 22, 1998 — Wichita *Eagle* — Letter to the Editor
"Choice Support"

This brings us to a highly controversial topic that demonstrates Greta's compassion for the human condition — that of reproductive freedom. It can be so easy for people to impose their beliefs onto others, but she asks people to turn the tables to really consider the differing circumstances of other women. The following letter to the editor beautifully encapsules the concept of looking at the issue of choice from many perspectives:

I write in honor of the 25th anniversary of Roe Vs. Wade. I support reproductive choice. I hope for the abolition of abortion but not by restricting access to safe, legal and affordable abortion services.

When the circumstances that call for the choice of abortion no longer exist, abortion will no longer be chosen.

When rape and incest cease; when there is no sexual ignorance, seduction or exploitation; when no one loves carelessly without contraceptive precaution and when no contraceptive device fails; when no accident or illness or genetic impairment occurs; when women no longer bear a disproportionate share in the care of children; when women are valued equally with men throughout their lives and have the same chance for lifetime partnership; when children are accorded the same societal support; when poverty ceases — then we will be well on our way toward the abolition of abortion.

Greta W. Crosby
Wichita

This is one of the most compelling letters to the editor I've ever read — I've even framed a copy of it for her. There are so many factors, circumstances and perspectives on this issue. Additionally, bringing it down to one more critical issue, whether or not abortion is legal, abortions *will* happen, and a percentage of those unregulated actions will be damaging and deadly for women.

There are still many machinations occurring across the country restricting both the use of contraceptives and safe access to abortion services. One of Greta's speeches that she presented to Washington's state legislature in 1991, expresses her sentiments about this:

> ... I speak out of my life-long experience. I speak as a woman, a mother, a lawyer, a minister, a human being in touch with the human condition. I believe that no woman, no girl, no child should be compelled to give birth against her will. I recognize the excruciating ethical dilemma in deciding whether or not to terminate a pregnancy, and I want that choice to be made by the one who is pregnant, with the help of the people she chooses. Her close ones, her moral and medical advisers.
>
> The same people who have brought us (the Gulf War), also war more quietly against women, especially on women's choice in the matter of motherhood.

Interestingly, when Roe vs. Wade was overturned by the Supreme Court in June of 2022, the Kansas legislature attempted to add an amendment to the State Constitution strongly restricting abortion services. Because it was an amendment it had to be voted on as a referendum, so it was added to the primary election on August 2, 2022.

Greta, at age 91, speculated that because it was a referendum from the voters, not just dictated by the legislature, it might not pass. She was absolutely correct. The vote on the referendum failed, with 40.84% in support and 59.16% against.

The Life's Work of Greta's Son Paul

After graduating from Bethel College in 1987, my brother Paul moved to Lawrence, Kansas, to study Psychology at the University of Kansas. He was a teaching assistant for a number of classes as he earned his Master's Degree in Psychology. For eight years, Paul lived at and helped manage a cooperative living space called Sunflower House.

Once he achieved his degree, Paul migrated from teaching classes to student advising at KU's Academic Advising Department. For several years he specialized in Pre-Med advising, guiding students to take the correct classes in the correct order to prepare them for acceptance into medical school. He also developed a class that outlined how to apply to medical schools. Additionally, for many years, Paul served on the National Association of Advisors for the Health Professions Communications Committee.

Over the decades, as KU's Academic Advising Department has reorganized, Paul has filled many advising roles. His years of experience provide highly valuable insights for students planning their academic training, as well as future careers. Greta calls Paul 'The Oracle' — the One whom students consult in planning their life's journey.

Just like her sister Paula, Greta's son Paul has remained single throughout his lifetime, though he has been pet-parent to a number of furry friends. At one point he had two feisty ferrets — Ping and Pong. His latest fur-baby is a sleek Russian blue kitty named Razz, short for Rasputin.

Over the years, Paul has dabbled with various hobbies, including brewing beer, mountain biking, hiking, camping, and playing on the Parks & Rec softball and adult kickball teams. Paul travels to our area to visit Mom and our family several times a year.

March 19, 1998 — Yaya Braves a Snowstorm to Greet a New Arrival

In the time since Miranda's birth in 1993, I had experienced problems with fertility as well as two consecutive miscarriages. In 1997, I was finally able to conceive and maintain a pregnancy, and the baby was due in March 1998. It was a terribly emotional time, because we didn't know if the pregnancy would go to term this time — fortunately, it did — but there were still worries all along the way.

On the evening of March 18, 1998, I was starting to feel contractions, but I wasn't sure if it was real labor. However, a snowstorm was moving in from The Four Corners that night, and whenever weather comes up from the southwest, it can bring significant snow. We lived in the country, about 45 minutes from the hospital and we didn't want to end up driving in heavy ice and snow. At about 10pm, we called Danny's grandparents and his mom. I called Yaya to let her know we were heading in. As soon as we arrived in the birthing room we heard ice pellets hitting the windows.

Shortly afterward, both Danny's elderly grandparents and Yaya came up to the hospital in the middle of the night! They braved the icy roads because they were so excited for the new arrival that had been so many years in the making. They took turns watching five-year-old Miranda in the waiting room. Baby Brett was born at about 4:00 in the morning. Miranda was so excited to meet her brother. When she first saw him, she cheerfully observed, "Ohhh, he's cuter than other babies!" Which he was!

After staying up all night, it was finally Yaya's and Danny's grandparents' turn to meet the handsome baby Brett. They could not have been more thrilled to hold him and welcome him into the world. The ice had turned to snow overnight and by daybreak, the Four Corners sent us 12 inches of snow, which is unusual for March in Kansas. We're grateful that all the grandparents made it home safely.

As Brett grew, we quickly observed his mechanical magnetism. We joke that hydraulic fluid pumps in Brett's veins where blood should be. His first words were "BBBBrrrrrr" as he drove his toys trucks over rugged terrain. He would always steer the conversation to trucks, cars, or anything mechanical. At the age of three he drew a chart of the tire tread patterns of Dad's truck, the go-cart, my car and the riding lawn mower — and his sketch included both front and side views.

Clearly Yaya is not a gear-head, but she loved learning what made Brett tick and she customized his toy collection to his interests. Brett remembers a blue Datson and a yellow truck among several toy vehicles that were parked on a shelf at Yaya's place. On the linoleum floor in the kitchen, Brett would roll the cars backward, then release them and watch them dart away.

Brett was also intrigued by Yaya's kaleidoscope collection. I actually forgot about Yaya's child-like enthusiasm for kaleidoscopes until Brett mentioned this in his recollections. He would experiment with each one, pointing it toward the window, observing the colorful shifting shapes. Each one revealed different combinations of colors and viewpoints, providing an endless array of entertainment.

Brett also recalls the silence within Yaya's place. At times he felt it was too still and quiet, but Brett observes, "I also remember a side of it that was very peaceful. I remember looking through the blinds at the trees and just embracing the quiet time. It was pretty valuable."

Ch 27 - The Late 1990s

Snack-time always appealed to Brett. He remembers that the cheese sticks at Yaya's had a very different taste and smell than any others he has ever had, and he loved them. Another snack that has special meaning for Brett is pretzels. Yaya would ask him "What kind of pretzel should I get for Bretzel?" There were the regular pretzel shapes, the little sticks, the big sticks, and she liked to buy him different kinds to take home with him.

When they walked to the Chinese buffet, Yaya would ask him what he'd like to get. He always answered, "Eggdropsoup!!!" He liked it because it came out piping hot.

Naturally Brett had recollections about Yaya's car, even though he didn't get to ride in it. It was a Toyota Tercel with a rustic red patina — I can't recall what year it was, but it was too old. In Brett's gear-head way he recalls, "But I think I actually really liked the boxy look of it because it reminded me of some of the race cars I had seen growing up." Fortunately, Yaya finally purchased a new red 2007 Toyota Yaris, which was cute as a button.

Brett shares, "I remember when I was first learning to do math, something clicked and all of a sudden, I knew how to do it. I was really excited to tell Yaya I was becoming interested in math and getting good at it. Not necessarily because she liked math, but it was more: math = smart and smart = Yaya."

Yaya also gifted Brett with books about airplanes, cars, trucks and the like, of course geared to his mechanical gear-head. However, one of the books Yaya gave him was different. Here is Brett's description of his experience with Yaya's unique gift: "There was this dictionary that I received as a gift from Yaya. It was at a 3rd grade reading level. And I remember then, kinda thinking, 'Okay, whatever, it's a dictionary.' It wasn't the kind of gift I was used to receiving. But then I would just read it. I was sort of infatuated with it actually. It had a ton of information in it and I remember being surprised at how much I actually liked it and used it."

As a side note, she once gave me a book called *A Browser's Dictionary: A Compendium of Curious Expressions and Intriguing Facts* that appealed to my English-teaching roots. I felt the same as Brett described, infatuated with it and surprised at how much I liked it and used it.

Then Brett observed, "Later in life I remember her sitting and reading. Always learning and always absorbing new information. It sort of reminds me of Odin's mission of wisdom: 'Wisdom is more valuable than wealth and worth the burden of bearing it.' And it seems as though she was trying to give him a run for his money."

Brett concludes his reminiscences with, "I do love Yaya and I'm very proud of her. She has many accomplishments that I am aware of and I'm sure several more that I'm not. Her 'Love you Lots' always warmed my soul."

Not surprisingly, Brett grew up to be an Airframe and Powerplant (A&P) mechanic. He works on airplanes for a company called Executive Airshare at Jabara Airport in Wichita. As of October 12, 2024, Brett will be married to Katelynn, his girlfriend of many years. It warms Yaya's soul to know that Brett is partnered with such a smart, capable and well-matched life companion.

June 9, 1998 — Wichita *Eagle* — Letter to the Editor
"Term's Time is Up"

In the 1990s, the term 'politically correct' or 'PC' was being used quite sarcastically and derisively when discussing culturally diverse people or issues. It's another example of a societal tendency to emphasize and criticize the differences between people, rather than finding common ground. Here is Greta's response to this disrespectful trend:

It is time to retire the term 'politically correct.' I am not suggesting censorship but voluntary abstinence from its use.

'Politically correct' is not simply a cliche. It has become a term of abuse applied to efforts to deal fairly and sensitively with situations involving people denied respect and opportunity because they are members of discounted groups. Such efforts deserve thoughtful consideration, not a mocking, thought-stopping label.

Greta W. Crosby
Wichita

December 10, 1998 — Wichita *Eagle* — Letter to the Editor "Don't Kill Killers"

An article in the Wichita *Eagle* entitled "U.S. execution rate picking up" appeared on January 9, 1998. The article explains that the number of executions nationwide had increased from 14 in 1991 to 74 in 1997.

Kansas has not performed an execution since 1965, but in 1994 the state legislature approved the use of capital punishment by lethal injection. Throughout 1998, the state was working to establish protocols for execution through lethal injection. Many religious and community leaders oppose the death penalty, and some were speaking out against it throughout the year.

An editorial by Rhonda Holman appeared in the Wichita *Eagle* on December 3, 1998, and Greta submitted her letter to the editor in support of Rhonda's well-reasoned article:

I share columnist Rhonda Holman's doubts about capital

punishment ("How soon will the killing start?" Dec. 3). Leading reasons to oppose this penalty are the possibility of mistake and the bad example of vengeful violence set by the state in its premeditated killing of prisoners.

Capital punishment is also unevenly imposed, as it is applied more often to people who are poor or otherwise discounted than to people of wealth, status or celebrity.

Those whose mother tongue is money sometimes argue that it burdens taxpayers to imprison people instead of killing them. Executions, however, cost as much or more than imprisonment, even in money.

Capital punishment has been rejected in most developed countries because it impedes rather than furthers justice. Let Kansas return to its former civilized position by rejecting capital punishment.

Greta W. Crosby
Wichita

May 1999 — Visits to the UU Congregation of Lynchburg

Greta had returned to Lynchburg, Virginia in 1981 for the installation of a new minister at the UU Congregation of Lynchburg. Then in May 1999, Greta was invited to be a guest speaker at the church. Her Commentary was entitled, "Time and Memory." I don't know the content of this sermon, but I can imagine that she shared her appreciation for the dramatic improvements in Lynchburg since her first experiences there in 1960.

July 21, 1999 — Yaya Becomes a Yaya Once Again

In July 1999, when Brett was 16 months old, along came Tiger, the caboose on our family train. Danny's grandmother had passed away about a month before Tiger's birth, but we know she was with us in Spirit. Yaya and Danny's mom populated the waiting room this time. They watched the kids, while I walked the halls with Danny because I had opted for natural childbirth.

Tiger arrived in the early afternoon, and Yaya was so happy to meet her third and final precious grandchild. Our shared first observations came in succession: Our delight with his curly red hair, a birthmark on his right foot that looked like a paw-print, and his enormous Tiger paws (hands & feet), forewarning us that he's gonna be a big guy. Which he is! [Brett and Tiger are now 6'4" and 6'5" respectively.]

While at the hospital visiting Tiger, Yaya brought 'unbirthday' presents for Miranda and Brett. She always did that for Paul and me — on the day one of us was celebrating our birthday, the other sibling received an 'unbirthday' present.

With our family expanded to three busy bodies and with my mom's low energy reserves, we couldn't have her watch all the kids concurrently. However, we still coordinated opportunities for her to spend time with each of them individually.

Young Tiger marched to the beat of a different drum. Yaya was fascinated with his endless imagination. He would take a piece of toast hold it up and call it a spaceship. Then he would take a bite, hold it up and call it a boot. Taking another bite, it became a choo-choo train trundling along a track. Then it was a bat with wings flying through the air. He wasn't pretending they were those things, in his mind they *were* those things.

From a very young age, Tiger was a biological scientist. On their walks, Yaya would step back and observe Tiger observing the natural phenomena unfolding around him. He loved watching ants industriously scurrying along a pheromone trail, carrying tidbits to their anthills — and he very conscientiously avoided stepping on the ants while studying them.

Tiger's true passion was dinosaurs, so naturally, next to Brett's carport, Yaya stocked the toy shelf with a wide variety of dino-figures. Tiger also remembers other toys, such as the figurines that had a button at their base. When he pushed the button, the figurine would collapse then re-animate when the button was released — he had fun reminiscing about the little things that were so entertaining.

Tiger also commented on Yaya's delicious cheese sticks and applesauce. He has fond memories of walking to Braum's and the Chinese buffet with Yaya too. Sometimes Yaya, the kids and I would go to another Chinese buffet that stocked small, previously-frozen octopi in a serving bowl on the buffet. Young Tiger would wrap one of the little octopi up in a napkin and put it in his pocket to dissect at home.

Yaya was sure to gift Tiger with dozens of books tailored to his interests. He especially loved *The Magic Treehouse* books, the Percy Jackson series and *Harold and the Purple Crayon*. I'm sure Yaya thought it should be titled *Tiger and the Purple Crayon*! Tiger also treasures Yaya's "Love you Lots," and he knows that Yaya really does Love him Lots.

One of the most salient memories for Tiger was seeing how the mail system worked. Tiger specialized in drawing ocean and marine creatures, dinosaurs, and anything else that popped into his vivid imagination. We would put the drawings in an envelope, stamp it and write Yaya's address on it. Then we would walk down our long gravel driveway and place it in our mailbox, raising the red flag to indicate there was a letter to be picked up. The next time Tiger was at Yaya's, he would see his artwork prominently displayed on her refrigerator. This concept of mailing his drawings to Yaya blew Tiger's mind. What happened? How did they get there? Who did it? Ironically, Tiger now drives for Amazon Prime, so he's the delivery guy who gets things from 'here' to 'there.'

CHAPTER 28

The Early 2000s to the Present

The Early 2000s

ON SEPTEMBER 11, 2001, the twin towers of the World Trade Center, as well as the Pentagon, were hit by airplanes that had been hijacked and crashed into the buildings. These disturbing events shook the country to its core.

Blame for the attacks was placed on an Islamic terrorist group called Al-Qaeda. Sadly, this caused accusations and hate crimes across the country against many innocent groups of American citizens. Here is Greta's letter to the editor in response to these hurtful injustices:

> **October 7, 2001 — Wichita *Eagle* - Letter to the Editor**
> **"Cultural Help"**
>
> I commend the Wichita *Eagle* for its efforts to educate the public to prevent hateful acts directed toward people of Islamic and Arab heritage and those who resemble common images of them.
>
> Hate crimes are always unjust, but it is particularly important now to avert such hostile acts, because the heritage of these citizens and friends constitutes an essential reservoir of language skills and cultural understanding essential for

countering the present terrorism. Persons who commit such hate crimes aid and abet the September terrorists by alienating those whose help our country needs in preserving lives and liberties.
— Greta W. Crosby
Wichita

First UU & Sunday Lunches with Yaya

Though I took the kids to First UU's Christmas celebrations, we did not attend church regularly. However, after the 9/11 attacks occurred, I felt compelled to connect more closely with our First UU community. I began attending more regularly and I brought the kids to participate as well. Mo, Brett and Tiger had fun hanging out at the old church building on Fairmount, which was built in the 1800's. In my own childhood, I remember endless hours of play at that church when my mom was in meetings. I knew every single square inch of the building and grounds. It was heartwarming to come 'home' to my church home, and to know so many people who had been there since I first arrived in 1975.

Since we lived an hour away from Yaya, we didn't get to spend as much time with her once the kids were attending school. However, a wonderful advantage to attending First UU is it gave the kids an opportunity to have lunch with Yaya after church. We went to several favorite family-owned restaurants. There were a couple of Thai restaurants, a couple of Eastern Indian buffets, and a Mediterranean place that we enjoyed. Miranda, Brett and Tiger all have fond memories of delicious meals with Yaya on Sundays after church.

In Yaya's apartment, Tiger vividly remembers a large, framed watercolor of First UU on her living room wall. The church moved to a new location in 2007, but just the other day, Tiger felt prompted to drive by the old building, which brought up so many heart-warming childhood memories.

October 9, 2001 — Wichita *Eagle* article
"Benefits Proponents Cry Foul"

In October of 2001, the Sedgwick County commission mishandled a situation that involved their employee health insurance benefits program. The following is an excerpt from an article appearing in the Wichita *Eagle* on October 9, 2001:

> When retired Unitarian minister Greta Crosby heard that Sedgwick County commissioners were considering not allowing domestic partner benefits for unmarried couples, she wrote a speech urging the officials to leave the benefits in place.
>
> She never got to deliver her remarks — and neither did anyone else who came to last Wednesday's meeting to comment on the most controversial issue to confront the commissioners this year.
>
> "Had we had the opportunity to speak, the result might still have been the same," Crosby said. "But what I do know is the process would have been democratic."
>
> In the wake of the commissioners' 5-0 vote to revoke the benefits, the process has become as controversial as the decision itself.
>
> Supporters of domestic partner benefits are accusing the commission of manipulating its agenda so that only those opposed to the benefits had a chance to be heard.
>
> A lawyer who specializes in open-government law says the commission might have violated citizens' constitutional right to petition their government...

Greta's letter to the editor in November further explains the mishandling of the situation by the Sedgwick County Commission:

November 20, 2001 — Wichita *Eagle* — Letter to the Editor "Fair Play?"

A public hearing on the matter of benefits recently denied to domestic partners of Sedgwick County employees could be helpful to the County Commission in understanding the issues involved.

The commissioners initially recognized that the business decision to offer such benefits was within the purview of the county manager. Under fire from a conservative segment of voters, the commissioners lost their sense of proportion and fair play. They privately decided to rescind the benefits offer, then put the matter on their meeting agenda with only a day's notice.

This did not give supporters of the benefits extension an opportunity to be heard in time to influence the decision. The commissioners subsequently refused a request for a public hearing, losing the chance to have important issues clarified — issues such as fair play for employees (equal pay for equal work) and fair play for all citizens (democratic process in which notice is given and time provided for public input before such decisions are made).

What of the future? Will the commissioners allow fear of this conservative segment of voters to exercise a silent veto on any proposal that might possibly concern this segment? I urge the media to alert the public to any further sign of undemocratic exercise of power.   —Greta W. Crosby
Wichita

January 2002 — The Peaceful Passing of Greta's Mother

In January 2002, Greta's mom, Emma Jane Worstell, passed away at the age of 101. She had lived in Rancho Santa Fe, California since the 1980's, and she was pretty healthy for most of those years. It was sad to say goodbye to Grammer, but her passing also inspired a joyful celebration of her life. As is evidenced by her mom's longevity, Greta has good genes, so at 93, she's doing quite well, too.

August 31, 2002 — Wichita *Eagle* — Letter to the Editor "Religious Agenda"

I am deeply concerned about the future of religious freedom in Kansas. The Republican candidates for governor and attorney general, among others, have promised to use the power of the state to impose their religious doctrines on other citizens. They would not hesitate to support state actions that interfere in the most intimate of personal and family matters.

For example, they proclaim that they will do their utmost to limit reproductive choice, requiring women, even children, who become pregnant to give birth regardless of circumstances of pregnancy, the prospects for responsible parenthood, and the religious, ethical or medical concerns of those involved. I appeal to all citizens who value religious freedom and reproductive choice to reject these candidates in the Nov. 5 general election.

We are fortunate in having the saving grace of well-qualified, humane candidates such as Kathleen Sebelius for governor and Chris Biggs for attorney general, who can keep Kansas free of religious coercion backed by the power of the state. I urge citizens, regardless of party labels, to vote for them in November.

— Greta W. Crosby
Wichita

Kathleen Sebelius was voted into office in that election and she did a very nice job as governor of Kansas. Unfortunately, in 2011, Sam Brownback became governor, and Kansas became known as 'Brownbackistan' until 2018. Greta's concerns about the future of religious and personal freedoms in Kansas are valid. The state continues to experience power-plays from both legislative branches with unconstitutional agendas that deny basic human rights to Kansas citizens.

March 30, 2003 — Wichita *Eagle* — Letter to the Editor "Loyal Protest"

In March 2003, despite objections from many world leaders, George W. Bush and Tony Blair declared war on Iraq as a 'pre-emptive strike.' They claimed Iraq was producing weapons of mass destruction, though those weapons stockpiles never materialized. They started bombing Iraq beginning on March 20, 2003, followed by a ground invasion of the country.

Greta responded with the following letter to the editor, published on March 30, 2003:

> I am one of many loyal Americans who support our troops by protesting their use in the pre-emptive strike against Iraq. I deeply resent being made an accessory against my will to a war that violates the United Nations charter and is unjust according to 'just war' doctrines.
>
> I join the vast majority of Americans who support our troops by hoping that they will bring a quick end to the actual war and that their dedication and sacrifice, their suffering,

will be honored even in the endless aftermath of our leaders' ill-advised, untimely, illegal and unjust war-making.

I hope against hope that some good — somehow, somewhere — will come of this tragic course of events.

— Greta W. Crosby
Wichita

January 2005 - Focus on Equality

One of my daughter's proudest childhood memories occurred in January 2005 when she was in 6th grade. Several members of First UU and other UU churches around the state were converging on our state capital in Topeka, Kansas. We were gathering to protest a proposed amendment to the State Constitution that would ban same-sex marriages. I took Miranda out of school that day and we drove two hours to Topeka.

When we got there, there were about a hundred people present for the protest. Filtering through the crowd, we were stunned to discover that Miranda's Yaya, who was 74 at the time, had ridden up to Topeka, too! With Yaya being less active at that age, we had no idea that she was planning to attend.

So there we were, three generations of women standing together for a common cause. We had a photo taken which now sits proudly displayed on my mom's bookshelf. We're standing next to a rainbow banner, and the three of us are holding up a sign proclaiming: "Focus on Equality." In cherishing this memory, I'm reminded of Simone Weil's "flashes of justice, of compassion, of gratitude which rise-up sometimes in human relationships in the midst of harshness and metallic coldness."

In January 2005, the Kansas State Senate passed an amendment to the State Constitution which would result in banning gay marriage. In February 2005, the House of Representatives passed it, and it was sent to the Kansas voters as a referendum in order to be added to the State Constitution. In response, Greta submitted the following letter to the editor:

March 11, 2005 — Wichita *Eagle* — Letter to the Editor "Gay Marriage Ban Should Alarm Us All"

Every Kansan has reason to be alarmed at the proposed marriage amendment. The first part would insert into the Kansas Constitution a definition of marriage limiting it to one man and one woman, to bolster an 1867 law already doing so. It is unwise and unjust to use the state constitution as a device to block the quest of same-sex couples for access to equal protection under the laws.

The second part is pure folly. It would be a legal land mine ready to explode in anyone's life, regardless of one's marital status, sexual orientation or religion. It would create an undefined monopoly of 'rights and incidents of marriage' only for people in a relationship of marriage recognized under Kansas law. No one knows exactly what rights and incidents would be included. The precise boundaries of the monopoly would not be known until after years of litigation at both public and private expense.

The area of health care is of particular concern. Loss or denial of health insurance to domestic partners may occur if the amendment passes, increasing risk of bankruptcy, homelessness, disability and death.

Everyone faces uncertainty here. I encourage everyone to think carefully and caringly about the proposed amendment. I urge voters to vote 'no' to this incredibly flawed proposal.

—Greta W. Crosby, Wichita

The above letter to the editor was Greta's last published letter to the editor that I have been able to locate in my research — and what a compelling letter to conclude with. She knew how detrimental these actions were to basic human rights and she was deeply concerned.

Then on April 5, 2005, Kansas voters approved the amendment by 70%. Our State Constitution was amended in such a way that rights were taken away from a specific group of people. This is unusual because amendments usually grant and protect rights.

Imagine our profound surprise and joyful celebration in 2015, when the U.S. Supreme Court ruled that the right to same-sex marriage is protected under the Constitution of the United States of America! Like Greta, I choose to hold on to my Inner-Vision of Truth, regardless of temporary outward appearances. Once again, we see evidence of Dr. Martin Luther King, Jr's. Vision: "The arc of the moral universe is long, but it bends toward justice."

References to Greta's Writings

The last of the newspaper articles that I located referencing Greta W. Crosby were each unexpected little surprises of people quoting her writings from the UU hymnal and also her meditation book, *Tree and Jubilee*.

On December 12, 2009, a Vermont newspaper article written by Erica Baron appeared in the *Bennington Banner*; it was entitled "The Gifts of Darkness." Erica quoted Greta's "Winter" meditation that appears in the UU hymnal (which can be found on page 39 in this book). She wrote, "...Darkness is an invitation to introspection, to imagination, and to regeneration. 'Let us not wish away the winter,' begins a reading by Greta Crosby. 'It is a season unto itself, not merely a way to spring.'"

The Rev. George A. Burn was the director of pastoral care at Nittany Medical Center in State College, Pennsylvania. He was a co-facilitator of a bereavement program called, "Growing Through Loss." He quoted Greta from an entry in *Tree and Jubilee* in *Centre Daily Times* February 2004 and in March 2006: "Loss makes artists of us all as we weave new patterns in the fabric of our lives."

In May 2012, *The South Peace News* in High Prairie, Alberta, Canada, referred to the same quote on loss while describing the resiliency of their town when a wildfire had damaged or destroyed several homes in the area.

And finally, in March 2013, Tom Carpenter from *The Arizona Daily Sun* in Flagstaff, Arizona, referenced the same quote from Greta's meditation on loss. Tom listed 18 quotations from people that he relied on for mindful insights, and hers was included in that list.

Meditation 24 in *Tree and Jubilee*, where this quote appears, has two entries and it is entitled, "When the Bottom Falls Out." The first entry (a), is a Zen story told by Paul Reps; the second entry (b), was written by Greta:

(a)

There is a Zen story of a nun named Chiyono:

"... she was unable to attain the fruits of meditation for a long time.

"At last one moonlit night she was carrying water in an old pail bound with bamboo. The bamboo broke and the bottom fell out of the pail, and at that moment Chiyono was set free!

"In commemoration, she wrote a poem:
"*In this way and that, I tried to*
   save the old pail
"*Since the bamboo strip was*
   weakening and about to break
Until at last the bottom fell out.
No more water in the pail!
No more moon in the water!"
(b)

Sometimes when the bottom falls out of our life, we are set free. We attain enlightenment, or an enlightenment of sorts: Some perspective, some clarity, some sense of reality, some sense of dealing with things as they are, some relief from anxiety and perplexity because something profound has happened.

Whenever that profound thing happens, we can expect to go through a process, sometimes a long process, a painful or at least uncomfortable process, in which we let go of something and slowly learn how to live again. This is true no matter what we lose: a loved one, a work, a hope, a vision, an image of ourselves, a part of ourselves. Loss makes artists of us all as we weave new patterns in the fabric of our lives. – GWC

Greta's Current Way of Life

As mentioned in the Preface, my husband Danny and I have been living with and caring for my mom since 2015. In 2019 we decided to find a home where I could consolidate my office so I didn't have to leave her for many hours in the day. My Vision was to find a home with green-space for Greta to view from her bedroom. For about six months, I had been looking for a home that ticked all the boxes; then Covid came into full swing in March

2020, which complicated the house hunting process.

Fortunately, we were able to find just such a location and we moved in June 2020. Greta now has a large picture window and two side windows where she can see the sunrise through a stand of trees, as well as seasonal changes, shifting shadows, cloudscapes, and blue skies.

For meals, her dinette table places her at a large picture window for sightings of birds, squirrels, rabbits, and turkey gathering around the birdfeeders. In the summer, hummingbirds hover at their feeders. If we're especially lucky, we'll spot a deer, fox or coyote wandering through the wooded area.

For indoor entertainment, she has Midnight, her silky black cat companion, who loves her Momma Cat very much. As in her youth, Greta spends the majority of her time in her room reading books. Her preferred genre is now almost exclusively mystery books. Jamaica is mom's in-home helper who does a wonderful job of caring for mom while I'm writing, working or running errands.

A surprising advantage that we never expected when we bought the house is that the neighbors in this particular location are fantastic. I've assured Mom that if she ever had to push her 'Help' button while we're out for a short time, we have a long list of neighbors who would be there in a heartbeat. It's so comforting to know she would be well cared for, should the need arise.

Greta's memories of times gone by have faded, but sometimes something jogs her memory and she comes up with interesting details I didn't know. As mentioned in the Preface, she still reads the paper every morning, keeping apprised of current issues. In her own gentle way, she quietly continues her humanitarian Vision of care and compassion for the human condition.

Closing Words
June 4, 1961

Lord of farewell, who sets limits to everything under the sun, give us a due sense of life's fragility that its beauty and dearness may touch us to the quick, and touch others through our brief lives. Balance this sense of fragility with a due sense of sturdiness, that we may trust also in life's power of endurance. Lifelong, let us be like the little child: fragile yet durable.

— Greta W. Crosby

CREDITS AND LIST OF WORKS CITED

For the sake of convenience, sources have been cited and listed according to their order of appearance within each chapter. The source will be noted the first time it is referenced, then any further references within the chapter or in subsequent chapters will not be noted.

CHAPTER 5

Hackworth, William, H. *The Unitarian Universalist Church of Roanoke 1954-2004: Fifty Years of Service to the Larger Community.* Roanoke, 2004.

Williams, Mary Frances. *Another History of the First Unitarian Church of Lynchburg, Virginia.* Warwick House Publishing, Lynchburg, 1990.

Brumfield, Dale M. *Closing the Slaughterhouse: The Inside Story of Death Penalty Abolition in Virginia.* Richmond, Abolition Press, 2022.

Johnson, Mack. "Opposing Pickets Converge on Store." *The News and Advance,* Lynchburg, 15 February 1961, p.8.

CHAPTER 6

Davies, A. Powell. "The Urge to Persecute" by A. Powell Davies. Copyright © 1953 by A. Powell Davies. Reprinted by permission of Beacon Press, Boston.

Weil, Simone. "Intimations of Christianity Among the Greeks." Boston, Beacon Press, 1958, p 196.

Brecht, Bertholt. "St. Joan of the Stockyards." Bertholt Brecht Plays: Vol II, Methuen & Co. Ltd., London, 1961, p 194.

Spencer, Anne. "For Jim, Easter Eve." Appearing in *The Poetry of the Negro 1746 – 1949* by Langston Hughes & Arna Bontemps. Doubleday & Co. Inc., 1949. Permission to reprint poem courtesy of the Anne Spencer House and Garden Museum, Inc. Archives

CHAPTER 7

Crosby, Greta W. "'Issues' in the Wansley Case Receive Discussion." [Letter to the editor] *News and Advance,* Lynchburg, 10 March 1963, p. 32.

Staff. "Race Unit Urges Unitarians to March on Washington." *The Daily Advance,* Lynchburg, 25 July 1963, p.17.

CHAPTER 8
Sandburg, Carl. "Sand Flat Shadows." *Rootabaga Stories*. Harcourt Brace & World, Inc., 1st copyright 1950.
Stevens, Wallace. "The Man with the Blue Guitar." Copyright 1937 by Wallace Stevens; from THE COLLECTED POEMS OF WALLACE STEVENS by Wallace Stevens. Used by permission of Alfred A. Knopf, an imprint of the Knopf Doubleday Publishing Group, a division of Penguin Random House LLC. All rights reserved.

CHAPTER 9
Braden, Anne. "The Wansley Case: Seeing Injustice Whole - For the First time a Locally Initiated Campaign." *The Gazette and Daily*, York, PA. 5 June 1963, p 19.

CHAPTER 11
Crosby, Greta W. "Unitarian Minister Sees Ruling Justified." *Richmond Times-Dispatch*, 30 June 1962, p.8.
Staff. "Paster Declines Speaking Offer." *The World-News*, Roanoke, 10 April 1964, p.13.
Staff. "Pastor Explains Action in Rejecting School Bid." *The World-News*, Roanoke, 14 April 1964, p.9.
Staff. "Woman Pastor has Yule Baby." *The World-News*, Roanoke, 26 December 1964, p.2.
Staff. "Slain Minister is Remembered for his Enthusiasm." *The World-News*, Roanoke, 12 March 1965, p.11.

CHAPTER 13
Roszak, Theodore. "Dream Exploration Among the Senoi." *Sources: An Anthology of Contemporary Materials Useful for Preserving Personal Sanity While Braving the Great Technological Wilderness*. Harper & Row, New York, NY, 1972, pp.20-39. Based on Kilton Stewart's paper "Creative Psychology and Dream Education." New York, Stewart Foundation for Creative Psychology, 1960.
Garfield, Patricia. *Creative Dreaming*. Simon & Schuster, New York, 1974.

CHAPTER 14
Crosby, Greta W. "Support for Gay Ordinance." [Letter to the editor] Wichita *Eagle*, 22 September 1977, p.44.
Staff. "Wichita Ministers Split On Gay Rights Ordinance." *Longview News-Journal*, Longview, TX, 6 May 1978, p.28.

CHAPTER 15

Eiseley, Loren, "The Poets," From THE INNOCENT ASSASSINS by Loren Eiseley. Copyright © 1973 by Loren Eiseley. Copyright renewed © 2000 by Mabel Langdon Eiseley and Trustees of the University of Pennsylvania. Reprinted with the permission of Scribner, an imprint of Simon & Schuster LLC. All rights reserved.

Yashima, Taro. *Crow Boy*. Puffin Books, 1976.

Neavoll, George. "The Many-Winter'd Crow." Wichita *Eagle*, 8 January 1978, p. 2B.

Frost, Robert. "The Dust of Snow" from the collection entitled: *New Hampshire*. Henry Holt and Company, 1923.

Joseph, Magaret. "The Crows." *Poems by Margaret A. Joseph*. Mariposa Press, San Antonio, Texas 1977. Margaret is a former member of First UU and a longtime member of First UU San Antonio, TX.

Kalmbach, E.R. "The Crow, Bird Citizen of Every Land." *The National Geographic*, 1920, pp322-337.

Seton, Earnest Thompson. *Wild Animals I Have Known*. Bantam Books, New York, 1957, Copyright 1898.

CHAPTER 16

Stebbins, Frances. "Woman Minister Likes New Area Attitudes." *The Roanoke Times*, 7 May 1979, p.22.

CHAPTER 17

Crosby, Greta W., *Tree and Jubilee: A Book of Meditations Composed and Compiled by Greta W. Crosby*, UUA's Beacon Press, Boston, 1982.

CHAPTER 18

Anderson, Maxwell. "Thousands of Miles." from *Lost in the Stars*, a dramatization of Alan Paton's Cry, Beloved Country. William Sloan Associates, 1949-1950, p. 86.

Buson. "Lighting one candle with another candle/an evening of spring." *Haiku, Vol. 2, Spring*, by R.H. Blyth, Hokuseido Press, Tokyo, 1955, p. 55.

Richards, Mary Caroline. *Centering in Pottery, Poetry and the Person*. Wesleyan Press, Middleton, CT, 1964, p. 18.

Levertov, Denise. "The Depths." *News of the Universe*. Sierra Club Books, San Francisco, 1980, p.151.

CHAPTER 19

Hale, Edward Everett. "I Am Only One." *The Book of Good Cheer: A Little Bundle of Cheery Thoughts*. Edited by Edwin Osgood Grover. The Algonquin Publishing Company, 1913.

CHAPTER 20
Jowett, Benjamin. *Translation of The Republic by Plato*. Oxford University Press Warehouse, 1888.

CHAPTER 21
Crosby, Greta W. "Confrontation." *UU World Magazine*. Boston, March 1985.
Staff. "First China, then Newton." Wichita *Eagle*, 6 October 1985, p.50.
Davis, Andrew K. & M. Kay. "Bomber Art Contest Angers Parents, Many Others." [Letter to the Editor] Wichita *Eagle*, 26 August 1987, p. 31.
Finger, Stan and Hurst Lavinia. "McConnell March Peaceful; 68 Held." Wichita *Eagle*, 26 May 1987, p.1.

CHAPTER 22
Crosby, Greta W. [Letter to the editor] *Yakima Herald-Republic*, Yakima WA, 22 November 1988.

CHAPTER 23
Crosby, Greta W. "Rainbow Ribbon." [Letter to the editor] *Yakima Herald-Republic*, Yakima WA, 8 February 1991, p.10A.
Crosby, Greta W. "Root Causes." [Letter to the editor] *Yakima Herald-Republic*, Yakima, WA, 5 May 1992.

CHAPTER 24
Bunting, Eve, *Fly Away Home*, Clarion Books, 1993.
Myers, Steven Lee. "Broadway's Newest Feature: The Cornstalk." *The New York Times*, New York, 13 August 1991, p.B12.
Channing, William Ellery. "Unitarian Christianity" Sermon 1819. Optional link to the full sermon: uuwestport.org/unitarianchristianity/

CHAPTER 26
Hopkins, Gerald Manley. "Pied Beauty." *Poems of Gerald Manley Hopkins*, 1918.
Pine-Coffin, R.S. "Confessions" (IV:8). *The Works of Saint Augustine, A Translation for the 21st Century*. Penguin Classics, 1961.
St. Exupery, Antoine de. *The Little Prince*. William Heinemann Ltd. London, 1945, 1951, pp.64-69.

CHAPTER 27

Crosby, Greta W. "Water Alert." [Letter to the editor] Wichita *Eagle*, 12 Aug 1997, p.6.

Crosby, Greta W. "Disney Boycott." [Letter to the editor] Wichita *Eagle*, 28 November 1997, p.10.

Crosby, Greta W. "Choice Support." [Letter to the editor] Wichita *Eagle*, 22 January 1998, p.6.

Crosby, Greta W. "Term's Time is Up." [Letter to the editor] Wichita *Eagle*, 9 June 1998, p.8.

Crosby, Greta W. "Don't Kill Killers." [Letter to the editor] Wichita *Eagle*, 10 December 1998, p.14.

CHAPTER 28

Crosby, Greta W. "Cultural Help." [Letter to the editor] Wichita *Eagle*, 7 October 2001, p.15.

Lefler, Dion. "Benefits Proponents Cry Foul." Wichita *Eagle*, 9 October 2001, p.20.

Crosby Greta W. "Fair Play?" [Letter to the editor] Wichita *Eagle*, 20 November 2001, p.10.

Crosby, Greta W. "Religious Agenda." [Letter to the editor] Wichita *Eagle*, 31 August 2002, p.6.

Crosby, Greta W. "Loyal Protest." [Letter to the editor] Wichita *Eagle*, 30 March 2003, p.13.

Crosby, Greta W. "Gay Marriage Ban Should Alarm Us All." [Letter to the editor] Wichita *Eagle*, 11 March 2005, p.8.

Baron, Erica. "The Gifts of Darkness." *Bennington Banner*, Bennington, VT, 12 December 2009, p.13.

Burn, George A. "Growing Through Loss." *Centre Daily Times*, State College, PA. Feb 2004 & Mar 2006.

Seraphim, Theresa. "'Resilience' a Good Word for Slave Lakers." *The South Peace News*, High Prairie, Alberta, Canada, 23 May 2012, p.34.

Carpenter, Tom. "My Little Bag of Platitudes." *Arizona Daily Sun*, Flagstaff, AZ, 3 March 2013, p.14.

Acknowledgements

BEING BORN into a Unitarian Universalist family, I feel deeply rooted in the UU church, however, years ago my search for truth and meaning led me to *A Course in Miracles*. Within that wisdom teaching, I have found my Calling and my Guiding Light, which is described in the Course as the Holy Spirit. Everything I do is now Spirit-led as I listen to my Inner-Voice and as I discern my felt-state, which helps me determine the best course of action at every decision point. Consequently, my first acknowledgement goes to the Holy Spirit for the comprehensive Guidance that has led to the publication of this book.

I acknowledge my mom, Greta W. Crosby, who is the epicenter of *All of Us Together*. Mom has always viewed me with her adoring Mom-Goggles and I feel so fortunate to have her as my mom. I have always appreciated her unique abilities and her kind nature, and now I'm even more impressed with her lifetime accomplishments.

My husband, Danny Pollock, has provided unwavering encouragement every single day. His message from the beginning has been, "You do You — just keeping doing whatever it takes to accomplish your Vision." Our kids, Miranda, Brett and Tiger, and their amazing Dear Ones, have also held the space for me to follow this path, for they know this is my Calling. I delight in their independence, and I celebrate that the time is now right for me to write.

I also wish to posthumously acknowledge my dad, Robert Crosby, who first planted the idea of publishing Mom's sermons. Though I was estranged from him for many years, the healing journey back to Love — seeing him for who he truly is — has been indescribably worthwhile.

I am grateful to the staff and members of the UU churches of

ACKNOWLEDGMENTS

Utica, Roanoke, Lynchburg, Wichita, and Yakima for their assistance with my in-depth research process. In particular, the Roanoke & Lynchburg churches forwarded the published histories of their churches, which provided excellent details for this book. I also appreciate the beautiful letters that UU members sent, rounding out our perspectives of Greta's ministry from different angles.

In the peer-review process, I thank my dear friends Tunara Frakes and her daughter, Lisa DeCow, for contributing wise and helpful input, greatly improving the book overall. Jamaica Belshe, my mom's helper, also assisted with proofing and peer review. Jamaica has been a vital tag-team member and we appreciate everything she has done for our family.

Two more members of the family must be acknowledged for their loyal contribution to *All of Us Together*. My 'writing team,' Riley Rose Marie, our 14-year-old Schnauzer, and Ava, our 7-year-old Great Dane, have provided couch-potato companionship every step of the way – lots of snuggles and warm fuzzies have gone into the making of this book.

D. Patrick Miller, owner and operator of the publishing company Fearless Literary, offers an entire array of self-publication services, which facilitate every aspect of the process. He is a Spirit-led answer to a prayer – Thank you Patrick, for your experienced input and patient support for this project!

Finally, a heartfelt 'Thank you' for anyone and everyone, my family members, my second mom (Bonnie Till), my beloved best friend Kris, all my other fabulous best friends, my amazing neighbors & Ladies Night Ladies, numerous church members and staff, my beautiful clients and colleagues, fellow retreat participants, my optometrist, my dentist, my chiropractor, my cranio-sacral therapist, my former students, utility workers, even seatmates on airplanes, who have encouraged me along the way. Everybody needs encouragement. We have no idea how helpful it is when we tell another person, "Hey, more power to you! You can do this!" Thank you All, for your Loving support for the publication of *All of Us Together*.

About the Author

Lara Pollock was born in San Antonio where she spent the first seven years of her childhood. In 1975 her family moved to Wichita, Kansas, where she has lived since then.

Being a sensitive-intuitive, Lara was often overwhelmed by the unkind ways of the world. Gradually she learned to manage her empathic abilities in such a way that she could serve the greater good. Lara feels her greatest good has been raising three amazing kids with her husband, Danny.

Additionally, Lara followed a widely varied career pathway. She was a dental assistant throughout high school and college as she trained in English for secondary education. From there she practiced therapeutic massage, facilitating hands-on healing, and teaching therapeutic massage classes. In 2005, she began training as a practitioner of Traditional Chinese Medicine (TCM), including acupuncture and herbology.

In 2008, Lara's life transformed as she discovered the great wisdom teaching, *A Course in Miracles*. Since then, in each of her roles in life, Lara's underlying goal has been to demonstrate the principles of *A Course in Miracles*, learning to Live the Golden Rule to the best of her ability.

In 2009, Lara completed her TCM certification and licensure. She then taught TCM and established a private practice from 2009 until 2020. Additionally, from 2016 to 2021, Lara taught a class called Introduction to Complementary and Alternative Medicine at Wichita State University.

In 2020, as with many people, the Covid-19 pandemic initiated a cascade of significant life changes. Lara's mom has been in Lara and Danny's care since 2015, and when Covid-19 went global in the spring of 2020, Lara's strong intuition prompted her to close her office to stay home and care for her mom.

In the years since then, Lara's priorities have transformed as her commitment to the Course continues to deepen. In 2023 she self-published a book called *Together Is Home* outlining the basic concepts of *A Course in Miracles*. Since completing that project, she has spent the last year compiling and composing her mom's memoirs into this book, *All of Us Together*. More writing projects are in the works and Lara looks forward to the next step in her Spirit-led journey.

Made in the USA
Monee, IL
17 October 2024

67996978R00194